LIVES ACROSS TIME/ GROWING UP

LIVES ACROSS TIME/ GROWING UP

Paths to Emotional Health and Emotional Illness from Birth to 30 in 76 People

Henry Massie
and
Nathan Szajnberg

KARNAC

First published in 2008 by
Karnac Books Ltd
118 Finchley Road
London NW3 5HT

British Library Cataloguing in Publication Data
A C.I.P. for this book is available from the British Library

ISBN: 978-1-85575-517-8

Printed in Great Britain
www.karnacbooks.com

DEDICATION

To the one human family, universal in its wish for security, opportunity, and kindness. To all of Sylvia Brody's "children" and their parents—the participants in this study of growing up who shared their lives with us for more than thirty years.

Henry Massie

To my daughters Sonia Aviva and Lily Rachel; to Elisheva; to my aunts and uncles (too many to name) who died in Auschwitz before reaching adulthood. And to the Jewish people.

Nathan Szajnberg

I learned . . . to follow the unforgotten advice of my teacher, Charcot: to look at the same things again and again until they themselves began to speak.

Sigmund Freud, 1914

But she had in her hand a cold key, and surrounding her, lives that were stranger than fiction, funnier than fiction, crueler than fiction, and with consequences fiction can never have.

White Teeth, Zadie Smith, 2001

Acknowledgements

LIVES ACROSS TIME/Growing Up has benefited greatly from many sources of essential support who are not mentioned elsewhere in this volume. Grants from the California Wellness Foundation, the International Psychoanalytic Association Research Advisory Board, and the Emmanuel Windholz Fund of the San Francisco Psychoanalytic Institue were critical. Our statistical consultants Karen Trocki, Ph.D., and Norman Turk, Ph.D., were indispensable.

Henry Massie and Nathan Szajnberg

Cheryl Colopy and Kathleen McGill have been wonderful editors bringing clarity to my often confusing syntax. My wife Bridget Connelly—a gifted writer—has always been my best wordsmith and problem solver. Finally my daughter Kate and my niece Clare have been my in-family joyous sounding boards and exemplars, first, on childhood, then on youth.

Henry Massie

Hank Massie invited me to collaborate on this study and offered an intellectual home. Paul Ekman has wisdom and defines good friendship with his thoughtful advice. Judy Wallerstein helped us clarify our writing. The Firefighter's Foundation and the little firefighter who is anonymous offered financial support that permitted me to commit my time to this work until the International Psychoanalytic Association honored me with their support.

Nathan Szajnberg

Preface

NATHAN SZAJNBERG

Mere air, these words, but delicious to hear

Sappho

Writing fixes the evanescence of sound. It holds it against death.

Edward Hirsch

THIS BOOK—WHICH I co-authored with my friend and fellow psychiatrist Henry Massie—reports the results of a 30 year study of 76 people, participants in a longitudinal study of mothers and infants begun by Sylvia Brody in 1964. Dr. Massie assumed responsibility for the study in the early 1990s, and in 1994 the work entered my life.

Hank had telephoned me in Wisconsin, where I was directing psychiatry at the Children's Hospital, to ask for ideas about what to include in the interview for the 30 year olds who had been followed from birth to 18 years. Among other suggestions, I recommended the Adult Attachment Interview; I thought that would be the end of my involvement. Within the year, Hank called again. The interviews of all 76 people had been finished; each interview was on videotape and lasted 2 1/2 to 31/2 hours. Would I watch and rate each person's life functioning and the structure of their internal worlds?

I am grateful to Hank for adopting me into this study, this story of lives. I am a psychoanalyst; I listen for hours to people's inner lives. I also research how mothers and infants read and interpret each others' emotions and develop attachment relationships. I had found attachment a powerful way to understand how we develop intimacies within the first year of life, and how inner strategies can change that development throughout life.

At first we worked long distance, punctuated by my visits to Berkeley for long weekends of watching videotapes (relieving the concentration with dinners at Chez Panisse). I would trudge back to Wisconsin loaded with videotapes too precious to ship. After a year, I moved to the Bay Area, in a large part to collaborate on this research.

Our method was simple. Prior to reading their prospective life histories, I watched and assessed all 76 people on videotape. Hank read and summarized the histories. When we were both done, we compared notes. My reconstructions of the participants' childhoods were tested against observations made prospectively and enriched by retrospective accounts. We compared our interrater reliability. A third colleague, Erik Hesse, independently rated parts of the interviews about attachment. We then categorized the life courses and began writing the book.

To present our results, we have parsed 76 people into two categories: those whose lives were fairly continuous from early childhood to adulthood, and those whose lives were not. Children with continuous lives included both those who began with optimal parenting and achieved good life functioning, and those who began with less than optimal care and 30 years later had suboptimal functioning. Discontinuous children's lives revealed outcomes that went against caretaking predictions in two ways: those who started suboptimally but achieved fuller adult lives, and those who started optimally but fell from grace.

In creating these categories, we followed a common human impulse to see patterns in experience. To recognize design in nature—a path through the woods, constellations marking the sky, the lunar predictability of tides—is to gain the confidence necessary to navigate successfully through life. Yet it is also easy to elaborate patterns from our own imaginations and impose them on reality. Phrenologists in the last century "read" bumps on skulls and drew remarkable, intruiguing—and wrong—conclusions about character.

Yet in the course of our research, we found ourselves listening to something very basic: the story people tell about themselves. While a life may fall into a certain configuration—and even share characteristics with other lives in a group—the individual story is the compelling event, and to group is to some degree to de-humanize. So while as researchers we group, as authors we allow our subjects to speak at length in their own voice. We wish to keep these lives very human.

In the chapters that follow, then, are stories, life stories of 76 people clinically observed over 30 years. The parents in the study graciously agreed to reveal themselves and their infants, as did later the children, teenagers, and now adults—on film, in tests, and in interviews—to Dr. Brody and the earlier researchers who maintained the study until 1990, and then to Hank Massie, myself, and those who assisted us. The stories the participants tell are not always easy. Some are tales of deep delight. Others, however, plunge us into winter's dark.

While earlier follow-ups showed much about parenting and development, our thiry-year-olds revealed the role of memory. We also deepened our knowledge of the effect of mothering style upon outcome and coherence, conclusions that correlate with and elaborate the understanding of the significance of early relationships and the revisions that can come later which other longitudinal researchers such as Waters, Hamilton, and Weinfeld (2000) are also finding. In their two-decade studies, these investigators demonstrate the coherence of development by using carefully constructed measures of attachment and studying different types of families (middle-class, indigent, single-parent), showing that attachment relationships are predictable, providing one takes into account adverse circumstances. Our study complements their work, extending the number of years examened and adding the intricate details of life that we found from prospective, filmed observations and retrospective accounts. We say how and why lives move in certain directions, how and why psychiatric symptoms develop in some people, and how the internal thoughts and feelings of individuals accommodate external circumstances as people try to keep an even keel while sailing through life's waters.

In the five years we spent watching videotapes of these lives in infancy, childhood, and adulthood, we puzzled over how to make sense for our readers of what we saw. We thought about how to articulate a life story in a manner that was true to each—and also clear to an audience. We wanted to bring alive how active, how busy the participants were, internally forming and reforming themselves, sometimes productively, sometimes not.

Freud (1932) suggested that we would best learn about how we contruct our inner worlds using two apporaches: prospective observation of development, and retrospective narration of lifestory. Our work reveals the richness of this dual method. We found that neither way alone is sufficient or more valid. Prospective observations, in some cases, only became fully understood when retrospective memories told us what the child was thinking or feeling at the time: a three year old is frightened of the kangaroos on a psychological test, but only at thirty do we learn from him that he was terrified by a picture of kangaroos on his bedroom wall. Or, a research observer is impressed by a father-son Heathkit radio project when the child is six: at thirty, the former child recalls the project as a tedious chore. At the same time, retrospective memories are exposed as constructions when we compare them to prospective observations: an adult "recalls" a traumatic separation from his parents that occurrred when he was four and a half years old; in the prospective record, we learn of three major separations between three and a half and five. Or, memory "sculpts" the historical experience: a thirty year old describes his father as tough but loving; from his sister we learn that the boy was beaten to bleeding. Where is the loving in this?

From these retrospective and prospective approaches, viewed over 30 years, we suggest that certain factors promote psychological well-being for a child:

1. Parents' sense of calm, reflectiveness, and attentiveness—seeing their child as a person;
2. Mother's and father's fondness for each other, over and above a sense of love;
3. Maternal gentleness, affection, warmth, and empathy—i.e. her *Einfuhling* toward her child;
4. Parents' pride in the active (assertive/aggressive) ability of the child. As one mother put it about her crying baby, "She makes her feelings clear!"
5. Parents' pleasure in the child's initiative and independence;
6. Parental emphasis on discipline rather than punishment. Discipline, from the same Latin root as *disciple*, suggests that mothers and fathers model appropriate behavior, and that children follow the footsteps of how their parents live;
7. Parental close attention to, and involvement with their child for at least the earliest years of his life.

A brief word about memory. Astronomers debate whether the universe is uniform or clumpy. Memory is clumpy. Thinking about the day that has just passed, or a year ago, or your childhood, recalls clumps of experiences rather than a continuous line. This book explores the components of these clumps of memory: how and why feelings, thoughts, visual images, and sound are put together into a memory, like, for example, Reba's memory of being seven: her father driving home in a shiny new car, and asking her and all of her friends out to the Tastee Freeze. This appetizing memory captures her current presentaton: delightfully engaging and hopeful.

* * *

The word "preface" has a history. The preface to a book comes before the matter at hand to foreshadow what lies ahead. In Catholicism, the Preface is a prayer of thanksgiving to approach the more serious Sanctus celebration; in Judaism the Preface is the Kabbalat Shabbat which ushers in the day of rest as if she were a bride. In this preface, I hope to usher you, our readers into the work of many years, which was to bring to life the stories and experiences of these people so that we may all enjoy more informed and enriched lives. In this endeavor, our task, our responsibility, to both our respondents and our readers, is to inscribe our awe in the face of observing the evolution of the inner world of childhood. In this way these thirty-year stories may evolve again, into something more enduring, stories not just lived once in an individual's lifetime and forgotten, but remembered, read, reflected upon by others, coloring their life and understanding too. We are thankful to those who have shared their lives with all of us. Their stories endure in our minds and in our hearts.

I began this preface with a few words of ancient and contemporary poetry that speak to me about how this book emerged. These words hint at what we hope will occur with our readers as they follow the stories gathered here. Our study participants lived their lives. Without researchers—listeners, observers—their stories might be evanescent, their words but sounds. When we write down these stories, we try to fix their experiences and the lessons they provide more permanently. It is the reader, though, who breathes life into them. May these stories take root in your mind and heart—as they have in ours. May they enlighten and change your life.

Nathan Szajnberg
San Francisco and Beer Sheva

Introduction

HENRY MASSIE

THIRTY-FIVE ODD YEARS ago, in July 1968, I was starting the first year of my psychiatric training at the Albert Einstein College of Medicine in New York City. A raw and inexperienced Midwesterner, I had just finished medical school in St. Louis and driven East. St. Louis in those days was so rooted in the past and somnolent that when I wrote an editorial in the school newspaper supporting the Civil Rights movement, the administration questioned whether I belonged in the school and the student body yawned. New York jolted me awake with its jackhammers echoing off immense buildings, its traffic, jazz clubs, and hundreds of thousands of people marching down Broadway protesting the war in Vietnam.

My first psychiatric patients at Bronx State Hospital were equally exciting for me as I struggled to align the books, lectures, theories and terminology with the actual people I and my classmates were trying to help. Trying to make sense of the human mind, and doing it not in an ivory tower but on wards, in the emergency room, and in the little cubicle offices the hospital gave resident doctors was riveting. Our patients really believed we could help them, and through a combination of their optimistic naivete and our graduate student hubris and good will, good things sometimes happened for the patients. As students we often had a false sense that we knew more than we did, which lent me a certain bravado that has long since gone by the wayside.

I remember being on duty at night at the state hospital, the only doctor on the grounds for several hundred patients. The phone would ring in my on-call room as it so often did in the dark early morning hours, which brought out more desperation in people than did the first part of the night. I'd leave the doctors' bungalow and walk across the dark, silent campus to one of the three ghostly high-rises in which the patients lived.

The dimly lit elevator ascended slowly and when the door opened, bright light from the nursing station beamed into my reverie. Usually a nurse (or an aide who might have been one of Muhammed Ali's sparring partners because he had been chosen for his strength) met me and led the way to a seclusion room where there was a horrible din. Sometimes it was a man growling or threatening to tear his own and everyone else's eyes out. I would gauge everyone's mood and fatigue—staff, patient, and mine alike—and give an instruction like, "Yes, put him in restraints," because the nurse had said to me that she thought it was time for that. Or I'd suggest an alternative, "Give him 75 more milligrams of thorazine." Or it might be a woman in a hospital issue house-dress, her age and features overwhelmed by distress, sobbing about a baby an unnamed "they" had taken away from her.

If I had enough energy I would sit down with her and encourage her to talk while I listened, trying to apply the lecture from the previous day about distinguishing schizophrenia from a manic-depressive psychosis. Usually by the end of an hour the would have patient had wound down and be ready to go to sleep, and my head, by contrast, would be spinning with confusion about whether she had lost a real baby or a fantasized child. I knew that I'd never see most of the night-time patients again or learn the source of their anguish, even though sometimes I came back during the day, if I had a cancellation or by skipping lunch, to try to understand them better. But still, none of the lectures or books taught me in a convincing way why the patients had become sick; it also took me many years to learn how to really listen to patients and talk with them. To do this I had to gradually unlearn most of the jargon and cook-book like, step-by-step approach to technique I learned during those early days. Although the training made me feel in control of the clinical situations that came my way, in reality it was a crutch and a barrier between me and the patients.

Yet one part of the training stood out, and I never jettisoned it. It was the course on early child development, a section of which was based on Sylvia Brody's research which she had turned into a teaching film, *Forms of Feeding at Six Weeks and Mother-Infant Interaction* (Brody and Axelrad, 1970). Sylvia Brody was then a psychologist, psychoanalyst, and professor at City University of New York and Albert Einstein College of Medicine, who worked in tandem with her husband Sidney Axelrad, a sociologist at City

University of New York. Unlike the other instruction we received at Einstein, her film did not *tell* us about good and bad relationships, it *showed* us by focusing on the moment-by-moment interactions of mothers and babies, often in slow motion. No other researchers had done this up to that time.

The movie narration simply highlighted in plain language what Brody and Axelrad had spent hours deciphering by examining the films in real time, in slow motion, and frame-by-frame, a technique they pioneered for the study of infant development. The teaching movie showed us scenes of 17 mothers feeding their babies in ways that the researchers had recognized fell into distinctive patterns, some good and many destructive. For example, I recall a mother half-smiling, placidly watching her six week old daughter rhythmically sucking. The baby's fingers unclenched, stretched out on the mother's breast, the mother lightly kissed her child, and the baby slipped off to sleep.

Another mother held her son on her lap but never otherwise touched him, never changed her blank expression. Only the spoon and bottle touched the tiny boy's lips, and his fingers grasped vainly at thin air for something to hold onto. Still another case fixed itself in my memory like a recurring nightmare. The mother had placed her daughter in a carrier on a table and stood over her at arms' length holding a bottle in the child's mouth. The mother looked about the room bored and annoyed. Once when the baby lost the bottle the mother angrily jerked her daughter's head back into position. The infant's head fell forward and she grimaced as if to cry but couldn't because the bottle was forced too tightly into her mouth. There was a gasp in the room from all of us watching the film.

Various mothers were angry, apathetic, controlling, domineering, chaotic, inept, remote, awkward, mechanical, inhibited, and didactic, and others efficient, tender, joyful, thoughtful, tolerant, and empathic. Watching the films I kept thinking that surely such different early experiences must lead to very different kinds of emotional growth, and sometimes to psychiatric conditions. What I was seeing in the research movies made far more sense to me as an explanation for my patients' troubles than the theoretical abstractions taught at the time such as "oral phase trauma" and "fixation at the paranoid-depressive infancy position"; or the diagrams of abnormalities in dopamine neurochemical pathways. I came to believe that very early parent-child experiences must explain to an important extent the grim encounters I had on the wards of the state hospital and in the emergency room of Bronx Municipal Hospital. There I talked to young people about my own age who felt they didn't belong in the world when they woke up in the morning, and others who had already tried to leave the world with LSD or by slashing their wrists.

One of my first psychotherapy patients did succeed in his wish to die. An uncle had sexually molested him for years when he was in grade school, and his parents had refused to believe him. By the time he became my patient he was seriously addicted to heroin and ran away from the hospital one night to start using the drug again. Not long afterward I learned that he had tumbled to his death from his apartment window. Whether he jumped, fell or was pushed, I never knew, but I was grasping the humbling lesson that I couldn't prevent some childhood traumas from taking their toll.

While I was watching Dr. Brody's movies in my first year of training, I kept wishing that I could see how the babies on her film would grow up. Then I would have some real answers about life, I thought, and better tools to help patients.

Developing a Research Methodology

Three years later, in 1971, I had finished my general psychiatric residency, and following the trail that pointed to a child's early experience in its family as a main source of adult psychopathology, I arranged a fellowship in the newly emerging field of family studies. This gave me access to Eleanor Galenson's research nursery at Albert Einstein, a project that had yielded seminal publications on how sexual identity forms in early life (Roiphe and Galenson, 1981). Their methodology was to carefully correlate behavior and symbolism inherent in young children's play, genital awareness, events in the child's life such as illnesses, separations from parents, and birth of siblings, and ongoing, in depth, psychoanalytically oriented interviews with the parents that tapped into their own attitudes about nurturing children and sexuality.

In the nursery I began treating a three year old autistic girl, but after months of struggling to draw the child out of her fixation on endlessly spinning coins in a corner of the room and into a relationship with me, there was no progress. I lost patience with the psychotherapy process, and searching for new information I asked the parents if they had ever made movies of Joan when she was a baby. It turned out that they had—grainy, jumpy, silent, 8mm home films. Not knowing what I was looking for, following Brody and Axelrad's lead I projected the movies over and over, and one moment caught my eye: When the child was four months old Joan's mother is holding her at her shoulder and they are looking across a playground at the direction of the father who is filming. The mother nuzzles Joan. The baby begins to drool and smile, and then turns toward her mother. At the same instant, the mother turns away. Their eyes never meet. The baby loses her smile, her eyes become glassy, and her expression turns vacant. This sequence repeats several times.

By the end of the first year, the films showed that Joan was profoundly lost to autism. She avoided all eye contact; her expression had not matured to permit communicating moods and intentions; and she was endlessly rocking to and fro. After discovering the failed mother-child interaction at four months, I recognized several other scenes in the first six months of life—more fleeting than the one described above—in which the mother appeared unusually self-contained and limited in her initiation of eye contact with her infant. However, in spite of seeing this in the movies and shifting the focus of the treatment to working with the mother and child together, to my regret I never was able to help Joan.

I still don't know with any certainty what caused Joan's autism, for it is a condition that remains a profound medical mystery. Every few years there are tantalizing neurochemical, neurostructural, or psychological findings that may be related to its etiology, but still no answers. A very few children recover after intense psychological efforts by parents or therapists, but there are no reliable pharmacological or psychological treatments. It is possible that some cases of autism are the result of psychological trauma, others of organic factors, and others the consequence of emotional trauma coupled with organic vulnerability. In fact, Joan's case brings up one of the profound conundrums in psychiatric treatment and research. This is the question of how to work with families where there is a major psychiatric disorder that may be psychologically induced, on the one hand, or biologically caused, on the other; how to study the impact of disturbed parenting on children's development without blaming parents? In my youthful zeal to heal Joan, I had upset her family by focusing too strongly on the dyssynchronous eye gaze between mother and child and the possibility that it had originated in the parent rather than in the child. Since then I have learned to proceed with less self-assurance.

On the other hand many psychiatrists today are so fearful of offending parents that they avoid even implying that parents may cause disturbances in a child. Usually only cases of egregious abuse, negligence, or illegal drugs give psychiatrists the courage to raise questions about the parents' behavior. If the legal code says the parent is wrong, the psychotherapist is shielded from the charge that he or she is blaming the parent. Similarly psychiatrists who rely on the explanation that genes and chemical imbalances are solely responsible for a child's problems are also shielding themselves from having to question and try to change a parent's behavior.

The best approach I have found to working with and studying parents who may have unwittingly hurt their children is to proceed gently in treatment or research. Respect the fact that almost all parents try to do as well as they can for their children, and maintain deep concern for parents' emotional vulnerability when the lives of their children are not going well. I acknowledge to them that sometimes we will never know with certainty why things have gone wrong, but I point out that we have to look carefully for answers with our eyes wide open, and to consider all possibilities, even those that go against the conventional wisdom of the moment.

* * *

In June of 1972, still following the pathway back from adult psychiatry to early childhood, I left the East Coast to start a child psychiatry fellowship at Mt. Zion Hospital in San Francisco. There I also began a formal research project to gather a series of family-made movies of the infancies of children who were later diagnosed with autism and a comparison group of films of normal children. The first systematic study of its kind with home movies, the project documented the appearance of the initial symptoms of autism toward the end of the first year of life. This made it possible to recognize the onset of autism in a child at the earliest time, and begin treatment when it is most likely to be helpful before the symptoms become ingrained.

From the autism study my colleague Kay Campbell and I developed *The Massie-Campbell Scale of Mother-Infant Attachment During Stress* (ADS Scale) (Massie and Campbell, 1983; Massie and Campbell, 1984) to compare mother and infant reciprocal interactions in normal and atypical families in the realms of eye gaze, vocalizations, touching, holding (the mother), clinging (the child), facial expression (affect), and physical closeness. These interactions were often disordered in cases of autism, and seemed fundamental to parent-infant bonding and the ensuing emotional development of children in all families. My sensitization to them clearly owed itself to my exposure to Brody and Axelrad's films some years earlier. The ADS Scale proved useful to pediatricians in detecting disturbances in early parent-child relationships, and it also remained central to my future research.

My final years of training and early years of research at Mt. Zion Hospital were also important because of the formative influence on my thinking of Erik Erikson who was on the faculty there at the time. Erikson's own peregrinations are interesting because they illustrate the twists and turns life can take. Born in Germany, as a youth he had wandered in Italy painting and playing music, gravitated to psychoanalysis in Vienna as a young man where Anna Freud was his teacher, and come to America in 1933 to escape Hitler's fascism. Following a teaching post at Harvard and anthropologic research with the Sioux and Yurok Indians, in the 1940s he came to San

Francisco where, as part of a group of therapists working with traumatized soldiers from the war in the Pacific, he helped found the psychiatry department at Mt. Zion Hospital and the San Francisco Psychoanalytic Institute. During this period he was also active in the psychology department at the University of California at Berkeley.

In 1950 published his landmark book *Childhood and Society* (Erikson, 1950) which delineated the psychosocial stages of development, showing how individual identity and social roles mesh across the span of a person's life. A short time later, McCarthyism gripped the Berkeley campus, and Erikson, no stranger to Fascism's destructive potential, returned to Harvard and the Austen Riggs Hospital, only to come back to San Francisco at the end of his career.

A moment stands out from my contacts with him. During a seminar, the discussion turned to how the character of the American people was rooted in the mythology of the frontier, which accounted for Americans' restlessness, seeking, and obsession with "newness." Sitting as we were there on the edge of the continent, someone asked what would happen when the West was all settled and there was no frontier. There was a pause while Erikson, white haired, gentle, shyly humorous, and insightful, thought. Suddenly his hand shot up in the air. "Space," he said, "that is where we will go." Perhaps he meant outer space, inner space (which he had written about), or some other dimension. Ironically it was just 40 miles down the road in Silicon Valley that ten years later the world entered cyberspace.

Yet his answer captures the essence of what I learned from Erikson—avoid thinking linearly and mechanically about people. In case conferences he taught me to think about unpredictability in people's lives. He also shaped my understanding of how, in his terminology, we move from trust as an infant; to autonomy as toddlers; to initiative and industry in childhood; then to identity and intimacy in youth; and to generativity, integrity and wisdom in adulthood. By contrast he also showed how some people can't escape the pitfalls of confusion, mistrust, doubt, paralysis, isolation and despair. Whereas Sylvia Brody's films helped me understand the importance of the beginning of life—graphically showed infants confused and mistrusting—Erikson helped me take the long view.

It was both of their influences—as well as Galenson's interpretive techniques—that Kay Campbell and I built on when we began our own longitudinal research with twenty families in 1980 (Massie, Bronstein, Afterman, and Campbell, 1988; Massie, Bronstein, and Afterman, 1996). Our goal was to discover if a child's developing personality was connected with the specific pattern of gazes, vocalizations, touches, physical closeness, and affect that he or she established with its mother in infancy. These bonding behaviors lead to the psychological attachment that develops between a parent and child; they are in essence the behavioral building blocks of emotional attachment. Our work in this area put us conceptually in the center of the then exploding field of research on attachment, which the British psychoanalyst John Bowlby (Bowlby, 1969, 1973, 1980) had brought to the fore with his encyclopedic chronicling of the essential need all human infants have for a secure connection to a primary caregiver, and the emotional disasters that can occur when there is none or when security is lost.

Teaming Up With Sylvia Brody

A fall evening in 1987 was the moment that I actually met Sylvia Brody in the flesh for the first time. By then I was on the faculty of the University of California School of Medicine and directing the child psychiatry training program at St. Mary's Hospital in San Francisco. The children whose development I was following were eight years old, and Dr. Brody had come to the San Francisco Psychoanalytic Institute to present the just completed analysis of the 18 year followup of the children who had appeared in her original films. When I had seen the announcement for her lecture, I had no idea she was still in contact with the children, but of course it brought back vivid memories from my training years earlier, especially the image of the mother jerking her baby's head into position to receive the feeding spoon, and my feeling that if I knew how the children on film had grown up I would have important answers about the roots of psychiatric illness.

For me Sylvia Brody's presentation was an electric experience. In person she was small and incisive, her trim appearance still much the same as on the films from years ago, though now 76 years old. She showed a relatively new teaching film from her research that I had not seen, *Six Weeks to Six Years: Individual Differences in the Growth of Competence*, which featured scenes from the life of six children. The baby whose face had haunted me was one of the six. The same scene flashed across the screen with the baby wincing and grimacing when her mother twisted her head, and then we saw the girl, whom I will now call Vicki, at six years arranging a toy schoolhouse with her mother. She was wearing a print dress and had large, dark, worried eyes. She moved the doll figures tentatively, looking questioningly at her mother. However her mother was stony faced, just as in Vicki's infancy. The mother was dressed like a mod Soho fashion plate in a miniskirt, military beret, and dark glasses. She reached out her arm and moved a piece of furniture in response to her daughter's supplicating looks, but exchanged no words with her. The child wasn't able to sit at the toy table any longer; she grabbed her crotch and said she had to go to the bathroom. The anxious, fitful, joyless play came to an end.

Syvia now told us what the children were like at the end of high school. I made notes on all of them though my attention was focused on Vicki, my touchstone to the past and the most obviously maltreated child whose life raised the possibility of demonstrating direct connections between trauma and outcome. When Vicki was 18 she had not wanted to meet with Dr. Brody, and her parents bribed her to go because they wanted to help with her tyrannical rages at home. At first she had been sullen and tense with Dr. Brody but gradually warmed up. Quite intelligent, her grades in high school had been good, but the only thing that had really interested her was her German shepherd which she groomed and trained for presentation at dog shows. "We are like two minds in control together," Vicki had said about her pet, "It gives me confidence." She was afraid of coming into New York City from Long Island, afraid of the dark, and afraid of the night if nobody was at home. If it stormed and she was alone, she would take a bottle of bourbon from her parents' liquor cabinet and lock herself in her car and drink until she felt calm and fell asleep. In spite of her grim feelings, she did have a few friends and planned to go to college.

* * *

Later at dinner Dr. Brody had a hard time catching her breath and seemed frail, though her eyes glinted with excitement talking about "my children," as she referred to the research subjects. Because of her trouble breathing I thought she had a serious illness. My wife, Bridget Connelly, who teaches cultural identity formation at the University of California in Berkeley, was with us that evening. She pointed out how her work involves studying the wanderings of groups of migrants across continents while Sylvia Brody's and my research is a study of the internal migrations of the psyche across different stages of life. In private she asked me if Sylvia had anybody to take over her research when she couldn't continue. The next day I called Dr. Brody and offered to interview the participants when they turned 30 in 1994. Dr. Brody accepted, and she and I began a close collaboration that continues to this day.

Sylvia Brody and the Roots of the Birth to Age 30 Study

During our collaboration I gradually learned about Sylvia Brody's personal life, an odyssey in itself. Born in 1914, she had grown up in New York City, the youngest in her family of seven children. Her parents were Polish Jewish immigrants, her father a cutter of men's suits in the garment district who left home at 7 am and often didn't return before 11 pm; her mother's unending work was shopping, cooking, mending, and supervising the children.

Dr. Brody talked about her childhood when she was honored by the American Psychological Association in 1991 for her "distinguished scientific contribution to psychoanalytic knowledge." When she was small she said that she had felt left out of the excitement of her older brothers' and sisters' lives, and watched them carefully to see how it would be to be grown up; she also studied how they fought with her parents when they were adolescents, and decided there were better ways to be a teenager and a parent. Strikingly, she described sitting at the window in her family's basement apartment when she was too young to go outside by herself, looking at the children on the sidewalk. The steel grates over the window seemed to turn the children's play into fascinating, flashing movie frames, a visual forerunner of the movies she herself made years later to study play.

Brody graduated from high school during the Great Depression of the 1930s. She was too poor to go to college so she started working as an assistant in an elementary school in return for meals and the promise of pay for her teaching later if money became available. Ultimately the richness of the school was not measured in money but in the evening lectures it sponsored for the community by visiting speakers on the then avant-garde field of psychoanalysis. She learned that of all the psychological disciplines, psychoanalytic theory was the most rooted in understanding the child's experiences with its mother and father to explain subsequent psychological structuralization, character formation, and psychiatric symptomatology. Thus the lectures the young Sylvia Brody heard at this time gave her the intellectual framework to which she could couple her wide-eyed curiosity about children. After 16 years of assisting at the school, caring for her elderly parents, and going part-time to night school, Sylvia Brody finally had her college degree. With the help of scholarships she then embarked on obtaining her doctorate in psychology from New York University.

An internship took her to the Menninger Clinic in Topeka, Kansas, which was a flagship for training in child development and psychoanalysis in the 1950s. She returned to New York City, quadruply armed with her Ph.D., her psychoanalytic training, the manuscript of her first book, *Patterns of Mothering* (Brody, 1956), and her husband Sidney Axelrad, whom she had started dating before leaving for Kansas. In childhood, Sylvia Brody told herself she must marry an educated man who wouldn't have to work long hours for meager pay like her father; Axelrad answered this wish with his expertise in sociology and research design, and became her principal research collaborator. Ironically her geographic journey from metropolis to Midwestern cornfields in pursuit of education was the reverse of my own.

Patterns of Mothering was based on Brody's doctoral research at the Menninger Clinic, which was strongly influenced by the presence there of Sybille Escalona (Escalona and Leitch, 1952), a Menninger psychoanalyst noted for careful description of infant behavior. Sylvia Brody enlarged the field of infant examination by carefully studying the behavior of 32 mothers and infants in the first half year of life. She recognized that the way mothers and babies interact during feeding is a key to understanding their relationship. Studying feeding led her to create the now classic grouping of mothers according to their degree of empathy, control, and ability to organize their infant's feeding. "I began work on the surface with direct observations of behavior and found my way into problems of psychic conflict," she wrote. Her main contribution to theory was the description of how the mother deals successively with the child's three erotogenic zones—oral, anal, and genital—in the first years of life. The way very young children's oral, anal and genital behavior stimulates the mother (irritates, satisfies, or excites her) reflects the mother's own relative mastery and comfort in these areas. Thus the mother and youngster are tightly bound together in a psychological-behavioral process as the years pass. Mother and child gradually separate, physically and emotionally, but never completely because each has had the other for a psychological template.

Brody's special contribution to methodology was the microscopic examination of mother-infant interaction (which many other researchers began using in the 1970s). In 1963 Brody and Axelrad assembled a small team of clinically trained assistants and began a large scale prospective longitudinal study to try to pin down the unique significance of the mother-infant relationship for emotional growth. The Grant Foundation and the National Institute of Health provided financial support, and 131 mothers expecting a child responded to a call for volunteers for "a study of infant development." The families—who received no reimbursement except travel expenses—were a cross-section of society, coming from all of New York city's socio-economic groups and many ethnicities and religions. Most had never had significant emotional symptoms nor had they received any psychiatric treatment. They had a range of motivations for responding to the notices posted in their obstetricians' offices seeking volunteers. For example, some wanted to know more about their children, some hoped for help raising their infants, and others were curious about participating in a scientific endeavor. Brody and Axelrad were initially uncertain how long they would be able to follow their participants because of the unpredictabilty of funding, yet the project continues to this day, under my direction since 1992. The movie which so riveted me in my first year of training in 1968 introduced me to the babies whose adult lives I would study a quarter century later.

* * *

Brody and Axelrad's study was unprecedented, the first project to document a child's first seven years so completely. And only one project that has reported its results has done so since—the Minnesota Child Development Study directed by Alan Sroufe (Sroufe,1997; Sroufe, Carlson, and Shulman, 1993), which began in 1979 and focuses more on measurable behaviors such as the child's reactions to separations from its mother in set situations and school performance, and less on the emotional relationship of parents and children. In addition to filming the mother and infant during feeding, the Brody and Axelrad group filmed the mother playing with her growing child, and registered the child's neurological maturity at birth and cognitive growth almost yearly. The researchers also interviewed the mother several times during her child's first year of life, then periodically afterward chiefly to determine the parent's background, her trials and worries with her baby, her internal conflicts, her knowledge, beliefs and practices with her child, and her pleasure in raising her child.

To this the study added psychological testing and observation of the children, school visits, teacher interviews, and occasional home visits. Thus as the years passed the researchers documented how the children were establishing their particular panoply of defense mechanisms, their prevailing moods, their personal strengths, their conflicts and anxieties, and their relationships with their siblings, parents and schoolmates.

Fathers joined the project when the children were four years old. They were interviewed in-depth at that time, yearly afterward until the child was seven, and occasionally but not uniformly observed interacting with their children. Were we to design a longitudinal study today, we would bring the fathers into the project as systematic participants with interviews and observations at a child's birth, however when Brody and Axelrad conceived the study in the very early 1960s, most fathers had a relatively peripheral role in infant care. Contemporary families incorporate fathers increasingly into baby care, but the prevailing pattern is still for mothers to attend for the most part to the needs of infants. By four years of age the children were well into the process of psychologically individuating from their mothers, and by then the fathers had typically established their own unique relationships with their youngsters, drawing the eager children out of the dyadic bond with their mothers.

In addition to the project's pioneering methodology of observing parent-child interactions, Sigmund Freud's ideas have been central to the correlation of the interactions with insight into the family members' emotional life. Especially important has been his recognition of how fathers help children move psychologically into the larger orbit of the triadic mother-child-father configuration. Freud understood how this triangular relationship has a tremendous formative influence on development. It reaches the height of its psychic intensity for the youngster at about four and five years, leading Freud (S. Freud, 1900; Herzog, 2001) to call this age the oedipal phase after the tragic Greek figure who murdered his father and became sexually involved with his mother. The passions of the mother-father-child triangle have a unique effect on the emotional life of the human species, and color a child's fantasy life and all future relationships, in his or her ever widening orbits that include siblings, school, and community.

Freud's (S. Freud, 1922; S. Freud, 1915, 1940) two other over-arching contributions to the twentieth century understanding of the human psyche—his elucidation of defense mechanisms ("the techniques the ego uses to protect itself from anxiety arising from within or from threats from outside of itself," which generally smoothly facilitate healthy adaptation but sometimes disturb adaptation), and his description of a restless unconscious life that is dynamically inter-connected with conscious life ("the dynamic unconscious")—have also been central to understanding the development of the children in the project.

When the children were seven years old, the researchers said goodbye to the families, for the most part, until they were 18 years old. Occasionally some parents called in proudly when a child excelled, or sought advice when they were worried about a child. Three books have presented the project's findings to 18 years—on infancy (*Anxiety and Ego Formation in Infancy*, Brody and Axelrad, 1970), through seven years (*Mothers, Fathers, and Children*, Brody and Axelrad, 1978), and through adolescence (*The Evolution of Character*, Brody and Siegel, 1992). Each stage found that the adequacy of mothering in the first year of life had a continuing influence on many aspects of psychological growth. At one year the children of more effective mothers had significantly more advanced cognitive and motor development than children of less effective mothers, more positive moods and affects, more investment in their worlds, spontaneity, responsiveness, curiosity and frustration tolerance, and less anxiety and tension. At seven years children of more favorable mothers showed more favorable self-esteem, relationships and reality testing, and fewer anxieties and pathological defenses. Similarly at 18, the more enhanced course for children of more effective mothers continued: they had better views of themselves and their parents, more advanced psychosexual maturity, characterologic qualities reflective of more favorable superego development, better relationships and control of anxiety, less psychopathology, and more mature defenses and career aspirations than children of the less effective mothers.

The 30-Year Followup

A year after our meeting, Dr. Brody sent letters to all of the research participants she had interviewed at 18 alerting them that I would be contacting them for a followup when they turned 30. She had been able to find 91 of the original 131 at 18 years of age; and we located 81 of these 91 participants for the 30 year followup, most through their parents and some through a firm that traces missing people. The subjects were spreading across the United States like widening circles in a pond riffled by a pebble since their births at Lenox Hill Hospital in Midtown Manhattan between 1963 and 1965. Roughly one-third of the participants remained in New York City, one-third had moved to the New York suburbs, a sixth were on the Eastern Seaboard, slightly less in California, and the rest were sprinkled in communities across America. All but four of the 81 we located agreed to participate in the 30-year followup, though one of the 81 who agreed moved to Europe before we could meet with her and we lost contact, so that the total group we studied at age 30 numbered 76. The four who declined said that they were too busy or reluctant to talk about themselves at this time in their lives.

The California Wellness Foundation generously funded the followup, and a grant from the Research Advisory Board of the International Psychoanalytic Association and from the Emmanuel Windholz Fund of the San Francisco Psychoanalytic Institute supported the analysis of the data from the past and present. The San Francisco Bay Area psychologist Carl Norris joined the project to interview half of the participants, and when we met them in 1994, we purposely had no knowledge about their past so that we could approach them without preconceptions. This was similar to the contacts Dr. Brody's team had had with them earlier. Psychologists who tested the children did not know what impressions the parents and children had made on other interviewers and vice versa. I personally interviewed the California residents and most of those still living in New York City. Somewhat to my surprise most people were eager to talk about their lives, generously sharing their experiences, often using the opportunity to think about problems or uncertainties in their life. A handful asked for assistance in finding a therapist. Their dim but fond recollections of Dr. Brody eased the way, they said, as did a desire to finish something their parents had started. Only one, a woman, said she had been frightened about coming to a stranger's office. Most also were pleased to be able to contribute to a research study of development, as their parents had been before them.

Carl Norris interviewed most of the other participants in a back and forth odyssey across the United States. In a rough Philadelphia neighborhood his car was rocked by a gang of youths; in Florida his air conditioner stopped working, and when he opened the windows of his car for air his research notebook flew out across a freeway. He risked his life to retrieve it by running across six lanes of highway. Then in Arizona a flash flood stranded him in the Sonora desert. He nevertheless returned beaming from his trip, feeling that he had learned more about people and America from what he saw and heard than any classroom or book could teach.

The followup meetings lasted three to four hours. We audiotaped and videotaped them with a small camera that caused little or no self-consciousness for most of the people. For the first part of the interview we used the Adult Attachment Interview (George, Kaplan, and Main, 1985) developed by Mary Main and her colleagues in the psychology department at the University of California in Berkeley. This interview explores with the participants their memories of experiences which made them feel secure or threatened in early childhood, and conveys a picture of their *mental representation as adults* of the nature and security of their attachment to their parents as children. This is a research extension of the actual visualization of childhood attachment made by John Bowlby and Mary Ainsworth (Ainsworth, Blehar, Waters, and Wall, 1978) who were Mary Main's teachers.

The second part of our followup asked the participants about their lives since high school—education, work, and personal relationships. Then we discussed their anxieties, conflicts, and psychiatric symptoms, if any. Finally we ended with a question about their very first memories in life, recurring dreams or nightmares from childhood and adulthood; we asked about their ambitions for their future; and let the participants talk about their concerns for society. Along the way the interviewees digressed to talk about topics and thought associations that seemed compelling.

Fifty-three (70%) of the 76 participants were in stable relationships at age 30, but only 12 (16%), seven women and two men, had children of their own (an additional man and woman were expecting a child's birth)—a small number of children which is entirely in keeping with the shift upward in the age of marriage and childbearing in the United States since their parents' generation. We ended interviews with the 12 parents by videotaping them feeding or playing with their own children just as Dr. Brody had filmed them and their parents. This allowed us to compare parent-child interaction from one generation to the next. Then we left our interviewees with take-home psychological tests, which gave us further insight into their emotional functioning.

When all the interviews were completed, I had the good fortune to have Nathan Szajnberg join me as my principal collaborator in analyzing and synthesizing the findings from the 30 year span of data. He had already assisted in designing the followup interview from his position as medical director of psychiatry at the Children's Hospital of Wisconsin, and now relocated as a clinical professor of psychiatry to the University of California School of Medicine, San Francisco. A psychoanalyst and child psychiatrist, Dr. Szajnberg is also an experienced researcher in the areas of infant psychiatry and psychophysiological disorders of children and teenagers. He organized the diagnostic assessments and the outcome ratings of the 76 interviews, and helped conceptualize the statistical procedures. When it came to synthesizing the overall data, we debated the lessons of each participant's life constantly, each the other's sharpest critic, until 76 individual biographies of manifest family history and unconscious processes took shape—culled from approximately 350 pages of data plus archival research films on each participant. Then we turned to conceptualizing the lessons of the group data.

Of the 350 pages of data and history on each person, about two thirds consist of Sylvia Brody's group's documentation of the first seven years of life, the other third coming from her 18 year followup and our 30 year followup. Beyond this are the hours of film that exist for each person, some in our laboratory in Berkeley, and most in the Archives of the History of American Psychology at the University of Akron, Ohio. The task of pulling together the information from each life and analyzing findings from the whole group of 76 has taken six years since 1994. The job has been as rewarding as it has been daunting. Like a mine that has been worked for many years, most of the ore has now been extracted, we feel, though there is always the possibility of a new strike as we continue to examine the data and life stories.

To describe what we have learned, in this book we will let the participants lives speak for themselves as much as possible. We have taken care to protect the participants' anonymity by changing specific details of their lives that might identify them. For the most part we eschew discussions of theory and have saved details of methodology and statistics for the Appendix. The first chapter presents children whose parents Drs. Brody and Axelrad found among the very best, whose childhoods were mostly happy, and who at age 30 were contented and successful. They refute Tolstoy's (1875) dictum that "Happy families are all alike," nor do they show "the deeper design . . . of human misery," which T.S. Eliot (1936) thought was concealed in normal lives. But they do show common themes.

Chapters two and three discuss children with unhappy childhoods who dealt with unhappiness in two different ways. Children in chapter two externalized their distress as youngsters, mostly in the form of hyperactive and oppositional behavior, and we follow them into adulthood. Children in chapter three internalized childhood unhappiness, most in the form of depressions and anxiety. The distinction between internalization and externalization of distress is not always pure nor of fundamental importance in and of itself, but it provides a scaffolding for presenting the lives of the participants and understanding developmental processes. Alternatively we could group participants on the basis of their adult outcome and psychiatric diagnoses, if any, and work backwards into their early years. However because of our child psychiatry backgrounds and daily work with children, we chose to focus first on the earliest signs of disturbance in people's lives. Seeing the early signs clearly, and understanding their roots and implications for later growth, sets the stage for helping new generations of families.

Chapter four examines the lives of participants who were not doing as well as foreseen in view of their favorable parenting when they were infants, and chapter five looks at the children who have defied expectations and were doing much better at 30 than predicted at the end of their first year of life on the basis of adverse parenting. These two chapters ask what are the factors in their lives that participants to grow up in ways that are contrary to what was anticipated based on their experiences in their first seven years. Chapter six, Family Counts, synthesizes all that we have learned from the study, and discusses its implications for child rearing, for theories of psychopathology, and for treatment of emotional disturbance. An Appendix—Methods and Measurements—summarizes the research methodology and statistical analysis of the relationship between measures of the quality of mothering the children received in infancy, childhood traumatic experiences, and assessments of adult outcome in terms of emotional health and symptomatology for the 76 participants.

* * *

Throughout this introduction, I have outlined the many influences that underlie the understanding of the lives in this book. Some of them have been personal teachers, and others are such grand clinician theorists of the twentieth century as Sigmund Freud and Anna Freud (1936, 1965), who elucidated the intrapsychic functioning of children as her father did for adults; Erik Erikson, who defied his psychoanalyst Anna Freud by broadening the field into a psychosocial perspective that looks at how individual emotional stages relate to societal tasks; and John Bowlby, who righted the drift of psychoanalysis toward too great emphasis on internal mental structure and fantasy back to a recognition of how emotional life is founded on the actual security of an infant's attachment to its mother, and the fantasies and fears that grow from this bedrock.

Others not previously mentioned have also been very influential, such as Margaret Mahler (1975), who described how a child psychologically separates and individuates from its mother in the first two years of life through moving from mental symbiosis with the mother to the establishment of its self-representation distinct from its representation of its mother; Donald Winnicott (1962), the British pediatrician and psychoanalyst of the mid-century, who attempted to portray how infants feel in inimical versus safe families; and George Vaillant (1977), a psychiatrist who described the evolution of defense mechanisms in 268 men from their youth in the late 1930s to middle-age with an imaginative, demanding longitudinal study.

Through all of my involvement with the Brody study, thinking of my own life and family has enhanced my appreciation of the research participants' travails and accomplishments; and I am grateful to the subjects in turn for having increased my awareness of my own experiences and for their unselfish, committed assistance in providing a fuller understanding of emotional growth in general.

Sylvia Brody is now in her 80s. Her husband Sidney Axelrad tragically died without warning from a heart attack in 1976, in the midst of his work and writing. He and Sylvia Brody never had children of her own. "They never came," she told me not long ago, "But then I have 131 children," she added with a twinkle in her eye. She knows just about everything about the early life of the children in the project—their favorite foods, their battles with their parents, their toilet training, their school adjustment, their problems and triumphs—and cares deeply about them as individuals, in addition to what their lives have taught the rest of us as time has gone by.

What had seemed like a serious illness the night I first met her was a benign asthma attack brought on by the night fog sweeping in over the Golden Gate Bridge. Since we first met, the American Psychological Association and the American Psychoanalytic Association have honored her for her contribution to the field of child development, and most recently with the establishment in 2001 by the American Psychoanalytic Association of the Sylvia Brody Award for the study of infant psychology. And nowadays in the course of reviewing the data, whenever I have a question about one of "her children," I pick up the phone and call her in

New York where she has been at work on the just published book *The Development of Anorexia—the Hunger Artists* (Brody, 2002), based on the cases of children from the study who suffered from anorexia as children or adolescents. She remembers each of the participants and provides invaluable details about their lives.

Envoi

There was one 30-year interview I saved for the end of my stay in New York when I would be most experienced. That was the interview of Vicki, the woman whose image of being force fed in infancy had so burned itself into my mind in 1968, and set me on the course that allowed me to finally meet her. I felt a chill when she came into the office. She walked cautiously, still thin, and with eyes that were worried, though less so than in her childhood films. She had just come from her work as the office manager of a dog and cat hospital on the Upper West Side, and was wearing jeans, a white blouse and a Navy pea jacket. Her calm, careful, soft voice belied an inner tension, for she was one of the very few participants who couldn't look at the camera, as if it was something that might bite her. So she sat sideways to the camera but face to face with me.

"My parents never should have had children," she said. "It was a great mistake. They had the mistaken notion that they could have us and then they wouldn't have to do anything, that we would just grow up while they ran their business." Vicki had stopped fighting with her parents when she went to college and has little contact with them now. Her drinking has also stopped and she likes her work, though she wishes she had the energy to continue in school and become a veterinarian. Her sister, three years younger, has recently been hospitalized with a nervous breakdown, and the doctors have told Vicki that her sister is suffering from schizophrenia or manic-depressive disease. Vicki thinks that her own life has been saved by a special relationship with her aunt who lived with the family for several years after a divorce. As a child when she felt very bad, Vicki would go to her aunt's room, get in her bed, draw the blankets over herself, and watch television for hours on end. She even married a boy to whom her aunt had introduced her in her early 20s, but it didn't work out and they separated. Nowadays Vicki suffers from migraine headaches, a poor appetite, and periods of severe anxiety. She is just starting to date again and hopes that she will meet someone with whom she can make a life.

She is an impressive woman—gentle, competent, articulate, psychologically minded, and remarkably frank and clear headed about what she has been through in her family. Her ability to see the reality of her childhood and not mince words about it is also something that has saved her. As you will see from the lives of other participants who had difficult childhoods, those who can't or will not remember what they have been through seem not to have not done as well as Vicki. When she left, I felt okay about her. In spite of the toll her traumatic childhood has taken on her, she is a person of quiet spirit, perceptiveness and hope. I don't think that she will become a casualty of her circumstances.

Vicki's life in many ways is emblematic of what can be learned from following lives across time, whether it be reflecting on ourselves, people we have known, or participants in the research study. On the one hand, it reaffirms what we intuitively grasp or have learned about how we are profoundly shaped by relationships in our families. On the other hand, it shows that there are many surprises in the way emotional growth unfolds. Trauma and early parent-child interactions are buried in our personalities. Trauma can smolder like a fire that only appears to be extinguished, and then bursts into flames again in symptoms that we can't anticipate. Lives can also take turns that appear to defy logic, but when we have enough information about them to examine them closely they show a deeper logic.

Chapter 1

SUCCESSES

Family exists only because somebody has a story, and knowing that story connects us to a history.

Fae Myenne Ng, Bone

IN 1963 WHEN Sylvia Brody and Sidney Axelrad began the Evolution of Character study, they asked the parents in the project what they most wanted for their newborns. Most simply wished for them to be happy and successful people. In 1994 we asked these same children, now adults, what would give them the greatest future happiness in the world, and they almost always said it would be raising a family with contented, confident and competent children. Thus in spite of the passage of a generation—a period that has seen many men become more involved in the lives of their children and many women more invested in what were formerly male quests for achievement outside of the family—the central wish remains the well-being of their offspring. Yet as with treks of old, the question remains how do you get there from here.

Raising children is still one of life's fundamental journeys. The dilemmas of how mothers and fathers should act with their children, so that their wishes for them become a reality, bedevil even the hardiest parents. The profusion of advice, research, and books about such questions as how much gratification and how much discipline to give a child, and how much difference it makes anyway, signifies our culture's preoccupation with doing the best by our youngsters. As child psychiatrists know, parents worry a great deal about raising their children because they seek help even when their children have no symptoms. They frequently come for consultations simply because they are anxious about how they and their children are doing in a chaotic society with more stimulation and less structure and authority than in the past.

This chapter describes three men and four women who, as adults, are living very fulfilling lives. Their experiences show what parents can do to launch their children into such lives. Selected from the entire group of 76, these seven people formed the subgroup who had mothers and fathers who were among the very best in early childhood—empathic, involved, thoughtful, organized, affectionate and responsive to their children—and who now 30 years later are among the group of grown children who are doing the very best in life. By this we do not mean that they are famous or wealthy, rather they have achieved several very important things that are basic to a good life. They are personable; delightful to be with; do not presently experience emotional distress (although two benefited from past psychotherapy); successful in their work; concerned with the lives of others; and are happily married. We will let their lives speak for themselves and listen to the actual words of the parents and children. We believe they show something essential about the paths to follow in raising children well. Still, no parent is perfect and no life is without rough times. They show us how they navigated through their problems and how difficulties also shaped them as people.

For this chapter we could have chosen several other exemplary people who are not currently married or in a partnership, and whose parents also had been excellent. However each one felt that something was missing in his or her life and was looking for a relationship, and we wanted this to be a discussion about people who were content with their lives. Additionally, some children with inauspicious infancy parenting are now doing very well as adults, and others whose early parenting was favorable have not done well. Their lives are the subjects of chapters 4 and 5. Here we follow the course of life of the seven whose early parenting was auspicious and who have lived up to their promise.

Nicholas

We asked Nick when he was 30 years old to describe his relationship with his mother and father when he was a young child growing up. A well built, red-headed man, he leaned back comfortably in his chair and loosened his tie, having just come from his work as an economics professor. Then he spoke clearly and firmly, eager to teach from his own experience and to learn about himself from participating as well.

"I think my parents and I were very close. I didn't really think about it much, I took it for granted. I spent more time with my mother although my father did a lot with me, reading stories to me, making up stories at night, doing little puzzles with me. It wasn't as if there was a set time, it just happened spontaneously. I don't recall hiding a lot of things from them but I didn't always tell them everything. I had a sort of perfectionist streak then, still do, so if there were things I wasn't too proud of, those were the things I set aside. But for the most part we did a lot together."

In his opening comments, Nick established three things that mean a lot to him: First his closeness to both parents; second, his excitement in sharing intellectually oriented activities with his father; and third, his independence from his parents. We asked Nick to go further and give us specific adjectives to describe each parent and memories of events that would illustrate the adjectives. After a few moments of thought he responded.

"My mother was loving, protective, happy and energetic. One of the earliest memories that I have is going to the square near where we used to live. It was fun because of the slide and sandbox and other kids, but this day I lost sight of my mother and panicked. I must have been about three. I wandered around for a little while looking for her, getting more and more scared, and then all of a sudden I saw her and had this tremendous sense of relief. And then she picked me up and hugged me and the whole thing was over. There was also the time from about the same age when we were driving and there was one of those real dramatic hail storms. It was an unusual event, like being in the inside of a drum. I don't recall my mother's reactions but I do remember a very strong sense of her presence and that made it all right. I also recall the excitement of big family dinners like Thanksgiving with everybody coming and how happy I was when I could first help out and set the table, do the dinner together with my parents and older brother. I mean I was just tall enough to reach the table so I was obviously doing something trivial, but the feeling of being appreciated for what I was doing was so good that it sticks with me."

We asked Nick in what way he recalled his mother as energetic and happy and he continued with his memory of family gatherings, "Well, she's not shy but it's not that she wants to be the center of attention. She just comes into a room full of people and she'll get excited, and suggest something to do or talk about and her enthusiasm has a contagious effect. That also made me want to please her because I admired her. I remember another event that had a profound effect on me from about seven or eight. Some kid had hurt me on the playground and I was trying to do the same thing to my little brother, you know, take out my anger on him, and my mother came up and took me aside and told me that that was not the right way to behave. She didn't yell at me or hit me. She didn't even embarrass me because she did it discreetly, but I felt a profound sense of disappointment that I had let her down."

Nick then elaborated on his memories of his father in early childhood, "He used to get into bed with me sometimes to put me to sleep and he would tell me a story, or we would make up a story together, something fantastical. It probably happened until I was about five or six. I looked forward to the story game; it was so exciting, and my father is really a very soft spoken person so it was not our usual way of playing together. For example, he was not at all a sports fan but he knew I was, and every year for my birthday we used to go see the Yankees play. It was terrific, like we were a team doing something together. Like that, he took an interest in me and my development. He'd inherited a truck engine rebuilding business from his father and knew about all sorts of things like the history of manufacturing in America, the labor movement, economics. So in high school he'd help me with my history papers and give me more advanced questions to think about than the teachers did. Again it was the sense that we were doing things together."

"My father was very slow to anger. In fact I'm not sure if he has ever really been angry at me, but I know there were times that he would express disapproval or speak sternly to me. Once I must have gotten a really bad grade on a test where it was assumed that I would do okay, and I was sort of dreading showing him the paper, not because I expected him to yell but I expected him to be disappointed. Instead he just said, 'Okay, well you'll do better next time. Let's see what you did wrong.' There's another fuzzy memory I have. I was supposed to go to the playground and meet a friend but I had broken a toy or I was doing something I wasn't supposed to do, and my father said, 'Well you know you can't go out now,' and I was crushed, I had been looking forward to it so much. I don't recall the whole process of what happened then, but I do recall that my father and I ended up at the playground and I had to make up in some way for what I had done wrong because he didn't just want to let me off the hook. I remember having a terrific time and thinking what a great dad I have to let me go after all."

* * *

Much that is important in the shaping of a child appears in these memories. The infectiousness of a mother's happy spirit comes through strongly; the infectiousness of the father's delight in thinking about things with his son in their turn-taking, make-up-a-bedtime-story game, and in sharing how his engine rebuilding work fit into American history. Nick's memories also convey the parents' sense of authority and their judicious discipline with compassion. The parents' interest in, and affection for their child; their protection of him; their participation in their child's life (via their empathy for his emotional life, and the actual activities they shared with him) all come through strongly. The parents modeled competency for Nick in their own lives and expected him to do well. In turn Nick's admiration for them made him want to please them by doing well.

How accurate are Nick's recollections? In fact, we found that most of the participants in the study had fairly realistic memories of their childhoods at 30 years of age, ironically far better than they had at 18. This is likely because at 18 they had an inordinate need to disengage themselves from their parents as part of the normal process of growing up, and so also disengaged themselves from remembering. Memories at 30 were nuanced, multidimensional, and reflective for the most part; at 18 they tended to be cartoon-like in their unidimensionality and to bring forth conventional aspects of family experience.

Let's turn now to the actual record of the beginning of Nick's life and see how it meshes with his recollections. Nick was born after an uncomplicated pregnancy and delivery, and in the earliest interviews the researchers had with his mother in the days and weeks after his birth they noted her thoughtfulness, calmness, confidence with the baby, and her attentiveness to him. The mother had worked as a schoolteacher before the birth of Nick's older sister and envisioned returning to teaching after the family was completed and the children were all in grammar school. Both parents were somewhat reserved and both firmly valued education. They had known each other in high school, and then became reacquainted and started dating in college. Their affection for each other was evident.

As the weeks and months went on in Nick's first year, his mother was proud, gentle, sweet and playful with her child. She breast fed him for several months then switched to a bottle and solid foods. The father helped out when the mother asked him, and played actively with his son. But the mother was the most involved in Nick's care and later in his discipline. As an infant Nick was lumpy and chubby—not the most physically appealing baby—however he was very alert and happy, and ate voraciously, chuckling all the while. He loved to look intently at his mother and visitors with his big green eyes. He was a vital, persistent boy and his developmental testing was always above normal. By the end of his first year and into his second he was so energetic and curious that he often jumped quickly from one activity or toy to another. In her feedback to the mother when Nick was one year old, Sylvia Brody urged her to help her son delay more and lengthen his span of attention, even if it meant frustrating him at times. Nick's mother listened carefully and agreed. She feared that it would be hard to not give in quickly to her son's forceful requests because it might make the happy boy moody or angry, but she agreed that it would be a worthwhile challenge. Many years later Nick's mother gratefully recalled making use of this advice, and credited it with helping her son develop the capacity to endure frustrations and set difficult goals for himself.

Almost all of the families in the study had crises which threatened their physical and emotional well-being, and Nick's was no exception. Toward the end of the first year during a routine well-baby medical checkup, the pediatrician discovered a kidney abnormality. Specialists advocated following his condition with yearly urinalyses and X-rays, saying that he might require surgery as he grew older, even raising the remote possibility of a permanent handicap. When Nick's mother told her interviewer the news, she cried. The parents tried to shield their son from their anxiety and from knowing that his checkups were anything but routine. In fact he was a fully active little boy, making them proud of his physicality which grew apace with his size. They even admired the temper tantrums he sometimes threw when he was very tired or hungry. His mother liked to soothe him by kissing and blowing on his neck. He gurgled happily, and she sighed languorously.

Nonetheless the parents' efforts to protect their boy from knowledge and anxiety about his kidney condition were unsuccessful. He responded to their fears unconsciously, and once when he was in first grade he complained of pain in his side at school and insisted that his mother bring him home. He had trouble returning to school for several days. It turned out that Nick was having an anxiety attack for there was no physical basis for the pain. The doctor determined that his kidney condition had not progressed, and in fact invasive tests such as catheterization or biopsies never became necessary. By the time Nick reached adolescence his physicians decided that the abnormalities on Nick's urinalyses represented a harmless anomaly that occurs in a small percentage of the population and would not affect his health.

In spite of the parents' caution, Nick had internalized their profound apprehension which their best efforts couldn't conceal. The anxiety had broken through Nick's own defenses leading him to feel pain and fear going to school for several days. Even careful parents can't hide their feelings when they are strongly buffeted by an illness, marital problems, or frightening events in the community. Anxiety infects children and resonates within them—even though they may say nothing about it—often establishing itself as an emotional current in a child's personality and unconscious. Thus when Nick visited the project when he was six years old (months before his pain and anxiety attack), he played out a story in which a child became sick and was taken to a "crazy school nurse" who gave the child an overdose of medicine, making the child worse. At this point in his play, Nick paused and went to the bathroom (the interruption coming probably because the story line of his play was making him anxious, as well as because he must have realized that his parents' fears were connected with urination). On his return he said he had flushed the school medicine down the drain so the crazy nurse couldn't get hold of it anymore, dramatizing his wish to be rid of his yearly visits to the kidney specialist.

When he was 18 years old he reported that he was in fine health though he did recall that he had been told of a concern with his kidney when he was small. Significantly, his psychological tests showed that he was struggling with unspoken worries about whether his body was intact, which impaired his self-confidence even though his accomplishments in high school were superb. Nick was most comfortable in the world of ideas; for athletics he had picked a non-contact sport, swimming. The theme of underlying worry about his body continued in adulthood. In his human figure drawing on the House-Tree-Person test (Buck, 1966) at age 30, he pictured himself with a full-bodied upper torso, and eyes looking downward to where the lower half of his body should have been but was omitted from his drawing, suggesting that he was worried or embarrassed about his physical adequacy.

Chapter 1, Figure 1.1.

Nick's Draw-A-Person, Age 30

Nicholas' concern about his body is like a leitmotif playing in the background of a richly orchestrated composition. It may in fact have bolstered his dedication to intellectual pursuits, and contributed to his becoming an active supporter of causes on behalf of people facing handicaps and prejudice in life.

* * *

Even though he had an anxiety attack at seven, Nick was not at all a timid school boy. In his first foray into school—actually pre-kindergarten—he found himself in a class with a harsh and critical teacher. After a few days Nick put his foot down and said, "I won't go back there unless the teacher is dead." His parents found a second school and Nick was enchanted. "My new teacher is so nice. She must be a mommy," he reported, charmingly equating goodness with his mother. Nick's tender devotion to his teddy bear also showed his affection for his parents, "Teddy's mine the way I'm yours," he told them. As for his self-love, he trumpeted it at four, "I'm the strongest. See how handsome I are." Later at 18 and 30, he spoke of having to be cautious to not be too impressed with the successes he had had, "As a kid and teen I was somewhat self-centered. I try to guard against that."

In school Nick was a leader among other children, and not averse to standing up for himself even to the point of hitting another boy with a plastic baseball bat. He sometimes played "like a wild Indian." Twice he "ran away" from home after he had been disciplined for being too rough with his brother and sister, and hid in the backyard for 30 minutes. Overall he was happy, cooperative, witty, original, diligent, and advanced in his schoolwork. Sometimes when he was pressing himself to succeed as a youngster he blinked his eyes involuntarily. He still showed this mannerism as an adult. In spite of this tic, a member of the research team wrote when Nick was seven, "I am hard pressed to find signs of conflict in Nick. He is one of the most relaxed children I have tested to date." His IQ at this age was an extremely gifted 136.

Nick's parents truly appreciated him and said when he was in grammar school, "We didn't spoil what was there," a richly profound stance and a gift for parents to offer a child. As we shall see in troubled families in the next chapter, it is far too easy for parents to project their own needs and shortcomings on to a child. Parents who see their child through the prism of their personal desires or feelings about themselves (for example, see a child as a genius, a "bad seed," a "cross to bear," a compensation for past hardships, or a helpmate, as the case may be) attempt to mold a child to their wishes and often end up confusing reality for themselves and their child.

Nick's parents were remarkably level-headed, valuing of decorum and humor, warm, gracious, permissive yet also firm and organized, devoted to their children and thoughtful. Recognizing their boy's intellectual potential they nonetheless decided *not* to push him beyond his age group or make special schooling arrangements for him so as not to interfere with his social development. They offered some of their views on child-rearing over the years. The father said, "The main thing parents can give a child is the feeling of being loved and secure in his own family where, regardless of how the world is, things are not arbitrary and capricious. My main strength, I think, is being able to turn the kids away from anger because I can be patient and I feel a challenge in doing this."

This was not a father who talked one way and acted another. He gave his son the care he espoused, which is no mean feat for any parent when a child tests his or her limits by being unruly as Nick certainly did at times. The mother was Nick's main disciplinarian, relying on reason and restriction when he acted up. Two or three times a year she resorted to spanking him on the bottom. Gradually she drew Nick's father into a more equal role with her in discipline, which was harder for the father because he felt he had been hit and controlled too much as a child.

Once when marveling at their boy's gregariousness with other children, Nick's parents said that he didn't seem to belong to them because they were so shy. Yet Nick was very much their child even though his parents didn't always see it. He was picking up different qualities of his parents to imitate, assimilate, and internalize, as all children do. The bits and pieces of his parents' behaviors, moods, defense mechanisms, and general style became the building blocks of his personality. When he was grown up, he spoke of how he had gotten his self-assurance and friendliness from his mother, described his admiration of her ability to walk into a room of people and generate enthusiasm; from his father he told how he had gotten his intellectual excitement and sense of justice.

Once as president of his high-school debating society, Nick had a major confrontation with the principal—actually a shouting match—over permission to use the assembly hall to debate the topic of birth control, which the principal felt was inappropriate. Nick was briefly suspended. This did not deter several colleges from offering him scholarships. On the eve of his departure for college he met with Sylvia Brody who described him as "a very unusual young man. He presents himself sturdily, directly, clearly, with pleasing dignity. He smiles easily, warmly with good humor, and is reflective and sincere. His high estimation of his parents is probably related to his own wholesome self esteem. He did not have to ponder, as many teenagers do, about values or goals, having thought them out a long time before now. There was genuine optimism in his communications. He was a pleasure to talk with."

When he went to college Nick did not stumble as many people do. Major transitions such as junior high school, entry into high school, leaving home, and graduation from college often bring out the weaknesses in a person's character while at the same time providing an opportunity for repair and growth. But Nick was solid while also open to youthful experimentation. In college he had his first relationships with women and got drunk a few times. Like 90 percent of his peers in the study he tried marijuana, and like them it never became a habit for him. He also returned home the summer of his junior year to help care for a well-loved grandfather during the final weeks of his life. Nick's major in college was engineering, but he shifted gears and went on to graduate school in economics because he found engineering too isolating and wanted to be more involved in social issues.

He has achieved this desire in an exceptional way for a young man. His graduate schoolwork was so thorough and dynamic that after he earned his doctorate he gained a highly coveted internship on the President's Council of Economic Advisors in Washington, D.C. He arrived in Washington at the time the North American Free Trade Agreement was being negotiated. He was assigned to research the positive effects of free trade on U.S. steel workers but found himself unable to do this and instead documented the negative consequences. He fought tenaciously for his findings and they were incorporated into the final agreement. After his internship he moved into academia at a university in Philadelphia and has since written a major textbook.

Is Nicholas sad about anything? Does he have any regrets? We asked him when he was 30. A wistful look crossed his face. "I'm more settled than I thought I would be at this age. My wife and I live in suburbia with a cat and dog. Not exactly what I hoped but I guess what I expected," he chuckled. Nick's fine successes at an early age and his agreeableness have been possible because of his tendency to conform, without sacrificing the ability to think and act independently. He acknowledges his conformity and wonders what he may be missing in life because in general he has followed his parents' and teachers', as well as society's and his wife's eminently reasonable expectations, he told us. Then he caught himself and added that he doubts that if he gave up all that he loves and respects in his work and marriage, that it would be worth it just to find out if he were missing anything such as knowing other women or "dropping out." "Somewhere along the line," he said, "I realized that my parents anticipated that I would do well. I was always encouraged that I could do well—achieve their expectations—by the knowledge that my parents liked me." It appears that Nick was so well treated and rewarded as he went along that there was no impetus for him to rebel. "I'm very much the product of a happy loving childhood. I would like to be more comfortable with the prospect of not being the best, be less perfectionistic. I'm moving toward that now, I hope."

He and his wife hope to have children in about two years when she is through her tenure review at the university where she also teaches. His aspirations for his own children are for them to know who they are, to have a sense of independence, and to know that their parents are always there. In a sense what he will offer his children—which he says he currently offers his students—are those qualities of his parents that Nicholas invoked at the beginning of his meeting with us: protectiveness and freedom to be separate. This to and fro exchange between parent and child is at the core of most people's lives, and Nick in his own life demonstrates its benefits and articulates them very well.

* * *

Toward the end of the interview we asked participants to tell us their earliest memory in life for it often encapsulated the whole story they had been sharing with us. Nick's earliest memory went back to his second or third year. In it he is running down a hill with his father. "The thrill of doing it was like a day dream. It was like flying over the ground," he recalls. Nowadays he and his parents talk a few times a month and he still invariably calls them up when he has good news to announce. "It is not as if they are peers," he says, "And I am more circumspect about calling them up if I have bad news. In fact I feel a little pressure from them to be in touch more often, to make the drive to New York City more often than major holidays, but I am grateful that they are careful not to nag me. I wish I could talk with my parents about who I am as an adult more openly like I can talk with my wife, or like we're talking right now."

Ironically, in view of this minor discomfort Nick and his parents feel about their closeness, Nick owes a great deal of his strength and success as an individual to his parents' very ability to understand and negotiate the boundaries between intimacy and distance—in essence the boundaries between generations. When he was small his parents nurtured him, didn't expect him to be more than a little boy, and knew when to set limits with him. However Nick's parents could also blur the boundaries at times when they played with him, as when his father created fantasies with him during their bedtime ritual, and when his mother invited him to share setting the Thanksgiving table. These experiences gave Nick a sense of almost magical shared omnipotence with his parents, like the memory of feeling he was flying over ground as he ran with his father. Ultimately his parents knew both how to push him toward accomplishment and let go of him as he grew older.

Tatiana

Tatiana found her way to maturity in a family with religiously devout parents who had immigrated from South America and had little formal education. Thin, dark haired, with a patient demeanor, Tatiana works for the New York Public Interest Foundation reporting on how government policies affect consumers. She has also almost earned her law degree by going to school at night, and is happily married to a junior college history teacher. Her large rectangular glasses are a bit awkward for her face but they don't obscure her warm smile which breaks out often. Similarly, she doesn't enhance her speech with gestures or body language, but she has a far reaching vocabulary and organizes her words carefully.

Talking about her mother brought tears to her eyes, "We were very close. My mother was so friendly and loving; and yes she was also challenging, demanding. She was always there. Excuse me for crying but I was thinking of the time in grade school when the other kids were teasing me because I worked hard and did well on tests. Once they stole my book bag and were passing it around the class and I couldn't deal with it any more so I left the classroom and told the principal that I didn't want to come to school anymore. She lived in the parish, close to us and knew us from church, so you know what she did, she said, 'Tell your parents I'm coming over for dinner tomorrow.' So we all sat down and the principal explained that it wasn't anything I was doing, but I was a challenge to the other students and that was good but it made me different. And my mom was there to reassure me as she always was—my dad's English wasn't good enough to talk with the principal and me together—and said that things would certainly change and get better.

Tatiana wiped her eyes and laughed. "My mother usually knew how to handle things. Do you want to hear the story about the oranges? Being from Venezuela my mother believed in fruit and always gave us fresh orange sections at breakfast and dinner, and we were raised to eat what was on our plates. But I had taken it in my mind that I didn't like oranges so I decided the best place for them would be behind the kitchen cabinet where nobody would ever find them. Of course my mother was cleaning one day and found the rotten oranges and obviously knew where they were coming from because my sister was too small to be doing it. She came to me and said, 'You know, I've been finding oranges behind the cabinet. Do you have any idea how they might have gotten there?' And I started to hedge and then realized she knew that I was doing it, so I told her. And she said, 'I trust you, and if you really don't want to eat them we need to discuss it and see what we can do. When you throw things behind the cabinet you're not lying to me outright, but it is a lie in another way because you're hiding something, and we should always be able to discuss things even if we don't agree. I may ask you to eat oranges and you may not like it but there are times that you are going to have to do things that you don't like, and it's things that are good for you. I don't mean to do things to harm you but rather to do things that are good for you."

"I have other memories also, like being tucked in every night, getting lots of hugs and kisses, having her there whenever we needed things. My mother went back to work full-time as a saleslady at Macy's when I was in fourth grade and my sister and I basically walked ourselves home from school each day. Then we were alone except for a neighbor who sometimes looked in on us. Apparently I must have been scared at first when my mother went back to work, because I went to the principal's office at school and said that I was sick, but I don't think I really knew why I was doing it. And the principal called my mother who left work and picked me up right away at school, took me home, gave me soup, and started reading to me. I knew then that things were going to be okay and whenever I needed her she would be there."

About her father, Tatiana said that when she was growing up he was low key, understanding, loving, well-balanced, and strong. "Because of his work as a mechanic he had to leave before I got up, and came home at night exhausted. We always waited for to arrive before we started dinner because it was the only time we really got to talk during the week. Regardless of how tired he was he would always listen to our stories even though he didn't really make that many comments. Then after dinner he would get into his recliner and I'd be jumping up on his lap and throwing my arms around him and he would always give me a hug and kiss back. He never said 'Get away, I'm too tired,' he just gave that warm comfort. When things went wrong in the family, when there was an argument, my sister and I fighting for example, Dad was the one who tried to calm things down while my mother was the one more likely to yell. My father would more likely say, 'What's going on here?' We'd respond more quickly to him because he generally didn't say too much so when he did speak, we'd take notice."

Sports as a medium through which fathers and their children bonded (not just sons but also daughters) figures over and over again in the recollections of the 30 year olds. Tatiana describes it this way, "My father was—still is—a great baseball fan. I remember him trying to teach me how to bat and play ball in the street. He's a huge Mets fan because we lived just across the expressway from the stadium. During the season whenever there was a game our TV was on. I remember being a little girl and asking him to explain the game to me which he did. Then I learned all the names and the batting averages of the players. He was so proud that his little girl showed an interest in something that he enjoyed, plus was able to remember all that stuff. We'd go to St. Jerome's on Sunday and outside after the service his friends would be talking about the game and I would come up and say, 'So and so made a great play last night,' and they were just amazed. I can just see him smiling down at me from way up high saying to his friends, 'She just knows it all, she can tell you anything you want to know about the players.' That sense of feeling that he was really proud of me because of something we shared was marvelous."

Tatiana's account shows how her father gave her not just a sense of feeling good and self-confident about herself but also praise for learning about things—in this instance baseball facts and figures. This carried over into pleasure in doing well in school. Tatiana's mother also supported her academically, and by high school she was outstripping both of her parents educationally, which pleased rather than threatened them. Tatiana speaks about how dependable and emotionally protective her parents were when she was growing up, to which she attributes much of her inner security and productiveness as an adult. She adds that her mother's firmness and her willingness to challenge her were also very beneficial to her. The story of the oranges shows her mother's conviction that Tatiana would sometimes have to do things she didn't like but which her mother felt were good for her. Instead of destructive, unblinking rigidity, Tatiana's mother offered her daughter the option of talking about disagreements; her firmness gave Tatiana a framework of values, expectations, limits and controls.

Tatiana's memories of protection, love and excitement recall Nicholas's memories with his parents; and her memories of throwing herself in her father's lap recall the descriptions of Nicholas' mother's mildly erotic reactions to her baby son. However compared to Nick's account, she emphasizes the *warmth and closeness* of her family; she recalls her fear of being separated from her mother in fourth grade when her mother returned to work full-time, and her unwitting need to feign sickness to test if her mother was still available. By contrast Nick's early memories emphasized *separateness* as a counterpart to his mother's protectiveness. In this difference Tatiana illustrates how women value close relatedness to others more strongly than do men, a gender divergence which Chodorow (1978) and Gilligan (1982) have elucidated over the past three decades. This notwithstanding, in adulthood Nicholas valued his closeness to his wife as strongly as Tatiana respected her intimacy with her husband.

In addition to illustrating how women may respond differently from men to separateness, Tatiana's anxiety when her mother returned to work was multiply—determined for it was likely also part of a long-lasting posttraumatic reaction to a six week separation from her parents when she was eight months old. As an adult she had no conscious recollection of this separation, nor an understanding of how it might continue to affect her in her relationships. However the temporary loss of her parents in the infancy of her life seemed to be controlling aspects of her adult existence in a way that was well out of her awareness. To understand more about this we need to turn to the early record of Tatiana's life, see how the project staff experienced her parents first hand, and learn more about Tatiana's separation and reunion with her parents.

* * *

The first researcher from the project who met with Tatiana's mother wrote that she was friendly, open and expressive. The young mother was 20 years old then, and had been a store saleswoman since finishing high school. She also had had considerable experience taking care of her younger brothers and sisters. She reported that her parents had been firm and good natured, and she spoke fondly of her husband, who was ten years older, as a handsome, polite, hard worker.

The father's interviewers came to know him as stiff because of his limited English, but they wrote, "There is warmth and gaiety in his eyes. He knows his child well and fills us in on a great deal of good detail about her life. He is a straight-forward man who is pleased with, attentive to, and interested in his daughter." The father had come to the United States in his late teens, never graduated from high school, and immediately began working as a mechanic's apprentice. Neither parent had aspirations for more education for themselves and spent their leisure time walking, going to movies or sports events, and watching television; still they clearly wanted their children to have educational opportunities. Tatiana's mother stopped work when her baby was born, and bottle fed her daughter because, in her words, "It was more modern, more convenient . . . too many mothers have bad milk which gives their babies allergies."

The early months of her pregnancy had been hard and full of morning sickness, and as a further trial she said, 'I am happy to be having a child but my mother is making me sad because she thinks I got pregnant too soon. Gradually, however, the grandmother got used to "losing" her oldest daughter, warmed to having a grandchild, and joined in caring for the baby. Neither Tatiana's mother nor the grandmother expected or wanted the father to do more than help with the household chores. Early in Tatiana's life the interviewer noted, "The mother appears remarkably free of conflict and at home with herself and in her life. She is very agreeable, even a bit ingratiating; the most important mobilizing principle for her seems to be that she wants to be 'a good girl' and to have good children."

In her first months of life Tatiana was calm, not particularly vigorous or persistent, and relaxed easily into her mother's arms. Describing the mother with her baby, the project record reads, "She is one of the most thoughtful mothers, attuned to her child, perceptive, even tempered, reserved but frequently pleasantly smiling and spontaneous. She attends to her child's needs efficiently, economically, gently, and with composure even when the baby is fiercely crying. The mother is smoothly competent with a minimum of fuss but also responsive in a deliberate and measured way. She obviously is enjoying her child even though she seems tired. She seems able to identify with Tatiana and maintain her own place and pace as a mother."

Once Tatiana was fussing during an interview because her mother didn't respond as quickly as the child wanted. When the mother picked her up she told Tatiana gently, "You must have felt that I was a mean mommy for awhile.'" With her interviewer the mother talked earnestly and listened intently, often appreciatively exclaiming, "What a good question that is."

The baby's cognitive and emotional growth proceeded more rapidly than in most children. By six months she was very alert with a sober gaze that was reminiscent of both parents' reserved demeanors. The researchers also conjectured that the child's sobriety might also be due to her response to her mother's attitude which was becoming more didactic, if not reproving, for she regularly urged Tatiana, "Be good . . . eat what is offered . . . keep still . . ." Nonetheless in the observers' eyes the mother never reached the point of being over-controlling.

When Tatiana was eight months old her mother's capacity to identify with her baby failed her in one major respect. At the urging of her extended family, the mother left the baby with her parents in New York City while she and her husband went to Venezuela for six weeks to get to know her husband's family. When the parents returned Tatiana quickly greeted her father with a smile and went right to him; however, she scarcely acknowledged her mother. She neither smiled at her nor went to her; just looked curiously at her mother from a distance. Finally her grandmother said, "Where is mama?" The child pointed at a picture of her mother on a table; the mother started crying and picked up and hugged Tatiana who hung limply in her arms, the mother reported. After many minutes Tatiana started responding to her mother. For many weeks after this Tatiana clung tenaciously to her mother and was upset if her mother went anywhere without her.

The mother reported to project staff that she was shocked at how much she had missed her daughter while she was away and would never go on another trip without her, a vow she kept until Tatiana was in college. Manifestly also, Tatiana had badly missed her mother. The pain of the separation had led her to mobilize her emotional defenses, for even at this very early age Tatiana had the beginnings of a repertoire of mechanisms (as all children do) for managing threats to her psychological equilibrium. Thus Tatiana had blocked her mother's image from her awareness in order to reduce the pain of loss; at the reunion with her mother she wordlessly denied recognizing her mother through her unresponsiveness, exacting revenge on her mother for going away. Her father escaped this harsh treatment paradoxically because he was less involved and important to her at this age.

For many months after the reunion Tatiana was subdued and remote. In her second year some of her spontaneity returned but then her mother had to return to work and the little girl became stolid. The mother continued working for another year and a half until the next baby arrived, and from this point she remained at home with the children full-time until Tatiana was in fourth grade.

Even during the difficult time in her life after her parents' absence and while her mother was working, Tatiana could warm up and have fun when she was given time to get used to new situations. Her mother—fundamentally proud of and tolerant with her child—was also learning to tone down her requests of her daughter. She sermonized less, stopped making Tatiana worry about "making stinky," and postponed toilet training from the end of the first year until the end of the second year (still an early age). She also stopped saying "bad girl" and slapping her hand when the child did something risky like poke at the gas stove. She relied more on explaining dangerous situations, especially after she saw her daughter starting to criticize and slap other children. Thanking Dr. Brody for the opportunity to reflect about her child's growth, Tatiana's mother described how she herself as a child had been valued for being very mature, quiet and controlled, and had been trying to mold Tatiana in this direction, which she was beginning to realize may have been taking a toll on her daughter's spontaneity.

By the time Tatiana entered school she appeared very feminine with gold hoops in her pierced ears. Extremely competent for her age, she attacked her developmental testing with determination and seriousness. Her IQ was a bright 120 at seven years and would have been higher if some immaturity, over-disciplined thinking, and dependency on her mother hadn't inhibited her performance. For example in answer to the test question, "What would you do if you cut your finger?" She said, "Tell mommy." And "What would you do if you were sent to the store to buy bread and there was no bread?" She responded, "I'd have to tell mommy." Like her parents she was conscientious and conformed to expectations so she could not imagine taking independent action such as bandaging her own finger or buying a substitute for bread. When Tatiana and her mother played they enjoyed each other, talked, smiled, exchanged ideas readily, and shared fun. While they played with the dollhouse, the mother positively reinforced her daughter's placement of figures here and there, but she couldn't entirely refrain from teaching, for when Tatiana put band-aids on the dollhouse bookcase, her mother interfered with the child's flight of imagination and said, "You don't put band-aids on a bookcase."

Composed and dignified, occasionally joking, Tatiana's mother was proud that her daughter at seven had had only one tantrum, and this was when she was two and a half years old. While shopping Tatiana had wanted candy and the mother had no change, so the child threw a fit. "I dusted her pants and told her to never act that way again. I couldn't have her being temperamental the way I was as a child, sulking and keeping it inside."

When Tatiana was in first grade, the research observer reported after a school visit, "Tatiana has one of the sweetest faces I have ever seen. She occasionally breaks into a wide grin that expresses expectation and shyness. Her schoolroom is incredibly regimented, run by a woman with an abrasive voice and chastising manner which subdues all the kids. Tatiana handles this the best, with the longest attention span, the best behavior, and an impressive ability to work on her assigned projects. She has an intense desire to impress the teacher and is somewhat too goody-goody, raising her hands a bit too frequently to answer questions. Though at times too didactic with her classmates, she is also generous and helpful."

Tatiana the schoolgirl was a happy child—playing with friends, enjoying winning, accepting losing, admiring herself in the mirror, and wanting to be a teacher and a mommy when she grew up. Like her mother she had a strict conscience and powerful respect for authority. Reflecting on her daughter's development, the mother still worried that she might have been too strict when her daughter was very young and perhaps had overdone her emphasis on politeness.

* * *

A decade passed, and when Tatiana came for her visit at the end of high school in 1982, she was poised, calm and direct. Dr. Brody observed, "This is a girl of uncommon worth. Her cultural interests are not broad but they are very wholesome. Her relations with people are sound and reflect a pious, loving home. There is a somewhat provincial quality or restrictedness in Tatiana, but certainly an unassuming simplicity and giving quality that is uncommon for these days. I cannot but feel that there are strong repressions of feelings, fantasies and impulses in her but they are wholesome repressions and may allow her to use her energies productively and with much gratification because her relationships with people are so positive."

Tatiana had done very well academically in high school, had danced with the school's Ballet Folklorico, and worked part-time. She had loosened up with schoolmates, she said, and had not been teased for many years, even getting herself reprimanded in junior high school for throwing water balloons on April Fools Day. Her psychological testing at 18 confirmed that she had internalized her parents' high regard for doing well, but there was a price to pay for this: She was inwardly torn by a desire to declare herself independent of their expectations and controls, and by her loyal desire to please them. Her tester concluded that she had well developed obsessive-compulsive defense mechanisms and a personality style that went along with these defenses.

Tatiana chose a medium-sized, not overly competitive college close to home. She majored in business because it related to her parents' work. Both of them had moved up into managerial responsibilities, and commerce was often a part of family conversations. She also felt that she could do something constructive for society with the knowledge a business major would provide. In spite of the inner conflict her psychological testing revealed, she insisted that her parents' strictness had not felt overbearing. She liked her own level-headedness, but wished she didn't take things as seriously as she did, and felt she sometimes let people walk over her. She wanted to be more outgoing but also well knew that her cautious way of only letting people she knew and trusted get to know her worked against being more outgoing.

Now, after 12 more years Tatiana has emotionally matured. As Dr. Brody had anticipated, her progression through life had continued well apace for she had enjoyed college and entered the world of work successfully. It is interesting how she met her husband-to-be in her senior year of college. They had been in a course together and after a lecture one morning he introduced himself to her by saying, "You look upset about something today. Is there anything I can do to help?" This harmonized with her fondness for her parents' supportiveness, and she responded to him. They began a very satisfying relationship in which she credits him with bringing a lot of laughter and less seriousness to her life. For two years they had a commuter relationship when Tatiana returned to New York City to take her job with the consumer foundation and lived at home, and her boyfriend stayed at the university to obtain his master's degree.

The high value Tatiana's parents placed on self-control continues today in her inner emotional life and outer behavior. Her fiance was her first (and only) sexual partner, and they waited until they were engaged. Unlike the vast majority of the participants in the project Tatiana has not tried marijuana, for she says it doesn't interest her. She does have an occasional alcoholic drink though she says that she has never been drunk because "I don't care to not know what might come out of my mouth."

Nonetheless she does feel free to make up her own mind about ethical decisions. She was raised attending Catholic church regularly and going to parochial schools, but says she is willing to come to her own conclusions about Church doctrine, explaining "Abortion is not for me, but I realize for some people it is necessary so as not to bring a neglected child into the world."

Tatiana concluded her interview with some thoughts about what her closeness to her family has meant to her, "My parents are a source of strength but sometimes I think it may have held me back. I really had to learn to say, 'Okay, I have to do some things the way I want them to be done not as my family wants me to do them.' For example, my husband was not Catholic which was especially hard for my father, and many times I felt terribly disloyal and guilty about how bad I was making him feel. Dad did get used to the idea gradually, and then Jack said he'd convert to Catholicism because it would be better to raise our children in one religious tradition, which of course helped with my parents. Sometimes also I felt too well understood by my parents. It was as if my mother knew me better than I knew myself. If I was going to make a cheesecake, my mother might have already bought the ingredients. So it was a struggle learning to make myself think about what I really wanted for myself, but in many ways the struggle with this has made me a better person."

Brief Examples

There are many other successful participants, though they have not necessarily achieved Nick's outstanding academic success or Tatiana's professional training. Five other participants illustrate different kinds of family backgrounds, different courses in life, and one the weathering of her parents' divorce later in childhood. They share common denominators with Nick and Tatiana—strong, healthy personalities, high ethical values, and the contentment and vocational satisfaction they have found as adults.

Rose is the youngest and first to go to college in a hard-working family. She has just completed her primary school teaching credential, while also working as a dancer in an Off-Broadway show and as a waitress to support herself. She laughs infectiously, describing with wit and wise detail her family's foibles and strengths, and the challenges of student teaching in a public school. Her husband works a printing press during the day and goes to school at night.

Another participant, Yvonne, speaks with authority of her administrative work with the Red Cross, continuing a tradition of social responsibility that her well-to-do family emphasized. During her college years she rebelled wildly against the standards of decorum with which she was raised. When she was 21, she was experimenting with living on the other side of the tracks, so to speak, and her boyfriend—a much older, alcohol abusing sculptor—left her without warning. Yvonne cut her wrists superficially with a razor blade. She told us how the self-inflicted cuts and pain brought her inner emotional pain and anger to the surface (literally showed her how bad her boyfriend had made her feel), which was a turning point for it made her realize that she was mistreating herself by letting herself be mistreated. She decided she could make far better decisions about managing her life. Setting herself on that course, it was about a year later that her father introduced her to the man she would later marry, with whom she has now lived happily for several years.

Another man, Victor, is one of but a handful of children in the study whose fathers shared the child-care more or less equally with the mother. After going away to college, Victor has returned to his parents' rural community. Strikingly like his father (a part-time local newspaper reporter and house-husband), Victor is a part-time art teacher in the local high-school and takes care of his two children, while his wife works full-time as a nurse and is the primary wage-earner (like Victor's mother). Also like his father, Victor built his own house with his own hands. He is one of just 14 participants in the study who already have children. The infrequency with which the participants in the followup have had children in their twenties is in keeping with the majority of the young adults in the United States today who postpone marriage to their mid-twenties (from the early twenties a generation ago) and children to their thirties.

Next there is Brad, raised like a prince by an adoring mother, a doting father, and three admiring sisters. At 30 he gives off a courtly aura—handsome, informed, assured, relaxed, casually dressed in well-tailored clothes, open and generous. His parents' work was importing designer building tiles. Brad built upon his exposure to art and business that came from growing up in his family, and founded his own successful company that provides a computer data base on world textile design and production. His wife runs an art gallery.

Finally we come to Julia whose parents divorced when she was eight years old, one of the nine children in the study whose families broke up before they were 18. Julia was the only one of the nine whose mother and father were both effective, dependable, and very nurturing before **and after** the divorce. In contrast to the too common pattern in divorces, Julia's parents did not turn their separation into a struggle for personal control or possession of the child. Despite their underlying disappointment and lingering hard feelings, the grownups continued to behave agreeably and tolerantly with each other. The father came to the mother's house to play and visit with Julia regularly at midweek, and Julia went to her father's house most weekends (not at the behest of a court but because Julia, the mother, and the father desired it). When she was a teenager, Julia came and went as she wished between her mother and father, developing a distinctive relationship and activities with each parent, for example helping decorate her mother's house and taking long hikes with her father.

"I never felt a lack of love from my parents," she reported. "My father traveled a lot in his work, but when he was in town I saw him all the time." Her parents' supportive presence and her mother's modeling the role of a disciplined, professional woman paid off. Today Julia is serious, reflective, articulate, open, and ready to laugh. After many qualms about whether it was safe to trust marriage because of her parents' divorce, she has now been happily married for some time, anticipates raising a family, and enjoys her work as a director of marketing for a mid-sized manufacturer. Nonetheless she adds, "I can't begin to describe the ways the divorce affected me. It was—and is—the most difficult experience of my life. I always felt pulled inside of me in both directions, to be with both parents. When I was with my father, I felt guilty about leaving my mother, and when I was with my mother I felt I was betraying my father. I never got over wanting my parents to be together. I think I felt unusually close to them because at a young age I found myself talking through feelings with my mother and father about their troubles with each other."

The effects of Julia's internal tug-of-war that lasted more than a decade show today in her personality. She feels that she may be overly conscientious about her actions, and turns to her husband for help in relaxing. She also recognizes that she may unreasonably project her self-demands to be a responsible person onto others, becoming too harsh with them, and too moralistic about other people's behavior. She has never had psychiatric symptoms and has never sought psychotherapy, but had she had therapy in the years after the divorce that addressed her conflicts about her parents, it may have softened some of the harder edges of her personality. In Julia's moralizing there is also suppressed anger at her father for leaving her mother for another woman. That relationship failed and today both of her parents are single. Because of the financial hardship the divorce caused the family, Julia feels that as an adult she worries too much about earning a high salary. She hopes one day to be secure enough to volunteer her time in caring for others.

Although Julia is successful professionally and emotionally in spite of the trauma of her parents' divorce, she is the exception in the group of nine project participants whose parents separated when they were children. All of the others have Global assessment of Functioning (GAF) (American Psychiatric Association, 1994b) scores diminished to the point of at least some psychological symptoms. Even Julia continues to register the tensions of the dissolution of her parents' marriage in her subdued, cautious emotional response to life that sets her apart from the other high functioning children of effective parents. What allowed Julia to do as well as she has done despite the divorce was her parents' continued, positive participation in her life after the separation (mediated by their civility with each other), and the fact that Julia did not encounter additional traumas growing up (see chapter four, Promise Lost).

The group of seven participants show by their lives what facilitates children's emotional growth. They also illustrate that neither high intelligence nor family wealth is a prerequisite for success, though some subjects have used financial support from their parents and their intelligence well and not squandered their gifts. Nor is it necessary to conform to a standard path or model, for their lives show abundant variation, even detours through periods of unhappiness.

PART TWO

The Bedrock of Success

For all of the participants described here who did well the bedrock of their auspicious development lay in their fine relationships with their mothers in infancy. For rating purposes, these participants who are doing very well in life all have Global Assessment of Functioning (GAF) (American Psychiatric Association, 1994b) scores of 91 or above (superior functioning); and their mothers had all been classified as belonging to the Group A mothering group (favorable) by the original researchers (see appendix for rating details). What actually constitutes successful early mother-child relationships is difficult to render in words. The participants' recollections of their early lives with their parents convey the emotional climate in the homes; the films of the mothers and young children during feeding and play show the early relationships; and the research team's descriptions of mothers with their babies chronicle the actual behaviors. Descriptions of mothering from two of the families expand the picture.

"I only go out for weddings, funerals and bingo," averred Rose's mother when her daughter was quite young. She was a full-time housewife whose husband worked a 15 hour day to support the large family. She rose at 4:30 am to fix tea which she shared with her husband before he left for his dawn work at the Fulton fish market in New York City. Then she went back to bed until 6:30 when it was time to get the three older children ready for school. By late morning the husband returned to New Jersey to work in an auto supply store, and finished his day tending bar in the neighborhood for the after-work rush. Staying at home gave the mother time to be with Rose whom she heartily enjoyed. Here is how the study record described the mother and daughter playing together with a doll house: "Rose's mother has a way of validating her child's decisions and statements by echoing and labeling them. She is patient, supportive, relaxed and attentive. She seems genuinely interested in her daughter, knows her daily experiences—as does the father—and *seems to be able to see the world through her child's eyes.*"

At 30 Rose, finishing her primary school teaching credential, said she feels quite close to her mother emotionally, and lives but a few blocks away. She spoke with some amazement about how well she and her mother have always communicated, an intimacy that the mother's interest and delight in her child's world made possible. Her enjoyment of her young daughter wasn't limited to play or good behavior for she laughed and took pride in Rose when she was feisty and rebellious. In the mother's words, "She is the best at beating me up, this one. She has a lovely imagination for trouble."

Brad's mother elicited the following comments from project staff, "Her sensitive and joyous response to him shows when he is six weeks old and continues in the feedings at six months and 12 months. The remarkable leaps in the growth of this little boy in less than a year provide a glimpse of the sturdy relationship between this mother and infant. For this baby eating has become a happy game with his mother. Unlike for many children at one year, feeding does not generate tension between the mother and child. Brad and his mother are able to be sociable and at ease." The mother even spoke of her fascination with her little boy's penis and how she enjoyed washing it and noticing his erections.

Then some months later when he was into his second year, she said that maybe she was becoming a little too excited with him, and perhaps she should be a bit more reserved and distant. Her thoughts then went to the fantasy of having a new little baby boy every year so she could keep repeating the experience she had with Brad, and her eyes welled with tears. Part consciously, part subconsciously she realized she needed to be cautious to not make her relationship with Brad overly erotic, and one way to do this would be to turn her attention to another baby.

As occurred with the parents of all seven children in this chapter, Brad's mother's affection for her baby led her to blur the boundary between parent and child at times (to the point of nearly allowing herself to be sexually over-stimulated by her baby, and over-stimulating him in return). Nonetheless she kept to her fundamental role of providing protection, affection and guidance for Brad.

The Parents of Successful Children

Comparing the parents who raised the children with the best outcomes with parents whose children grew up troubled pointed to a number of qualities which distinguished the parents of successful children from their less successful counterparts.

Parental Confidence

Parent's confidence with their children was the *sine qua non* of effective child rearing. In the early life of the children **maternal confidence** was perhaps the single most essential ingredient in good care. It in turn bred self-assured children. However, maternal confidence does not imply maternal omniscience or self-certainty that one has all the answers and that the child is always wrong when there is a conflict. The next chapter shows some of the consequences of such attitudes.

The self-assured mothers of the successful children readily sought and accepted advice. Additionally five of the seven parents of the children in this chapter had already raised babies through toddler-hood and so had gained a measure of security from prior experience. Several of the mothers had, in fact, learned much from difficult times with first children. For example, Brad's mother had used psychotherapy in the year before Brad's birth to separate for herself her role as a mother from her own father's expectations that she work with him in his business, a conflict that had made her terribly uncertain with her first child.

Parental Optimism

An extremely important bedrock of the good nurturing that characterized the parents of all seven children was **an optimistic parental**

sensibility toward children and the future. Yvonne's mother brings this to life. "Our children will blossom if we give them the chance," she said, speaking also for her husband. After visiting with Yvonne and her mother when the child was 12 months old, Sylvia Brody wrote, "This mother is very mature with a capacity for empathy, firmness and standards. In her quiet way she seems to be able to make demands on her children to take care of themselves, bear frustration, and do things for each other in a natural way." The mother's belief in the future blossoming of her children is much akin to Nicholas's parents' attributing his success to the fact that "We didn't get in the way of the good that was there."

Parental Calmness

Also at the core of success in all seven parents was **parental calmness, reflectiveness, and attentiveness** with the very young children. These qualities were necessary simply for understanding the baby, reducing tension, and responding to the child's mood in a way that enhanced growth. The qualities also paid off in a secondary way, for the children learned to be calm, to reflect and to be attentive from their parents, and made it part of their own repertoire.

Maternal Affection

Maternal affection, gentleness and warmth was also present in the life of each baby. Sadly this is not given to all children for there are a great many things that can interfere with a mother's freedom to be warm toward her child. For example in other families that we will describe, parents feared spoiling their children with kisses, and mothers took out their anger at fathers on their children.

Parental Empathy

Parental empathy was present in a very large measure in the families of the six children. Empathy, from a Greek root, literally means "to feel into" another person, as opposed to sympathy which means to "feel with" another person. It contains elements of calmness, thoughtfulness, attentiveness and warmth. However the actual process of empathy requires the parent to execute a series of psychological and behavioral steps. First, there must be affection which is the motive force behind empathy; and second there must be perceptiveness which is the tool that makes it possible for a parent to project herself into the child's experience. Once projected into the child's experience—that is, identified with the child—the parent can understand the youngster's state and mood, and grasp what the child needs and wants. Empathy often takes place in the twinkling of an eye, and the parent through projecting herself into the child's experience literally translates it into grownup parent language and then deconstructs it once again into baby patois in the form of coos, baby talk, grownup talk, touches, broadly exaggerated facial expressions, play, and care-taking such as feeding and keeping the child warm.

Parental Pride in Child's Activeness

In each family there was great **parental pride and pleasure in their children's activeness**. Going beyond pride in their youngster's activeness, four of the seven parents of the children who have grown up very well (Nick, Rose, Julia, and Brad) also valued their child's capacity for anger and assertiveness. Thus Brad's father said about his son, "He always had a good temper." His mother added, "He makes his feelings clear," and in valuing his ability to speak up for himself, albeit at times with a temper, she was fostering it.

Parental Pleasure in Child's Independence

Parental pleasure in a child's independence and separateness allowed mothers and fathers to appreciate a child's high energy and hi-jinks. For example, Brad's mother spoke about how she wanted him to be self-sufficient physically as fast as possible; she delighted in his eating by himself and managing things on his own quickly. She fostered his independence with her pleasure in it, but did not push him away nor prevent him from being dependent on her for she also generously indulged him. Brad's father added, "We want to keep the family close. We spend as much time as possible doing things all together. Having a regular dinner hour means a lot to us." Aligned with appreciation of a child's independence was **parental pleasure in allowing children initiative**. All of the parents of these successful children were sufficiently free of anxiety and secure enough to permit their children autonomy even when it involved letting them have minor accidents and letting them make mistakes and messes.

Discipline

Questions of parental permissiveness raise the issue of how these emotionally mature parents went about disciplining their children. The word "discipline" comes from the same Latin root as "disciple." In the Biblical narrative, Jesus' disciples followed his way of living. In the narratives of the project participants' lives, the parents of the children who did well lived disciplined lives, an example which their children followed so that they did not require a great deal of punishment. When it was necessary, in each family **parental discipline was careful, present and measured**. There was a remarkable similarity in how the six families went about it, as if they had gotten together to compare notes, ask questions of each other, and devise strategies. The families generally *did not believe in punishment or training their children's habits in the first year* but waited until their second year when their toddler's ability to move about could put themselves and others in danger. Before that the parents' focus was protecting and nurturing their children rather than limiting them. Putting it succinctly, Brad's mother said, "I don't believe discipline is important in the first year but later the child will run you if you are not firm enough."

As the children grew into full-fledged toddlers, nursery schoolers, and schoolgirls and boys, they attempted to assert their autonomy and test and break rules, as all children do at times. They needed regular intervention and watching on the parents' part, but their parents' response was not vigilante vigilance. The mothers and fathers typically consulted together about how to respond to the more egregious acting up of their children. They didn't lose their tempers and strike their children. Their discipline was judiciously tailored to the child's actions. The parents didn't take their children's misbehaviors as personal insults and defeats. Consequently they didn't hold grudges, and could show compassion and adjust the consequences they gave their children.

When a child acted badly the parents responded stepwise. **First**, the parents *modeled moderation* for the children in their reactions to the youngsters' misbehavior. **Second**, each parent attempted to reason with their child and explain the importance of a rule, and listen to the child in turn. **Third**, if reasoning was not effective they offered rewards and incentives for cooperation and promised restrictions such as losses of pleasures and privileges if a child did not heed warnings. Reasoning occurred often daily or multiple times daily. For example the daily refrain in several of the homes went something like, "Don't hurt your sister. Don't throw your toys." Restrictions and rewards occurred more at weekly intervals. **Fourth**, when children were still heedless, parents needed to work harder to get their attention. The most frequent way of doing this was to forcefully raise their voices, which might occur several times a week. Sometimes parents escalated to yelling. In general, these very mature parents were able to control their yelling so that it occurred less than about once a month. Their yelling was not passionless; it clearly expressed real feelings of exasperation; and it clearly communicated the next consequence to the child such as, "I've warned you too many times. I'm fed up and if you do that one more time you are not going out to play, and if you think you're going to watch TV, you've got another thought coming."

The parents did not turn mean and curse at their children; they did not tell them that they were evil or hateful; and they did not threaten to leave them or send them away. Their yelling, like the other measures, had the point in an overall scheme of getting a child's attention, expressing standards of behavior, and making clear what the consequences were going to be if the child continued to act badly.

Fifth, when reasoning and restrictions failed, and raising voices was insufficient, parents isolated their children in their rooms or an out-of-the-way corner in the home (not in frightening places like dark closets or basements). Isolation might last until the child calmed down and agreed to cooperate. Sometimes it lasted until a child apologized. Sometimes isolation was for a fixed amount of time ranging from five minutes to a whole evening. The parents' purpose was not the punishment, rather getting their child's cooperation. Room isolations were rare for the children, usually a handful of times a year, but sometimes they came in a flurry of two or three in a week or two. After testing how serious the parents were two or three times, the children inevitably got the idea of what they could get away with and what they couldn't.

Sixth, in this group of children of basically normal parents, all of the children received spankings when all else failed and their parents were truly fed up. But spankings were very rare, typically two or three times a year in the form of one to three whacks with a hand on the clothed behind of the child. None of the successful 30 year olds whose lives we have been narrating recall ever being spanked after fifth grade. In fact they typically say as adults that they are not really sure if they were ever spanked. Corporal punishment was so infrequent and without marked physical pain for these children that it did not clearly and permanently register in their memory in contrast to how fixedly the traumatic beatings we will hear about in other families did register in memory. Nicholas is typical of the group when he said as a grownup, "I think I was spanked once or twice when I was small but it didn't hurt. My parents told me I was spanked occasionally when I was small, but I don't really remember."

The historical research record of interviews with the parents coincides with their grown up children's memories. The parents reported that by the time the children were in grade school spankings were down to about once a year. For example Rose's mother—evoking the parents' teamwork approach to discipline—said when her daughter was eight, "The last time we've hit her was when she wandered off last year. Something bad could have happened her going out the front door and nobody knowing. Her father really dusted her pants then. It was the only time he hit her that hard. Rose wouldn't talk with him for three weeks. I finally had to tell her she had punished her father enough before she'd talk with him again." Rose's mother also offered how she had changed over time with her children, "I was 18 when I had my first child and 36 when Rose came along. With my first child I had an attitude toward him as a baby. It was my way or else. I was so strict. It was as if I was fighting back with my own mother then, for as much as I thought I was grown up, I wasn't. Rose got the best love."

None of the parents had a strong belief in the value of spankings. For them it was a regrettable last resort, not a form of discipline of which they felt proud. Neither they as parents nor we as child psychiatrists would recommend corporal punishment to other parents. Rather, the parents looked upon spankings as a failure on their part for not having been sufficiently patient, firm, or understanding; and we would concur with them that forbearance, firmness, and thoughtfulness are preferable to hitting. What the parents did convey to their children was a belief in tolerance, acceptance, love, fun and warmth; and basic standards of respect for others and for social expectations such as accepting school and family rules. These parents expressed their principles with love through personal example, discussion, firmness and consequences.

How did these mothers and fathers of children who grew up so nicely come to the point of being able to discipline so effectively? There is no universal pathway to mature parental judgment. The parents came to their abilities from different backgrounds. For example, Nicholas' father had been harshly spanked with a wooden paddle regularly as a child by his father and said, "That didn't help one lick." He decided to be different with his son. Other parents closely followed their parents' examples, and others decided that they had not been given enough discipline in their childhoods. Several of the parents learned to be more relaxed or firmer by raising older children first. What is consistent is that *each parent worked hard* at this aspect of parenting. It was time consuming, unrewarding, and often the most painful and difficult part of raising children for them. They all thought carefully about how to discipline and punish, and all felt bad when they thought they might have gone too far.

Maternal Affect

Happy maternal affect characterized each of these mothers who had a basic contentment which their smiles and amiable expressions highlighted. They were relatively easy going, jovial, yet hardworking with their children.

Each of the mothers of the seven children who did very well were full-time parents until at least their child's first birthday. Then all but Rose's mother returned to work or school over the next several years with varying time commitments. Two attempted to go back to work full-time in their children's second year, but when they saw the regressions in developmental attainments and distress in their children, they decreased their work to part-time for several more years. All of the fathers always worked full-time except Victor's who in his son's third year traded places with the mother. Because she had greater earning power in her profession as a nurse and the family needed the money, Victor's mother went to work full-time outside of the home while the father continued part-time work and became a house-husband doing most of the childcare and house work. His love of children extended beyond the home, and as the years went by he became a summer theater program director for the town's children.

In spite of her full day of work outside the home, Victor's mother relished her children. Illustrating the phrase "happy maternal affect," when she and her son played together during visits with the project she would laugh, "What fun this is." She, Brad's and Nicholas's mothers all delighted in kissing their boys almost (if not actually) erotically. The study describes six month old Brad's mother's "sensitive and joyful response to her son, kissing him all over, his genitals too." The parents' good spirits were contagious and they quickly became evident in the personalities of the children. When Brad was a year old, the researcher wrote, "He just vibrates with happy excitement." When Yvonne was a year old she took time out from taking her bottle in her mother's lap to stretch and wave her legs up in the air. Then she teased her mother and stuck her toe in her mother's mouth and her mother sucked on it for a moment, picking up that it was a game Yvonne was inventing about bottle feeding and affection. Then Yvonne limberly sucked her own toe for a second; and then mother and daughter had a great big laugh together. Bubbling with humor at 30, Rose excused her devoted father for his irascibility when he came home from his 14 hour work days with too many beers under his belt. His years of devoted support of the family and his tears of happiness for her when he walked her down the aisle at her wedding carried more weight with her than his bouts of anger had. She cried with fondness for him as she recalled this moment.

The mothers' happiness in these families closely linked to their relationships with their husbands. In six of the seven families there were strong, affectionate bonds between the mothers and fathers. The parents respected and supported each other even when temperamental differences existed between the mothers and fathers. When they sometimes didn't see eye to eye about raising their children, they were able to compromise. Even though one couple divorced, there was love and cooperation in the marriage for many years until the father suffered a serious depression following a series of business reverses and strayed from the marriage.

Chapter 1. Table 1.1 Qualities Of Parents Of Children Who Did Very Well

1. Confidence
2. Happy maternal afffect
3. Optimism
4. Calm
5. Attentiveness to the children
6. Thoughtfulness
7. Gentleness
8. Warmth
9. Reliability
10. Empathy
11. Pride in their children's activeness
12. Pride in their children's initiative
13. Pride in their children's independence
14. Careful discipline
15. Compassionate discipline

Three Levels of Mother-Infant Interaction

The search for specific components of healthy parenting has led us to the understanding that mother-infant interaction takes place on three different levels of experience. Telling the stories of participants' lives, we have focused thus far largely on the first level, termed the *global (or macro) level.* Here the positive components include maternal confidence, joyfulness, affection, consistency, organization, protectiveness, empathy and compassion. When these qualities come together for a child, the child experiences what our culture calls "mother love." The child internalizes and reciprocates these parental emotions and behaviors so that they in turn become part of his or her own personality and repertoire of responses. The child begins showing them as early as the first months and years of life; they continue into adulthood; and are transmitted to the next generation.

The second, deeper plane of mother-infant behavior is the *level of micro-kinesic interactions.* Careful second-by-second micro-analyses of films of mothers and children together breaks down global interactions into ever more specific micro-components of behaviors. Using the graceless jargon of the scientist, we can say that analysis of microkinesic mother-infant behaviors "operationalizes mother-love." For example, in our research we have analyzed the films of the mothers and infants during feeding, play, and reunions after mildly stressful brief separations on a moment-by-moment basis in order to determine and describe the core components of the microkinesic level of social interchange. These appear to be mother-infant eye gaze, mother-infant affective interchange, mother-infant touching for play and for contact, mutual verbalizations, holding and body molding one to the other, and the general maintenance of physical closeness or proximity. These behaviors follow suit with those at the global level; that is, when macro-interactions are healthy, so are the micro ones.

The micro-interactional experiences (propelled by emotions and responses that are innate in the human species) are also the ones by which mothers and their babies become bonded to each other. Each mother and child established their unique pattern of bonding through, a) The interplay of their favored micro-kinesic elements of social interchange (be they finger touches, vocalizations, kisses, gazes, expressions, etc.); b) The pair's particular timing and rhythm; and c) The pair's characteristic physical force. This bonding style is the substratum of the psychological attachment that the child and parent form with each other.

In good relationships, when a baby experiences a stress such as hunger, cold or fear, it signals its discomfort with its eyes, cries, distressed expression, hand grasps and touches, and attempts to stay close (that is, it communicates with the components of bonding). The parent replies swiftly with a range of responses in the same modalities. This interaction repeated thousands of times in the first year of life provides the foundation for the child's attachment, emotional security and subsequent growth into independence.

Thinking and feeling underlie the micro-behaviors of infancy; they are implicit in the mother's actions whether or not she actually verbalizes her thoughts to her baby, and they are evolving in the child as part of the interactions even though the baby is not yet able to verbalize them. Here is an example of a detailed research observation which leads us to understand the child's state of mind, using the paradigm of a brief separation and reunion, which Ainsworth et al. (1978) developed to assess the child's security of attachment to its mother. When we observe a 12 month old reunite with its mother after she has left the room for three minutes, we note particularly the child's body movements, for a child this age speaks in movements. If a child is insecure or ambivalent about the security of its attachment with its mother, it is likely to approach the returning mother crying, reach to be picked up, but then gaze down or away from the mother; hang limply like a sack of potatoes when she picks him up, perhaps reach its arms around the mother's neck, but raise its turn his hands upward to avoid touching the mother with his palms.

By contrast, the 12 month old child who has experienced effective parenting and not been separated from its parents in infancy feels secure in its attachment and approaches his mother after a several minute separation often tearfully but with his gaze upon his mothers face. He tucks himself into his mother's body when she picks him up, and puts his hands and palms full on her neck or back. Such interactions speak volumes about the pre-verbal youngster's state of mind.

The successful children and parents whose lives we have been detailing functioned very smoothly and positively in these microkinesic parameters when compared to parent-infant pairs in which the children had lesser outcomes later in life. We wondered whether these behaviors would continue into the next generation? Of the seven people in this chapter only Victor already has children of his own. We filmed him with his baby and three-year old daughter, studying their interactions, and saw that Victor had learned his lessons well from his parents. He had the same perceptive, gentle and timely responsiveness with his youngsters that his mother had had with him.

The third dimension of mother-infant interchange is at the *neuropsychological level.* Addressing this level in the course of comparing the cognitive and emotional growth of infants of depressed and healthy mothers, the research psychologists Murray and Cooper (1997) have reviewed the "... accumulating evidence that experiential factors influence the course of infant brain development. This is extremely rapid in the first weeks and months, with prodigious production of synapses, followed by extensive pruning, in which only functional connections are retained. Thus when parents repeatedly respond sensitively to recruit the infant's engagement and then modulate their behavior in response to infant arousal and interest to sustain the infant's attention, it is likely that they directly influence the process of brain differentiation and organization. Our own and other's research suggest that at two months postpartum there is still considerable flexibility in the infant's repertoire with, at best, a relatively modest generalization of infant behavior from infant interactions with the principal caretaker to those with others ... [the mother's] success in sustaining the infant's attention and involvement in face-to-face interactions, repeated over a period of some months, may, by four to five months, have influenced the infant's capacity to attend and process information in the wider social and the non-social environment."

As clinicians, when we work with parents and school children we focus our therapeutic efforts on the global (macro) level of feelings and behavior. When infants and toddlers are our patients, we also direct our attention to the micro-transactions that occur with their parents. When these transactions are troubled we may even attempt to bring microkinesic moment-by-moment behaviors to the conscious attention of parents, and thereby give them the opportunity to make purposeful changes. By contrast the realm of neurophysiological and neuropsychological structuralization remains the province of the laboratory scientist, although more and more findings from the "wet" laboratory, from clinical research, and from psychotherapy support each other and open new vistas of understanding.

For parents, the realm of feeling and thinking is the first, or global interaction level. The families who have modeled success in this chapter have all done well at this level. The mothers and fathers had an accurate awareness of how they related to their babies; when difficulties arose they could adjust their responses and feelings, ask others for the kinds of help they needed, and listen to advice. Their children were the beneficiaries. In short, good parental feeling and timing led to good moment-by-moment interchanges with the babies. Feeling and behavior in turn combined to facilitate neuropsychological development, and correspondingly good emotional development. Significantly, 30 years later the adult children of these successful parent-infant relationships all had positive, secure mental representations of their early attachment to their parents as indicated by Secure ratings on their Adult Attachment Interviews.

Too Hard an Act to Follow?

Are these parents of successful children too hard an act to follow? Is it asking to much of mothers and fathers to be truly self-assured, upbeat, sensitive, and alert? It would indeed be expecting too much if this group of parents who serve as models were flawless and their children perfect, but (fortunately) that is not the case. As good and competent as they were, each mother and father had weaknesses and problems, as do all parents. As well as their children have done, now these grown children as adults nonetheless have self-doubts at times, or have sacrificed strength in one area of their personalities in order to be very competent in other ways.

For example, Nicholas's parents unspokenly expected that he perform up to his ability and conform to social expectations. At times the project staff felt that his mother bordered on too didactic with him and missed opportunities to have fun ("schoolmarmish," they wrote of her). At 30, Nicholas echoed these concerns when he wondered what he might have missed out on. Tatiana's parents' expectations were more outspoken. They talked actively about their hopes for her to achieve and be very good and proper, sometimes to an extent that worried project staff. This made Tatiana sometimes isolate herself from classmates growing up because she needed to impress teachers. Happily by high school she felt more a part of her class, and now as an adult she describes how her husband has made her less serious by bring more laughter into her life.

Quite different, Rose's parents were relatively casual about what they expected of their daughter and she has a more light-hearted nature than Nick or Tatiana. But the counterpart of this is that she has not pushed herself academically or professionally. Consequently Rose is years behind Nick and Tatiana in her vocation, having had false starts in the past and only now at 30 is finishing college and getting her primary school teaching certificate.

Tatiana's parents also made the traumatic false step of leaving her for six weeks in her first year because they lacked knowledge about child development and had a serious lapse in empathy for their baby. This seems to have fostered an enduring anxiety in Tatiana about being physically apart from her parents and conflicted about acting independently of them.

Yvonne's mother struggled with a severe postpartum depression and anxiety during her daughter's first six weeks, a depression that was related to her having hoped for a baby boy after having had several daughters. The distress—unlike anything she had ever experienced before—was so intense that she thought at times she might lose her mind and need to be hospitalized. But she consciously willed herself to compartmentalize and suppress her distress. Her dedication to her baby kept her on track, and outwardly she did very well with her infant in spite of her depression. With the reassurance of friends and her family doctor, her depression had passed by the time Yvonne was three months old. Shortly after this a project interviewer observed, "The mother is radiant and a delight to watch with her children."

Nonetheless on rare occasions during Yvonne's childhood, when her daughter resisted good manners, her mother was harsh with her. An interviewer noted that the mother was "more comfortable living by predetermined rules of behavior and may lack some flexibility." These maternal characteristics may explain Yvonne's rebellion in her college years. They may also account for a similar lack of emotional flexibility in Yvonne herself that contributed to her feeling so bereft and cornered that she cut herself with a sharp object when her boyfriend left her. From this low point Yvonne righted herself—actually used her miserable feelings to decide to put a stop to her self-destructive behavior—and started making better choices in her life.

There was trouble also in Victor's family although things worked out nicely for him. Early in his life his mother was very upset by the family's poverty. The father was earning nothing while struggling to be a novelist, and the mother, who was caring for the three children and working part-time, considered taking the children and leaving the father. The stress took its toll on the whole family for Victor had several severe infections, the mother had a car accident, and the father developed hepatitis. The mother at one point told her interviewer, "My husband feels to me like having another child in the house." Still she remained sensitively attuned and playful with Victor. Finally toward the end of his second year of life, the parents came to a splendid compromise. They moved from New York City to a small New Hampshire town where the father became a writer for the weekly town newspaper, sacrificing his wish for fame on a worldly stage for local recognition and a small regular paycheck. He also took over the lion's share of childcare and housework while the mother began working full-time outside of the home. Twenty years later the town council honored the father for his contribution to the village cultural life with his feature stories and summer theater program for children; and Victor himself is a father, house-husband, and part-time art teacher.

Victor's parents' compromise was difficult. They needed to work with a family therapist intermittently to manage their feelings about their unusual household. As an adult Victor recalled some meetings he had alone with the family therapist in grade school, "It was awesome, being able to talk with somebody who was interested in how I felt about my mom working full-time and my dad being the one at home who cooked and cleaned. It helped me get over the notion that there was something shameful about it because the kids had teased me at times. I'm sure it made it easier for me to be okay with my wife and I setting up our life like my parents."

When Victor was four years old, an interviewer wrote, "The father is more aware of delicately shaded nuances of his son's feelings. The mother has more broad responses to her children's behavior." Curiously, this is a reversal of what gender researchers have found to be the typical pattern of male and female responses in relationships, illustrating how statistically based studies are generalizations that miss individual differences. In spite of Victor's family's basically sound adjustment, his mother had waves of guilt when she went to work full-time, was no longer fully available to her child, and saw him become less bold and more shy. This subdued quality endures in Victor to this day.

The problem in Brad's family was actually a mixed blessing. His mother was ebullient, physically affectionate, and had grand fantasies about her son. So much so that when Brad was one year old the interviewer was struck by the extent to which the mother's excited fantasies had formed her image of her son. In the mother's words, Brad was "self-willed, seductive, a genius, aggressive, and assertive." However this was not how the interviewer saw the little boy, for he appeared to the researcher sound and happy but not strikingly unusual. As time passed Brad adapted himself well to his mother's image of him; benefited also from his father's strong role model; and at 30 was in fact very much the vision his mother had of him as a baby. Nonetheless, the mother's dynamism and profusion of joyful talk with him as a young child made it "hard for him to get a word in edgewise at times," wrote an observer. Probably as a consequence, Brad developed a slight stammer or speech hesitancy in childhood, which is still present now.

Everybody has psychodynamics but not everybody has psychopathology, a phenomenon well illustrated by these seven successful children: They all have psychological conflicts, defense mechanisms, strengths, and vulnerable, less fully developed parts of their personalities. However none of them have psychiatric conditions or symptoms of any consequence. The extremely effective meshing of their emotional dynamics makes them admirable people.

The Bottle or the Breast, Siblings, Social Status & Religion

To conclude let us briefly consider the impact on the successful children of four factors thought to influence child development—breast versus bottle feeding, brothers and sisters, parents' education and economic status, and religion. Regarding feeding, we could not discern differences in the successful children based on whether a baby was breast or bottle fed. Brad and Victor's mothers breast fed, the others bottle fed. Further, the research project did not find any statistical effect of bottle feeding and breast feeding in the overall group of 76. What is clearly more important is what the mother brings to the feeding experience. Additionally one could hypothesize that had Tatiana's mother been breast feeding her daughter, she might not have suffered the lapse in sensitivity which allowed her to leave her baby behind and go to Venezuela when Tatiana was eight months old. Still her overall empathy for her daughter was more highly developed than that of many other mothers who were breast feeding.

With respect to the influence of brothers and sisters on the seven highlighted children, siblings did not significantly affect their contentment or accomplishment as adults in any way that we as researchers or the participants themselves could define. This not withstanding, the sibling relationships and the personas of brothers and sisters are etched into the emotional life of each participant. The siblings lent richness, substance and depth to each participant through their interconnected experiences, their sharing, and in some cases through their relative distance or rivalry. The brothers and sisters have helped teach the children in the project how to compete, win, lose, share, separate and return; and how to feel sympathy, anger and pride. None of these lessons, however, depended on siblings entirely for the children learned them first (as children without brothers and sisters do) in the course of finding a place for themselves in the triangular world of their relationship with their mothers and fathers—the oedipal situation as Freud termed it.

In some of the other 76 families, siblings did in fact have a more powerful formative role, but this was when there were unusual circumstances: for example; a brother or sister with a severe physical handicap or emotional illness, a sibling who was unusually competitive or hostile; parents who unfairly favored another child; and in large families when an older sibling provided considerable care for a child. If a child had a brother or sister who was ill, she had to deal with the guilt of being the healthy survivor and with the attention the parents focused on the sick sibling. If a child had an unusually dominating brother or sister, she had to learn to master her own competitiveness, anger, or possible passivity or sense of inadequacy in the course of being dominated.

What about the impact of the parents' level of education, economic circumstances, and the child's level of intelligence on his development? For the seven children profiled here—as for the group of 76—parents' financial status, education, and the children's IQ *did not* play a central role in forming personality and adult vocational competence and satisfaction. How parents raised their children, the parents' personalities, and their expectations for their children were far more powerful determinants of future emotional well-being and adaptation. By way of illustration, Tatiana's family was the least educated and poorest, and Tatiana will soon finish law school. All of the children in this chapter have either equaled or bettered their parents' economic and educational attainment.

On the other hand, intelligence (as measured by IQ testing) did help predict whether children in this chapter (and in the entire study population) would obtain advanced education. Of the four cognitively gifted children studied here, Nicholas, Tatiana, and Julia have gone beyond masters degrees; Brad achieved a masters in computer science and then started his own company. It was not easy for him to leave the security of the university for the uncertainties of independence and competition in the business world. A period of psychotherapy helped him make his decision to go off on his own, and things have gone very well for him since. The other participants (Rose, Victor, and Yvonne) are not gifted but are doing well in their work or studies, favorable parenting having allowed them to use their abilities well.

Finally, we considered the role religion played in the lives of these children. From assessing the parents' beliefs and practices, and from talking with the grown children, it appears that organized religion exerted a surprisingly strong influence in the formation of the adult personalities of the children who have done well. It was not so much that religious doctrines guided actions over time or taught the participants what to believe in. Rather when parents actively belonged to a church or practiced a religious tradition at home while their children grew up, the religion reinforced the parents' personal doctrines. Parents in these successful families typically valued respect for others, love of family, compassion for others, decorous social behavior, and self-sufficiency. Parents may communicate and model these beliefs without specific religious practices or affiliation, but the added framework of religious practice in these families seemed to bolster the parents' message to their children. It did not matter to which particular tradition a family belonged for several were represented—Catholic, Protestant, Jewish, and Quaker. Four of the seven families went weekly to religious services, though only Tatiana's were devout believers in Biblical miracles as truths rather than as metaphorical teachings. The two other families occasionally went to religious services but were more apt to practice rituals of their faith at home.

Now as adults three of the participants continue to attend services regularly: Yvonne and her husband join her parents every Sunday at the same church she went to as a child; and Victor and Tatiana go to church but with slightly less regularity and investment than their parents. Rose attends church much less frequently than her parents did; and Brad, Nicholas, and Julia follow their parents' example of occasionally attending services on special occasions and practicing some observances at home. The level of involvement in religion of these 30 year olds may very well change when they have children of their own and wish to pass on traditions and values. Only Tatiana unhesitatingly answered that she believed in God; the responses the others gave were more equivocal and intellectual about the question, holding out the possibility but not the certainty of faith in the existence of God.

In spite of Tolstoy's (1873) dismissal of "happy families" as alike and lacking drama, our journey through the lives of Tatiana and Nicholas and their five counterparts has offered new discoveries and reminded us of old truths seen in new ways. The next chapter focuses on families filled with tension, distress, even tragedy.

Chapter 2

CHILDHOOD DISTRESS EXTERNALIZED

I've done new things, but whether I've changed inside I don't know,
Neil, 42 Up

WHEN A CHILD is distressed, there are basically two ways to manage distress: externalize it physically with emotionally driven behavior that reflects the child's inner unrest (often extremely restless, over-active, defiant or inattentive behavior), or turn suffering inward with a shutting down of physical expressions of feeling. Pain turned inward appears as depression, anxiety and fear, which over time frequently disfigure a child's developing personality: a sense of inadequacy, compulsivity, obsessiveness, and sometimes even compensatory grandiosity or arrogance can mark the behavior of these children.

Most children in distress are predominantly either externalizers or internalizers, however it is not unusual for children to shift back and forth from turning suffering inward to acting it out, until a child's unhappiness settles into a relatively stable balance of symptoms and personality distortions. This process—like the compacting of layers of sand and clay into sedimentary rock over geologic time—occurred in the children in our study in their twenties, although for most of the children distinguishing features of their adult personalities were well prefigured, sometimes even apparent by seven years of age.

A five year old said, trying to please his demanding parents, "I'm trying to be good but I can't." It being virtually impossible to meet their expectations, he nonetheless refused to sink into passivity and instead had become physically driven like the motor with the proverbial battery that never runs down. He had countless accidents, each one showing anew how he suffered inside. Of the 76 children in the project there were six like him whom the researchers identified as hyperactive in early childhood.

Although it was some 30 years ago that the six were identified as pathologically active, their behavior *then* (reconstructed from their childhood research record) fit or came close to fitting present-day criteria for attention deficit hyperactivity disorder (ADHD), which today is the most common childhood psychiatric diagnosis. In some instances, their behavior in its excitement, restless driven-ness and flight from expressions of sadness, unhappiness and anger also had hypomanic features. In this chapter we will follow two of these extremely active children closely from birth to age 30, and the other four in lesser detail in order understand the meaning and significance of outwardly directed symptoms of childhood. The life courses of these six individuals illustrate a series of phenomena: a) Psychological mechanisms involved in externalization of distress, b) problems in the families of the hyperactive children, severe in comparison to those in the successful, happy families of chapter one, c) the manner in which the children's symptoms are a response to perturbation of early parent-child interactions, d) psychological defenses externalizing children erect to manage unhappiness, and e) the manner in which symptoms and defenses endure **and** transform over time, affecting the adult personalities and lives of the participants.

Chapter 2. Table 2.1 Criteria for Attention Deficit Hyperactivity Disorder

1. Fails to give close attention to details and work.
2. Difficulty sustaining attention.
3. Doesn't seem to listen.
4. Difficulty organizing tasks and activities.
5. Loses things necessary for activities.
6. Easily distracted.
7. Forgetful.
8. Fidgets and squirms.
9. Leaves seat excessively.

10. Runs and climbs excessively.
11. Difficulty playing quietly.
12. "On the go . . . as if driven by a motor."
13. Blurts out answers too quickly.
14. Difficulty awaiting turn.
15. Interrupts or intrudes on others.

(Adapted from the *Diagnostic and Statisctical Manual IV* (DSM IV), American Psychiatric Association 1994. Diagnosis required 6 or more symptoms of inattention or 6 or more symptoms of hyperactivity and impulsivity to a degree that is maladaptive and inconsistent with developmental level.)

Frank—"I'm trying to be good but I can't"

Frank's mother and father, owners of a Long Island produce farm, were stiff and poker-faced like the couple in Grant Wood's emblematic painting, *American Gothic*. Their hard work seemed to have taken the spirit out of them, and when his mother nursed Frank, she was wooden, grim and still. On film she was unsmiling, affectless, and mechanical, rarely talking to her baby during feedings. She moved only to clean or burp the baby, albeit gently.

The mother read her child's states poorly for she usually interrupted the child when he was quiet and made him tense. She said that she felt great love for her baby, and seemed to have underlying warmth, but she could not release it. In her passivity, she was paradoxically present yet absent. She did not even know what to do for Frank when he cried, and by the time she did pick him up, he was too tense to relax. The boy's father was like the mother—quiet, accepting and austere. On the positive side the parents were a remarkably peaceful, level-headed couple.

At one year Frank's developmental testing was quite advanced, he had much energy, and babbled happily when he saw other children. "All male," the parents said of him and imagined that he would be "nice and easy going when he grew up." However as he started walking he became more and more active, got into everything and was unable to sit still. Like his mother and father, he was more involved with objects than people. Imitation of, and identification with his parents had begun very early for him—as it does in general with children—and affect was already missing in Frank except for that which other children could arouse in him. **In his second year** he became irritable, too easily frustrated, hard to soothe, aimlessly driven, and apart from others. His aloneness gave him a false air of self-sufficiency which his parents mistook for maturity and contentment. **At two years of age** he ate rat poison, which led to an overnight hospitalization.

At three Frank clung to his mother more than children usually do at this age. When he cried on seeing his mother after a brief separation, she gave no response. During his third year Frank became increasingly negativistic and on-the-move, as if there was an unseen motor operating within him and overwhelming him. Human contact should have been the brake for Frank's out-of-control motor, but his parents were simply too affectless to connect with him. It was also possible that Frank was trying to enliven his parents' interest in him with his unremitting activity, or make himself feel alive in the face of his parents' remoteness, which would represent an early form of hypomanic defensive behavior against emptiness or against parental depression.

Frank also at times seemed to use his over-activity to resist involvement with people, perhaps because he was already angry at his parents' emotional distance. The little boy's emotional tone was flat; he was shy; and he had a hard time paying attention. He was happiest playing physically with his father, yet it was a strange rough-housing: His father lay passively on the floor while the boy bounced frenetically on him.

He learned how to use the toilet during his third year, but bedwetting continued for many years. At home he was a trial, for even when he appeared to be well-meaning, his activity often misfired. For example, he tried to help his mother clean the house only to spray water on wet paint with his toy gun, and wipe it off with a dirty shirt. His mother had urged him to stop but didn't restrain him until had made a mess; then she spanked him on the backside. At this time in his life his parents were spanking him briefly several times a day.

At four when Frank visited the project he was so restless and controlling with his peremptory demands for cookies that it was not possible to test him. He was so immune to verbal restraint that his tester had to turn off the water to the sinks to prevent him from flooding the playroom. Both the mother and father—still distant and didactic—had no idea that their boy was having difficulties, nor any awareness of his inner life. At five, Frank valiantly protested his spankings, pleading to his discouraged mother, "I'm trying to be good, but I can't."

In the next few years Frank suppressed his oppositionality and did become "good." When he accidentally knocked down a chalk board at the project, he readily said, "Don't worry, I'll fix it." He and his mother remained stiff and mechanical like robots together, but outside of the family Frank was friendly with grownups and could light up with children. His ability to avoid conflicts helped him relate to people and ward off loneliness. Nonetheless **at five years of age** his interviewer wrote, "He is plagued with much underlying aggression and a poor self-image." When he played fantasy games he was a monster or robot from outer space; in real life he was sweet.

By seven years of age Frank's parents had tamed his hyperactivity at home, and his spankings were down to once a week. Only very rarely did he really burst out angrily as, for example, once when his mother asked him to put away toys at the end of a visit, and he flung them wildly across the room toward the toy box. A doubly chilling lesson for Frank had been when a school mate was struck by a car and killed, and his father said it was because the child had not obeyed his parents. But unfortunately the process of teaching him restraint had also interfered with the child's impulses and arrested his aggression and spontaneity. As we shall see this led to an enduring, incapacitating conflict over the expression of aggressive impulses, including normal sexual ones. At home Frank's parents were satisfied because he was less wild, only required "a clout less than once a week," and maintained his seeming cheerfulness. When he asked them if they were going to die, the parents were puzzled, though the researchers felt this question spoke to his suppressed anger against them and his guilty fear that they might reject him.

As a school child Frank's tension and probable underlying anxiety drove him to bite his fingernails to the quick. He was frequently agitated, moving constantly, and awkward with classmates—sometimes inappropriately aggressive when he tried to make contact with them. Nevertheless he gamely kept up an air of friendliness. He didn't heed his teacher's instructions, yet he also sought her out for approval and earned good grades. By age seven Frank had clear obsessional traits which showed in his difficulty committing himself to single answers during testing, traits which endured. The researchers thought that his avoidance of commitment came from his poor self-esteem, and from his need to suppress any self-assertiveness, even to the extent of masking how smart he was.

* * *

Let's jump now to **18 years**. Despite his powerful appearance, Frank was meek and methodical. At moments he offered a warm smile or solicitous comment. He had done very well in high school, earning high grades in keeping with his high IQ. He planned to attend a small university near his home in order to be able to visit his parents on weekends, and thought of becoming a teacher.

His psychological testing at 18 showed him still trying to check impulses and affects, as in childhood. Rorschach (Exner, 1974) and Thematic

Apperception Test (Bellak, 1975) pictures that connoted aggression unsettled him, and showed him to be very inhibited and restricted. In view of how restless he had been in childhood, his stillness, soberness, and self-control surprised Dr. Brody, but to achieve it he had lost his emotional life. He described himself as unable to stay interested in anything, which he unconvincingly attributed to his school mates being away for the summer. He felt good about himself when he played basketball, he said, but lamented his inability to shake minor injuries. His boredom and preoccupation with his body indicated a gathering depression.

As with many teenagers, he didn't remember his troubled childhood. "I had the best parents in the world. Mom and Dad have always been there . . . they put no pressure on me. They just wanted me to do well," he said, adding that spankings had happened once in a while but they didn't hurt. The double-bind for Frank was that in viewing his parents so generously, he abrogated seeing the reality of how troubled was his parents' relationship with him. He was left to blame himself for his emotional deadness, and in protecting his parents he turned his anger inward.

Frank had only two bad memories from childhood. The first was his sense of remorse and shame when his parents restricted him to home for a month for playing with matches. Fire seduces children like Frank whose parents over-control them or are too remote (especially if it is the father who is absent from a boy's life). Figuratively, Frank's parents had been extinguishing his emotional flames, and he had been trying to make sparks.

The second bad memory was his family's move to a new community when he was 14. Deep sadness appeared on his face as he described how the boys and girls of the town in which he had spent his childhood had been the bright spot in his life. In his new town he had not been able to find new friends. As researchers we imagined that his childhood friends—even though there was some evidence that the friendships were problematic—had been like a surrogate family compensating for the deadness in his nuclear family. We also wondered if Frank's sadness over the loss of his community roots at 14 might not be a memory that screened for deeper, unremembered experiences of never having felt (or never having been) truly rooted to his mother and father in early childhood.

Frank talked earnestly in a run-on, associative way. This suggested to us that the out-of-control motor that had prevented him from modulating his actions in childhood now expressed itself in his being verbally out of control. He sat very still, rambling on earnestly from subject to subject about how he wanted to help people, oppose war, attack people who were disrespectful to him, and learn martial arts. He couldn't watch sports, he said, because he felt too restless, and couldn't play because minor injuries seemed to take so long to heal. He insisted he wouldn't smoke or drink alcohol, because it was illegal and unhealthy. Hyper-morality and self-criticism seemed to have transformed his former wildness into inner conflict and torment. When asked if he felt any emotional distress, Frank said no. But then he talked hypothetically and at length about whether suicide was justified if someone were depressed. Dr. Brody also thought that his rambling speech came from loneliness, for it helped him hold onto her. She urged him to find a therapist if and when he found himself unhappy.

* * *

Twelve years passed. At 30 Frank was gaunt. He wore khakis and a blue work shirt to the interview; his hair was in bangs over large spectacles, giving him a dazed look. He told us that his twenties had been like lost years. He had had a brief, asexual marriage during university with a classmate who, he said, had been mostly a study partner. She left for graduate school at another university and he had lingered on, taking an occasional course and going home most weekends. He had not dated another girl in ten years, and felt no sexual desire toward women or men. He had not sought psychotherapy although he realized his life was not going well. He still insisted that he had never felt depressed, but at times felt confused about what to do with himself. He still linked the loss of his childhood friends when he was 14 to his stagnation.

He had resisted his parents' invitation to return home and work their farm with them because he wanted work that involved more people and using his mind. His ability to earn money was a comfort. Since university he had worked in college restaurants and bookstores and in construction, always quickly getting promoted and then losing interest. A year before he had enrolled in theology graduate school because he liked the questions of morality and meaning that theology posed. He imagined that with the degree he could teach or even have a congregation, for he enjoyed being with people. However, he doubted how suited he was to this profession because he wasn't sure if he believed in God's existence.

At 30 Frank's psychological tests showed that his seven-year-old nascent personality style had crystallized. His primary defenses were reaction formations of kindliness against aggressive impulses, rigid repression, regression into sleep-like withdrawal, and obsessive intellectualization and rationalization which kept feelings at a distance. Also highly compulsive, he frequently double and triple checked to see if he had turned off the heat and lights when he left his apartment, which he recognized as mildly irrational.

Significantly, he no longer idealized his parents. He now recalled feeling lonely for more contact with them as a child, especially a keen sense of longing for more activities with his father. Remarkably, in a research film made 25 years earlier we saw Frank playing with toy figures. He says, "This is daddy, and this is me. I'm making a room for daddy where I can keep him to play with me." The adult Frank also now said that he wished his parents had "pushed" him to do more as a youth, but he couldn't say how they could have pushed him more. The wish seemed more a general yearning for greater past involvement by his parents in his life. His mother made him feel safe in childhood, he said, but she was so busy that she left him alone a lot. He could recall no hugs from the time he started school, and to this day he has difficulty talking to his parents about anything personal, which he still takes as a fault of his own.

Frank is evidently very troubled and we are quite worried about him. His first memory, which he places at about four years of age, is of being trapped in the furnace room of his house. He is now trapped in himself like his mother had been with him as a baby. He has a recurrent nightmare of being chased by a monster, but his gun won't go off. This may represent his misfired sexuality or his sense of inefficacy in the face of inner, monstrous feelings. He suffers physical symptoms such as frequent indigestion, and once couldn't move his legs to walk for three days, a paralysis for which no physical cause was found. His typical mood is "tired." Suicide is a question that interests him, but he doesn't feel that he needs psychological help because these thoughts are purely a philosophical exercise, he insists.

Dafna—Like A Wound Up Top That Has Been Let Go

The lives of restless, impulsive children are not always as grim as Frank's, nor do they inevitably portend troubled adaptations in life. Dafna's story is far more optimistic. She is the oldest of four, born when her mother was 19. Her mother had been a secretary in a law firm when she met Dafna's father, a young attorney. The mother was action oriented, not introspective, and had loved the exciting camaraderie in the law firm. Her own childhood had been like this, she said, joyful in a large, close, happy family.

The mother told her interviewer that she wanted to give her baby all the affection she had received, but the mother's energy and personality got in the way of her closeness with her daughter. The mother was still an adolescent, and as many teenagers are wont to be, her emotions were poorly modulated and her sense of patience not yet developed. Her relationship with her baby was "busy" rather than physically intimate. When she fed her child she was controlling and lacked empathy. Although consistent, she was also aggressive, dominating and self-certain.

At six weeks during feeding, the mother fussed over her child, talked loudly, and took a cheerful command that allowed no time for quiet, gentle moments. Baby Dafna couldn't relax during feeding and the mother was unaware that she could have slowed down the tempo. The mother's smile appeared intimate, her humor kept the mood upbeat, but mother and child were not connected emotionally. The research observer wrote that the mother was "like a wound up top that has been let go." Well-paced mother-infant reciprocity was missing; the mother didn't draw the child into interactions, and didn't allow the baby to bring the mother in.

By six months Dafna was tense, restless and often vomited during feeding. To engage and entertain her baby the mother made faces and talked constantly. Often tough and teasing, the mother rarely played quietly with her baby or left her alone much. Dafna herself now had many moods—she could be quiet and subdued, irritable, contented, and engagingly smiling.

By one year the mother often simply placed the food on the table and let Dafna run around and take what she wanted, because she felt her child was resisting her feeding. However the researchers observed Dafna waiting for her mother to join her in feeding or to offer food, but the mother didn't notice. At other times the mother pushed Dafna so tightly into her high chair that instead of running about the little girl shifted to social activity—waving a banana and making comical faces at her mother, expressions like those the mother used to engage Dafna.

Correspondingly, on developmental testing at one year, Dafna favored physical and social activities to the detriment of understanding relationships between objects. She was now walking, almost in constant motion, and when she put herself in danger her mother spanked her. **At two years** an observer wrote, "Dafna's high level of gross motor development, sustained intensity of activity, and unusual physical strength is unlike that of any other baby I have seen. She is the only one who has literally turned over furniture within a few minutes after arriving."

When Dafna was a toddler her mother often vacillated suddenly from permissive to controlling to emotionally and physically remote. She was proud of her child—predicting that the little girl would be a friendly, extroverted adult—but also quick to reject Dafna's unhappy feelings with a sarcastic, "Such a tough life you have." By now Dafna had identified with her mother's outgoing qualities—her assertiveness and excessive activity.

Around two and three years of age the child became shy in the presence of her talkative mother, but she warmed up to the examiner when her mother was absent. Dafna lingered on her bottle until she was three, and about the time she gave it up she started using the toilet, but like Frank bedwetting was a problem for her until she was 11. Dafna could be quite stubborn and she had temper tantrums, which especially vexed her father who frequently spanked her; however, she was also relatively easy to soothe. Overall both parents had affection for their daughter, and as more children were born, Dafna tried to help and even wanted to nurse the babies.

When she was four a dark cloud passed over the family. The mother became very tense, started chain smoking, and spoke angrily about what she said was her husband's "laziness". The researchers assumed at the time that the troubles were from the demands of two more babies. The father himself became distant in his interview but also talked for the first time about his father's alcohol problem and his mother's violent temper. Only years later when Dafna was 18 did the project learn from her that her father had begun having episodes of manic behavior and drinking at this time.

At five Dafna maintained her lively friendliness. On testing she challenged herself and succeeded well, but had developed the habit of avoiding conflicts and tended to be over-compliant. Although the mother continued to be distant and brusque at times, when Dafna played with her mother the youngster was excited and enjoyed it, and the mother responded actively.

During their interviews the mother and daughter reported a new baby and two near tragedies. With wry humor to control her tension and help her take life as it came, the mother said, "You missed all the fun. First came the baby, then our two year old fell down a cliff, and then we found my husband unconscious in the basement." At five Dafna said about the near tragedies, "You know, Ryan fell down a hill and he had to get so many X-rays you couldn't believe it." In his interview the father acknowledged somewhat evasively, "I've been acting like a child. I don't know how I got myself into having so many children, and I am getting help for my problem."

When she started kindergarten Dafna had headaches, stomach aches and other pains for many weeks. At school the research observer found her "robust, feminine, competent, accepted by peers, yet often alone." Her earlier hyperactivity was transforming into compulsive neatness with her school things in class and toys at home—a manifestation of a desire to create external order to manage inner turbulence, and also an attempt to be like her business-like mother.

Next year when Dafna was six the father was boyish and egocentrically dogmatic, upset that his daughter was not yet reading because he recalled already having been a reader in kindergarten. He said that Dafna had outgrown the need for physical discipline, but contradicted himself and revealed that he had just spanked her for slamming a door. The mother remained hearty and well-meaning, and enjoyed Dafna's sociability, though she was little tuned into the girl's inner life and quickly became brisk and cool when Dafna wanted to stay and play at the end of her project visit.

At seven Dafna's vitality *and* tension were especially present in her expressiveness. The psychologist wrote, "She is without a doubt the most animated child I have met. She has rapid speech, rapid movements, a broad contagious grin, theatrical behavior to the point of silliness, and myriad expressions. When she talks, her train of thought is broken by extraneous thoughts and a habit of changing words from those originally chosen." When asked what a stomach is, Dafna replied, "It . . . like . . . takes our food, and the part . . . you know . . . we don't need . . . you know . . . it goes away."

During her developmental testing Dafna worked hard to stay still with only partial success. She was considerate, perfectionistic, had trouble admitting failure, asked for reassurance, and doubted her ability. One of her comments alarmed the researchers. She said that the most pleasant thing she could think of was "going to sleep." This suggested that Dafna was pushing herself too hard to be grown up (and being pushed by circumstances and her parents). She was emotionally worn out, and wanted to regress to a changed state of consciousness (sleep), and to retreat.

There was apparently an imbalance in the child's needs for release, and needs for keeping herself under control. The mother said revealingly, "I see my own devils returning in the personality of my kids. They get wild and I lose control." She explained that when Dafna jumped on the couch, she responded like a tornado, giving her daughter many room restrictions, and spankings. Dafna's daily chores were making her bed, setting the table, feeding the cat, and keeping her room clean, a hefty order for a child her age.

* * *

Eleven years passed and Dr. Brody wondered how Dafna would appear after a childhood replete with problems as well as gratifications. She arrived smiling for her **18 year followup** and spoke quickly, openly, often tangentially, and didn't pause to reflect. She was colorfully dressed and handsome, and had enjoyed many high-school extracurricular activities, especially cheerleading. In her busyness she was like her parents, who themselves were involved in many community activities and were officers in the Parent-Teacher Association.

Her grades had been Bs, and her Standardized Admission Test for college was not up to that level. Her IQ at 18 was the same as at age seven, 112, a high average score. Although happy and successful in many ways, she also said she felt insecure about focusing herself on doing well academically in school. Her psychological testing indicated that poor confidence had lowered her performance.

It appeared that Dafna was so in need of companionship that she had not developed herself as an individual. Her childhood interviewers had worried about this possibility because of her desire to please others. We later theorized that the mother's lack of responsiveness to Dafna's cues in infancy, and her over-control of Dafna perhaps undermined her individual development. This problem between mother and child appeared to have created a lingering loneliness in Dafna. She had attempted to repair it by identifying with her mother, and by socializing compulsively. As she went off to college her adolescent aspirations were exhibitionistic and narcissistic—she planned to try out for lead roles in campus theater that would capture attention and make her feel good.

Dr. Brody also felt that the parents' strict discipline may have contributed to suppressing their daughter's personal development and pushed her to live emotionally through interaction with others. The father's alcohol problems seemed to have driven Dafna to support others in their problems, while at the same time she clung to supportive figures herself. At 18 Dafna recalled well her father's crises when she was four and five. She and her mother had found small bottles of brandy all about the house; the father had been hospitalized and, as her mother told her later, diagnosed as a manic-depressive. Every few years, Dafna said, "he stopped taking his lithium and went off the deep end." Most of the time the father didn't drink, and had been able to continue his work.

* * *

When Dafna was interviewed at 30, we saw that time had been good to her. Her interviewer wrote, "She is an impressive and lovely woman, a standout in the study—composed, thoughtful, accomplished, warm, and satisfied with her life." Anticipating the imminent birth of her first child, she was still animated as in childhood and candid like her mother. Now living in an attractive home which she had decorated in restful pastels, she reported that getting to this point had not always been easy, for as she said, "There were time that I didn't have a pot to piss in." A marriage in her early twenties to a man who became alcoholic had ended in divorce; and she herself had drunk too much during this marriage. She is now remarried and neither she nor her husband use any alcohol. Her vulnerability to drinking recalls how as a six year old she said that the most pleasant thing she could think of was going to sleep. Sleep as a child and alcohol as an adult defended her against her conflicts and unhappiness. "My addiction now is chocolates," she says.

Thinking back to childhood, her greatest satisfactions had been her many girlfriends and being "the little parent" to her younger siblings. She recalled her mother fondly in childhood as playful and comforting. This view of her mother, when compared to the research documentation of the mother's brusqueness and insensitive interactions with the young Dafna, raises important questions. Is her perception of her mother based on a mature appraisal that her mother was well-meaning and did the best she could? Is her perception distorted by amnesia for early childhood experience? How much of her affection for her mother comes from being provided for, her mother's own quality of upbeat denial, her mother's relative stability compared to the father, and limited contact with other mothers who nurtured differently? And did she need to protect her mother from criticism, or protect herself from guilt if she devalued her mother? These issues have implications for understanding development and the relationships adult children have with their parents, as well as for psychotherapy in adulthood, which we will consider further in chapter 6.

On the other hand Dafna said that life with her father had been like a painful roller-coaster. When he was happy and up, he was fun; when he was depressed, he was hostile. He had made her fear the unpredictable. Once when she was 11 and her father couldn't work, the mother had to farm the children out to relatives for several weeks and start working full-time until the father got on his feet again. Then characteristically the mother became active on the board of the local foster care agency as a result of her own personal experience. Interestingly, at 30, in spite of her relatively detailed recall of experiences with her father, Dafna had forgotten that he had ever spanked her. Perhaps this was because of a need to repress certain emotional states connected with aggression, for she said, "I'm a forgiving person; the downside is that I never learned how to get angry because I was scared to lose control. I couldn't take a chance on that after what my father put us through."

At university she did reasonably well as a theater major; but then turned down job offers in television to become a probation officer for juvenile delinquents. She could use her talent with people, and the work brought her into her father's profession. She laughingly says, "Hey, I'm familiar with lawyers and know how to talk with them. My dad was like a mentor to me, taking me around and introducing me to all the judges and lawyers. It was an easy job, and I was good at it." This was also how she met her first husband, a public defender. But life around the courts was too fast, there was too much substance abuse, and she realized she had to make a change.

"I felt terrible about helping myself by leaving my husband. And my father didn't help by telling me I should stay with him, that he would stop drinking." It was also hard for her to leave her first husband because she felt dependent on him, she said, and in fact beginning in her teens had always thought she had to have a boyfriend. Feeling desperate, she imagined suicide, which led her to obtain psychiatric treatment, which enabled her to move on with her life.

On one of their first dates, the man who became her second husband asked her what she was trying to run away from. This helped her start thinking about her fear of losing control of feelings and situations. Now that they have been together for four years, she says that he has made it possible for her to stop running. "He is practical like my mother, but calmer; not a kid like my father or first husband." With her husband she manages a garden supply company, and no longer feels the compulsion to be constantly moving. "I can sit down and think when I'm worried. All my life I had been hyper. I came by it naturally since those were the models I grew up with. I don't have that racing feeling anymore, that sense of a storm brewing. Up until we bought the baby's crib, I don't think I've ever had happy tears. I grew up with so much chaos that it is only now that I can be alone with one person, not constantly looking for some kind of excitement." Dafna's greatest sadness in her life is about her father. "I want to shake him and say, 'Deal with things! His own father died last year and he hasn't shown any feelings yet."

We ended by asking Dafna how she would change the world if she could. As with many of the research participants, her wish comes from painful experience projected onto society. She says, "The world is fear-based. The fear of not having enough, or of losing what you have. And then what people do to avoid fear or create fear in others. This is what needs to be changed. I'm fascinated with fear and what it makes people do."

Kevin—A Sticky Enmeshment

Kevin faced none of the family tension, drama and over-stimulation which Dafna did, nor the emotional vacuum and rigid standards that were Frank's lot. Instead he had to cope with his parents' confusion. Even before she returned home from the hospital with her baby, Kevin's mother (dominated by her own disapproving mother) spoke of feeling panicked that she wouldn't be able to care for her son. Her husband was little able to ease her anxiety, and in fact curtailed her breast feeding because he thought it wasn't as efficient as bottle feeding.

When Kevin was six weeks old, the researchers said of the mother, "She has not established a relationship with her baby. She is clearly eager for one but her inner conflicts and lack of support from her husband and mother wall her off. She suppresses feelings and substitutes being very organized. Often, however, she misreads her child saying he is hungry when he is actually resting; when he is curious she has said that he is 'too nosy,' and in this regard seems to be identifying her baby with her mother in feeling that they are both intruding into her life. When he is actually hungry she is slow to gratify him and inept in her attempts to comfort him when he is upset."

About the father they wrote, "He is uncomfortable with his wife's closeness to the baby, uneasy, restless, emotionally closed and avoiding eye contact. Still he is polite and not unappealing. The father seems to be in hiding, peering out timidly with positive feelings for his son but sadly shyness and with-holding conspire to prevent him from saying, except rarely, good things that he likes about his little boy."

In this climate, lacking the stimulation and support of a well-forged relationship with his parents, Kevin was a relatively inert, subdued, and inexpressive infant. By the second half of his first year, his interviewer could scarcely engage him and he appeared depressed. As he entered his second year the excitement of walking (his newfound mobility and adventuring) brought Kevin relief, even joy, which rubbed off on both parents who for the first time spontaneously had fun with their son. Still the mother couldn't maintain her pleasure, and often became apprehensive or cold and matter-of-fact. The father also retreated and never truly settled into a lively involvement with his son. Thus by the third year Kevin was increasingly restless, unanchored, and unable to focus on anything for more than a moment.

As the years passed he became quick, impulsive, wild with his toys, and often tried to hit his mother. He resisted his parents' entreaties, room restrictions and occasional spankings. Increasingly frustrated and by now convinced that their son had always been hyperactive and difficult, the parents pushed him prematurely to learn manners in the hope that this would civilize him. For respite they started taking one and two week vacations apart from him. Tense and whiney, Kevin was also a worrier about car accidents after his father experienced a minor injury from an accident, about robbers, and about bad news in general on television. Highly unusual for a boy, he cried at sad movies, and feared his own and his parents' death. Illustrating how children do not necessarily fall neatly into either the category of externalizer or internalizer, Kevin's fears were probably a response to anxiety about the many separations from his parents, combined with anxiety over his internally experienced anger at them for their frustrating lack of engagement with him.

In school he was bright, silly, sometimes fun, often inattentive, and sometimes uncontrollable, such as when he set off the fire alarm. Once when he leapt into a school-yard fight, received a bad scratch on the face, and came crying to the teacher, he said of the pain, "My tears did it," as if he knew that sadness underlay his aggressiveness. Academically Kevin's work was average as was his intelligence. At times the school recommended tutoring for him, which helped him overcome obstacles in his learning.

What remained of the little boy in adolescence and adulthood? When he was 18 Sylvia Brody wrote, "Kevin continues to be stickily entrapped in a family whose members are mostly at odds with each other. He wants to run from them but feels too isolated to flee. As time goes on he may husband his energies for sports and not be able to care for much else." His greatest pleasure in his late teens was an interest in golf he shared with his father; but he still was ill at ease with the way both parents compared him unfavorably to his younger brother and sister.

Dr. Brody's comments were prescient, for when we visited with him 12 years later he took little joy in life. He said he was contentedly married but he and his wife and parents were involved in a three way conflict over a joint real estate venture in which they each blamed the others for problems with the property. He seemed to be a person of deep feelings but also enduring resentments, halting and inarticulate, who made his interviewer feel as though he would say something wrong and Kevin would hold it against him. It was hard to win his trust as if he had been hurt badly, while at the same time he exerted a strong pull to be taken care of. When we asked him to describe his parents he first said that they were nice, protective and sharing. But when we asked him for memories of times that they had been this way, he could give none, and in fact could not recall ever being held or comforted by his parents. Memories he did have were of their teaching him hard work and responsibility, for which he thanked them. His only experience of unalloyed warmth when he was growing up was from an uncle who had taught him to play baseball and had often taken him fishing.

Kevin is now an assistant administrator of a social services agency which occasionally gives him satisfaction, and he also fantasizes going to graduate school in city planning, but doubts whether he has enough discipline for the reading and writing requirements. Golf still remains a pleasure for him and his father, while the idea of having children seems to him very remote. Periods of psychotherapy have helped him feel less shy, he reports, though he still is troubled by fears such as worries about his own and his wife's health. His childhood hyperactivity has receded so that as an adult he is able to sit and work steadily at a desk. His early life symptoms have transformed into a chronic, low grade guilty depression and anxiety (dysthymia), as well as into obsessional personality characteristics in which compulsive, restless worrying takes the place of his childhood physical restlessness.

Like the proper boy he was raised to be, he tried to spare his parents as much ill will as possible, describing them as nice. However when he let his guard down, he also said they were distant and demanding. Both statements are relative truths, for across the span of his childhood and youth his parents were concerned about him and took care of him, while on another level they could frequently be emotionally absent, uninvolved, and dissatisfied.

Farley—The "Bad Seed" of a Physically Abusive Father

Farley was one of but a handful of the 76 children who were physically abused. His story shows how physical maltreatment can shape a child, first making him look and act one way during his early, plastic years, and then another way as his personality solidified. His father was an insecure, angry, paranoid man whose own father had beaten him at a young age, then left the family and occasionally returned, promising that he would be dutiful, only to leave again. Farley's father attempted to control his inner desperation by tyrannizing his wife and two sons, and occasionally erupted into belt thrashings, which twice sent Farley to the hospital. During his 30-year interview he showed us a belt buckle scar on his shoulder.

Unfortunately the mother herself was too immature to protect her children until ten years had passed and she had found another man ready to take her in. At that point she finally gave up her peace-at-any-price detachment. She threatened to take the children and leave if her husband didn't stop his tirades, which did in fact cow him into a stolid submission.

The mother's immaturity also showed in her care of Farley as a baby. For example, during a feeding she and the child were in different worlds emotionally. The baby was sated from his bottle and uninterested in cereal but his mother continued to shovel it into his mouth. He became very upset yet even at moments when he calmed, she continued mechanically feeding him, re-arousing his tension which she mistook for hunger. There were frequent instances of such micro-misreadings of the child's shifting states of calm, hunger, satiety, irritability and responsiveness. They often happened very swiftly, and a casual observer who simply saw the feeding, the mother's unchanging rhythm, and her seemingly contented expression (which masked her disconnection) may have been lulled into thinking that the feeding was unremarkable.

The father's tyranny and the mother's mechanical insensitivity with Farley did not mean that the youngster was over-controlled, for he was also relatively neglected in infancy and early childhood. The parents spent most of the day at work in their small neighborhood cafe, letting their children run free a great deal. Casually watched by neighbors, teenage girls, and the father's kind sister who lived around the corner, the children had no set meal times and slept when and where they dropped when they were tired. As they grew older they took food where and when they wished—from the restaurant, from the apartment, in front of the TV, and on the front steps.

As an infant Farley was tense, stiff and restless. At six months an observer wrote, "There is a shocking lack of communication between the mother and baby as if each continually reads the other incorrectly. The child cries more during the visit than almost any other child. But he has a great winning smile, is enormously tough, and loves to use his body. By the time he was walking he was wrecking the house, and neither parent made any consistent effort to control him. For his part Farley seemed to be soothing his internal tension with continuous, changing activities, and was little related to people. Growing older, he hardly ever walked, only ran, and developed the school-boy reputation of being the fastest kid in his Brooklyn neighborhood. Perhaps he was running away from inner demons, for his father had labeled him "a bad seed," and Farley and his parents were fighting about everything—dressing, toys, orderliness, food, school work.

A project interviewer wrote, "I feel marked pessimism for this child who gives evidence of emotional problems and lives in a confusing environment that is lacking in security and physically threatening, which will lead to an exacerbation of emotional disturbance." This was the only family of the 76 in the study that prompted the researchers to alert child protective services (another child, Nita, chapter five, suffered equally bad physical abuse but the project was not aware of its severity at the time).

There were compensations for Farley, for his parents provided him and his brothers with all the art and music lessons their very modest means would allow. They enjoyed their turns walking the children to grade school. In class Farley was largely mute and inexpressive, and could scarcely pay attention for he was so vigilantly tuned into noises from the street that he regularly jumped up to go to the window when he heard them. With classmates he was unfortunately remote like his father, and rarely had pleasant interactions with them. Yet he tried to please his teachers by offering to do chores for them. "A little adult," said one teacher of him, adding that his mother was "a gentle soul." At seven Farley told his interviewer, "I love my parents a million dollars." Later when Farley became a stand-out competitor in track and field in high-school, one or the other parent was always in the stands.

When he was 18 years old, Sylvia Brody was apprehensive about his interview, but he presented himself forthrightly, modishly dressed like a clothes conscious hippy in a tie-dyed shirt, hair carefully cut to his shoulders. His early childhood effervescence was long gone, and the emotional blandness and impassivity that had appeared by the time he entered grammar school was still with him. His IQ had risen from mid-average (95) in childhood to high average (112) which probably reflected the decline in violence in the home, and Farley himself said he could do better but he became too nervous on tests. His distinction was sports and he was on his way to the University of Texas on an athletic scholarship. He wanted to major in business, an interest which he attributed to working the cash register and assisting in the family's restaurant throughout high school.

His psychological testing showed poor self-esteem, and a tendency to lose his identity and fall into a symbiosis with parental figures. As for his hyperactivity, he tried hard to inhibit his impulsiveness and felt ashamed when he couldn't keep himself still or in a chair. In terms of psychological defenses, he alternated between a Pollyannaish denial of emotions and irritability; he regularly used projection to displace his anger onto others; and he split people into camps—all good or all bad. In spite of his liabilities he had grown into an agreeable teenager but one who seemed to Dr. Brody as "too tamed" with his low, emotionless voice and prematurely narrow, fixed interests.

More years passed and Farley returned as a grownup. His appearance had changed with the times so that now, still eager to make a fashion statement, he was dressed in a Western style, with cowboy boots, a studded Western shirt, Levis, and a denim vest. However, he had not stayed long in Texas. He felt quickly out-of-place and homesick, and his college and sports career had come to a premature end. He returned to his home neighborhood and convinced his parents to convert the cafe into a more upscale juice and sandwich bar. He had also taken the initiative in opening two new locations in Manhattan, one which he runs and the other which a brother runs. The family was earning far more than they had ever imagined and with his leadership had more plans to expand.

Given how threatening his childhood had been, it was gratifying to see Farley make a satisfying life for himself in spite of such adversity. Yet his manner was still deadened; in a way, he appeared worn out. Farley says of himself: "I'm a hardworker and I'm realistic. I don't look for people to be perfect, I just try to hire people so that their good qualities balance out their bad ones." This approach also explains how he deals with his father now, for he is actually in business with him.

Two years ago Farley married his girlfriend of many years, the only girl with whom he has ever had a serious relationship. "We dated for ten years before I gave in. I knew she wanted children and I was too scared to be a father because I've seen how parents can lose it with their children. My wife has a temper also and it took me a long time to deal with that. I had some therapy in high school because I knew I had to talk to somebody about my father. The therapist had my mother and father join us for a few visits and my dad blew everybody's mind and actually talked about himself. It was the first time he said anything about having any feelings about his own father."

Farley still has vivid recollections of his father abusing him until he was ten. One beating came after he and his brothers ate a pizza the father had been saving for himself. He also remembers a trip to the hospital when he was slapped and his ear started bleeding. Sometimes if toys were on the floor when his father came home, he would punish the children because he assumed they had been playing rather than studying. There was a period in which he was hit every time he did something wrong, which was at least once a week. Once his father put him in a closet with his dinner and forced him to stay there until he cleaned the plate. Farley became hysterical but refused to eat hoping his mother would come home and calm his father; but she didn't and Farley ended up eating the food and throwing it up. "Always the next day my father apologized but we were so scared of him that I'd piss in my pants." Farley was still literally trembling at 30 as he talked about these experiences. "I'd constantly think of places to hide from him, but I also knew he loved us and wanted us to have the best; that's why he stopped hitting because he didn't want to lose us when my mother said she'd take us away. He's still strange. He works hard all day and never says much except a few words about work. I know he had a very hard time growing up so I can understand. I don't think I've ever really seen him laugh."

As an adult Farley has compassion and strength, though his high spirits of early childhood were long ago squelched. The father's rages, combined with Farley's stubbornness, anger and tension, and the absence of structure within the home all seemed to have been behind Farley's extreme childhood restlessness. He never contained it enough to do well in school, but he did channel it successfully into sports. His kind aunt's presence in the neighborhood must also have lent him the strength to stand up to his father rather than be entirely broken by him. Farley now sublimates his restlessness and aggression into expanding the family business.

As an adult he has identified with the good qualities in his parents, such as his father's assertiveness and both parents' dedication to the family and hard work. But he has not at all escaped his childhood unscathed. When he and his wife-to-be first became sexually involved in their early twenties, Farley had a period of impotence. Psychotherapy helped him through it. Throughout his adult life he has had occasional panic attacks especially when he feels a threat to success in his work or has to stand up to an employee or supplier. Once when his father was in pain from a kidney stone, Farley's own stomach began to hurt and he rushed to the emergency room afraid that he had cancer.

Farley's anxiety attacks are also a recurring, unconscious re-experiencing of his terror that he wouldn't survive his father's rages as a child—a chronic posttraumatic stress reaction. His vulnerability to anxiety is also likely linked to his mother's painful, detached relationship to him in infancy; however Farley is only aware of fearing his father. The past also lives on in his marrying a woman who has tantrums so that Farley must still work on strategies for handling another person's outbursts, though fortunately his wife is also protective of him. The family's terrors at the hands of the father from years past have made them mutually interdependent and unable to separate. But seen differently, their symbiosis has also created a family partnership which is prospering. In some respects Farley (like many abused children) is like a subject in a totalitarian regime. When given the chance for freedom, he choses to stay home with what is familiar and never truly becomes liberated.

Kandis—"The most unpleasant thing I can think of is me."

In the group of six hyperactive children Kandis was the other child who was badly abused; however the abuse was not physical but unremitting emotional torment by her mother. Also in contrast to Farley who knew his parents cared for him, Kandis was never sure whether she even mattered to her parents. A few days after the mother gave birth to Kandis she announced that she "would get rid of a child who wouldn't mind," and with this call to arms, she raised Kandis with just that kind of iron-clad mentality.

Nonetheless, there were inconsistencies in the mother's expressed attitudes, and also between her words and actual behavior that betrayed a serious inner confusion about firmness and love. For example, she chose to bottle feed because she said it was efficient, but said she would never use bottle props because, "Feeding is the only way to be close with the baby." Still, shortly afterward she started leaving Kandis alone in her crib to suck on the propped up bottle. She planned to indulge her daughter, she said, because, "Only lack of attention hurts children," but then shortly afterward she said, "Indulging children is a weakness and they will find you out." Listening to her talk of her baby was like listening to military and political leaders planning strategy. At other moments she feared her strictness would keep her daughter from loving her. Misguidedly she thought that she could quickly establish her baby's sleeping and waking patterns because, "It is just a matter of conditioned reflexes." Then in the midst of what she called "habit training the baby," she and her husband left the one month old with a sitter for a two week vacation.

Films show the mother tensely restraining Kandis when she tried to move during a feeding at six months. The mother spoke to her in clipped tones offering no respite for mutual cooing or play. These were painful films for infant psychiatry specialists to watch even though untrained viewers might have been lulled by the mother's seeming efficiency, purposeful gaze on the child, and lack of visible anger. In spite of her deprivations, for most of her first year of life Kandis smiled and gurgled, enjoyed being held by people, and was developmentally advanced, vital, and easy going.

By her first birthday, however, her pace of development was slowing and on testing she lost interest too quickly if she didn't solve problems on her first or second try. In her second year she lost her smile and became tense. She kept moving, couldn't relax, couldn't stay in her mother's lap or even close to her, nor could she place with a toy for more than a moment.

Unlike some parents who changed when they saw their children having trouble, Kandis' mother remained controlling, withholding, and fixated on cleanliness, wiping up after Kandis the instant food landed outside the dishes, shutting down the child's spontaneity. Because she couldn't stand messiness, the mother rarely allowed her daughter to eat with her, and often forced Kandis to wait for her meals until she had finished reading the newspaper or doing her exercises.

Why did the father allow this to go on? Did he not see how it was hurting his daughter? Like Farley's mother, he was meek and felt it better to keep the peace, though in the interstices of his wife's criticisms of Kandis, he found opportunities to play with his daughter. The father's interviewer wrote, "He is a timid person, but he can identify with Kandis against the mother as shown by the twinkle in his eye when he talks of her stubborness. This must be a great comfort to Kandis but the father's lack of spirit gives the child no alternative model."

As a toddler Kandis was destroying things by incessantly taking them apart and tantruming when she was hungry. She had grown to tolerate people and children in place of relating to them, though she never actually withdrew from people. She was continuously busy but without any sparkle. In fact her hyperactivity may have saved her from an autistic-like psychotic withdrawal, for had she not kept busy, had she slipped into passivity, she might have created a self-generated hallucinatory world to fill the void in her life. Her moods narrowed over time to slight, bland smiles and crossness. Her speech showed the impoverishment of a neglected child who was perplexed by what was going on about her, though unable to express her perplexity.

When she started nursery school, the mother returned to work as a travel agent, and Kandis's mood improved slightly. Slightly more satisfied with her daughter, and seeing her as a confident child, the mother felt she still needed to hold Kandis in check with spankings and room restrictions when she didn't meet such expectations as keeping her room clean, which was hardly possible for such a small child. At five Kandis was somewhat rebellious in kindergarten, but it was mostly in the form of passive-aggressive actions—surreptitiously cutting the hair off dolls and stealing from other children, and bringing forbidden candy to school in her pockets. In class she swung from excessive compliance to restlessness, with compulsive scratching, rubbing, hitting or pinching her legs, and masturbating. She appeared inattentive, depressed, vacant, awkward, and over-cautious. She was too frozen to join other children in play, but stayed in her place during group activities and was able to work alone. Her teacher said, "She's wishy-washy. She can follow rules but it seems like she does it out of fear." Poignantly Kandis once put her arm around another girl who had been bullied by a bigger girl and said, "I know how you feel," but Kandis was too inhibited to continue her overture and the girls drifted apart.

At six and seven years of age she was changing. She raced through her testing, talking non-stop and sometimes boasting how smart she was or belittling questions as stupid. It was as if a hypomanic defense had taken over, a defense that contained in it an identification with her mother's anger and aggressiveness. Playing with her mother at the project, they struggled for control, Kandis telling her when and where to put dolls and furniture in the doll house. When her mother chastised, "Stop giving me orders;" Kandis countered, "Then you stop doing things." In school she was clowning, grandiose, rude and bossy—even occasionally violent, hurling toys into their boxes during clean up. She talked too much, largely in monologues, apparently to control relationships and perhaps also to keep other children and grownups attentive to her.

At eight when her interviewer asked her what was the most unpleasant thing she could think of, she said, "Me, 'cause I'm mean to myself." She had learned to see herself as unpleasant and to criticize herself the way her mother habitually criticized her. Hapless because she couldn't please her mother, she was losing her capacity to fight back against her mother and life in general was aborting. Kandis was once again shifting emotionally and behaviorally; for last year's grandiosity (her hypomania) had dissipated and in its place was appearing a painful lack of confidence, more over-compliance, and even perfectionism in her school performance and test performance at the project. The little girl was becoming strikingly gentle and delicate as she calmly aligned blocks in perfect order and itemized every single test object during her research visit. When she couldn't do something right on her test, she bolstered herself by rationalizing mistakes and covertly cheating. There was much sadness in her eyes and a sense of the weight of the world on her shoulders.

Ten years later at 18 her eyes were still sad and she was pale and plainly dressed. She had ranked low in her class with a C average, and her IQ had dropped from very bright at age seven to high average. She was lonely and directionless, though a clue to her future was her part-time work as a student coordinator of the high school health center. Unlike many of the 18 year olds, she eschewed idealizing her parents or downplaying troubled relationships, saying that she could recall no joy in her childhood. She was well aware that her mother was very aggressive and had scarcely ever appreciated anything that she had done. She said she was closer to her father who was more generous but hurt deeply that he never openly took her side in the struggles with her mother. "It was not as if I felt deprived as a kid because I didn't know what it was to have anything. I used to get upset, slam doors or break something, mostly my own stuff, but I gave that up because it never got me anywhere. I should have stood up to my mother more but the few times I did she became more angry or started crying, and this made me back down. I guess I thought she would fall apart or something."

When Kandis was 18, about to embark on her life apart from her disturbed family, Sylvia Brody wrote about her, "She has a loving, gentle quality but her will has been squashed. She is emotionally starved with some awareness of this but doesn't know how to get out of it, her feelings are so tied up in rage and sadness." At 18 Kandis was relying on psychological defenses of avoidance, identification with the aggressor, inhibition, regression, repression, restriction, and turning of aggressive impulses against herself. Her most optimistic defense was reaction formation in which she took on the role of helper of others in order to ward off her feelings of being bad and deprived.

Now as an adult Kandis is far distanced from her parents, living in Canada and rarely in contact with them. Her appearance is still bland, her manner ingratiating, but her memories of her mother's rejection and hostility are vivid and stark. She also added new recollections she hadn't reported at 18: When she was 14 her mother had dragged her home from a Saturday morning football game after a sleepover the night before because she had not called home for permission to go to the game. She still felt guilty from soiling the entrance hall of her house with a nosebleed as a child. And she told us that she had run away from home and hid in her friend's house for several days in her sophomore year of high school.

Out of the maelstrom of her background, as an adult she has managed to grasp gratification in her work. She is a personnel benefits administrator for a mid-sized company. This is a continuation of her high school volunteer job at the health center, and an adaptation to life by being helpful to other people to demonstrate to herself and others that she is a good rather than bad or angry person, and that she is a giving rather than needy person—her defense mechanism of reaction formation. Having risen to her position even though she never quite finished college, she spoke of her company as her family in which she is the caring and benignly disciplining parent of the workers who come to her for help. "I work at doing a better job with the people who work under me than my parents ever did for me."

Given the promise of her lively responsiveness in the early months of her life, her personal life verges on tragic. She has hardly ever dated, feeling inexpressive like her father and tongue-tied with men. She had once felt excitement in a relationship with a man for several months, thinking that they would marry; but he disappeared from her life without warning or explanation. Kandis says that she doesn't know if she will ever date again. She is so muted and controlled that the only sadness she showed at 30 was when she talked about the death of her steady childhood babysitter when she was in high school. The elderly woman had been the only one who had unstintingly supported her, and Kandis still keeps with her the woman's favorite rocking chair in which Kandis curled up when the sitter was not around. To this day she has had only one longstanding friendship which goes back to grade school, the girlfriend who gave her refuge when she ran away from home. They keep in touch by letter.

"My childhood wasn't fun," Kandis concluded, a slight smile on her face, working at keeping her emotions and life in balance. "I guess I smile because I try to be calm like my father, and different than my mother who yelled so much." The price Kandis pays for identifying with her father is that she also avoids conflict like him. She is cloyingly nice to ward off anger, and is emotionally depleted. We felt great sympathy and sadness for her, yet also wanted to say to her, "Be real, be a grownup, stand up for yourself."

Ironically this is exactly what Kandis said she wanted to say to her father growing up, "Stand up for me, stand up for yourself."

Chuck—Compulsively Mothered and Kindly Fathered

Sometimes in pathos there is humor, and Chuck's life provides this. As a toddler charging about his house leaving a trail of toys, he looked like a future football player, and when we met him at 30 he could easily have passed for a stereotypic, slightly over-the-hill athlete—hearty, a bit tongue-tied, and chunky. Let's go back to the beginning. Chuck was the first-born of three children, and when he was six months old his parents left New York City to return to upstate New York where they joined his father's parents in running a small mill that made wooden items such as golf tees and swizzle sticks. While Chuck was growing up his mother managed the business books and his father ran the mill. His father grinned for weeks after his son was born, and because the mill was only blocks from their house he was constantly in and out to help care for the children. His easy going warmth was in sharp contrast to the mother's tense compulsivity. As a couple, Chuck's parents were more dissimilar to each other than any of the other parents of hyperactive children.

Not hostile to her baby, and readily speaking of her love for him, the mother compromised her effectiveness and potential by routinizing all aspects of her baby's life, from the details and precise minutes of feeding to the exact position of furniture, diapers and toys in his room. This hyper-organization substituted for emotional spontaneity.

Chuck was an easy-going baby with charming smiles who hummed while he played. But by one year he and his mother were in an open struggle over food. He was subverting his mother's schedule by holding food in his mouth for a long time before swallowing it, and often spitting out the food. When he got angry or upset he vomited, a habit that continued for several years. His mother responded with scolding and yelling; somewhat later she added spanking to her disciplinary repertoire. In spite of her continued remonstrations of love for Chuck, she was impersonal and unable to play with him; her favorite endearment was "my little slob."

Although Chuck remained generally sunny and agreeable like his father, by pre-school the tension and struggle with his mother had affected him in several ways. His speech was poorly modulated, he had a slight stutter that is still present in adulthood, and he was so restless he could not stay with anything for more than a few moments. He also had fears and compulsions about dirt on his hands which lasted many months; and in connection with them he held his hands stiffly and counted 1-2-3-, 1-2-3 until he or his parents washed them. When he was school age, Chuck's father commented that his son was "half-sociable and forward like me, and half timid like his mother." The little boy had developed an unusual demeanor. On the one hand he feared many things like dirt, finger-paints, park swings, and worried that his parents might die. But at other times his behavior might alternate between friendly excitement and episodes of aggressiveness. Mostly he was emotionally blunted (sad, stubborn, lumpy, passive) with little range in his facial expression or voice, though his non-stop squirming and periods of non-stop monotone chatter indicated that he suffered from a great deal of underlying tension. Sometimes when difficult tasks frustrated him, he beat his head against the wall and whined for his mother; then he countered his whining by bragging about how big he was.

In school Chuck liked to learn but his erratic behavior hindered him. Recognizing his emotional imbalances, the school suggested to the parents that Chuck needed therapy but his parents never followed through. Chuck was evidently stuck in a hostile-dependent relationship with his over-certain, hyper-vigilant mother. His dependency and inability to leave her orbit accounted to a great extent for his lack of self-control in school, his inability to modulate his moods, his trouble self-directing himself in class, his chafing against restraint, and his occasional angry outbursts. In school it was as if he were two children—generous and relaxed like his father, on edge like his mother. At times the tension between the two personas overwhelmed him and he seemed in a daze. Chuck's psychological testing at six showed him to be one of the most disturbed children in the project, especially preoccupied with whether his body was intact and physically sound. In this regard, he told his sister that everyone is born with a penis which mothers take off when they want a girl; and he told a girl at school not to worry because she would get a penis when she got bigger. Chuck's castration anxiety was so intense that he refused to play with broken toys or broken crayons. Intuitively Chuck's father provided a good counterforce to the son's and mother's enmeshment (for example she was still bathing him and sometimes wiping his behind after he used the toilet) by regularly playing ice hockey with him despite the mother's protests that they would fall through the ice.

* * *

Years passed and Chuck turned into a big, blunt adolescent, authoritatively emblazoned with a Maltese cross and a large peace symbol hanging from his neck when he came for his senior year interview. Similar to his mixed behavior in childhood, he was still labile and contradictory—at times friendly, even ebullient, at times guarded, passive and antagonistic. He concentrated well, liked doing well, and said that he was competitive, but when he encountered hard questions on psychological testing he called himself stupid or called the test badly written. He told Dr. Brody that he was quite satisfied with his low B average in high school, along with his many sports and girlfriends, and then told her of "a slump" in his junior year in which he lost interest in everything and his only friend had been his bicycle.

When Chuck was young, his mother had not been able to describe anything she especially enjoyed doing with him. Now Chuck was not able to think of any clear or specific experiences good or bad in his childhood. "I block everything out," he said, but he could describe his father as hard working and fun, and his mother as "the little woman, calm, collected, nice, and on top of everything. But when a light bulb burns out or something breaks she needs everybody to come running." After saying this, tension overcame him and he got up and started pacing for the rest of his interview.

Sylvia Brody summed it up, "He is a sincere, well-meaning youth suffused with a need to deny and bluff in order to avoid anything that might be uncomfortable. He has zero interest in introspection, yet there is much kindness in him. He presented himself as a hardy worker with no cultural or intellectual interests, emphasizing that he was his own person and needed nobody. His restlessness appears to be a flight from quietly thinking about himself or even quietly spending time with me, though he remembered me from childhood. He told me that his motto is, 'Never worry, be quick, be sure, get the job done.' He plans to study engineering in college and earn a lot of money. I can see him as a successful on-the-go worker as time passes, kind like his father, but with superficial relationships. I fear that he harbors a mass of unconscious fantasies of a very frightening kind, and is a candidate for a breakdown, a heart attack, or an aggressive outburst if things do not go well in his life."

His psychological testing at 18 elaborated the frightening unconscious fantasies. His tester reported, "His Rorschach responses are pervaded by dead, mutilated animals. When he stops his fantasies, he becomes apathetic and withdrawn. He reacts against this by becoming hypercritical, which escalates into paranoid and confabulatory thinking. There is no clear sense of self apparent; at his best he projects a narcissistic, grandiose, macho persona. At his worst he deteriorates into helpless dependence, angry at himself for feeling this way, and angry at others whom he blames for this feeling. In his human figure drawings he shows an unconscious uncertainty about his sexual role in life. He is lonely but likes people because they are important to him for meeting his needs. He defends himself against feeling anxious and depressed by keeping active and by attempting to control his environment.

* * *

Over the next 12 years Chuck avoided the disasters Sylvia Brody feared, and when we met him he was contentedly married and prospering as a construction project site manager in his hometown. Bluff and hearty, he was also wary and never really relaxed during his interview. His amnesia for his mother's strictness and over-control when he was growing up continued for he said that she had been loving, hugging, warm and caring; but he could not come up with memories of any specific instances when she had treated him this way. By contrast he brought his father to life by remembering them playing together, his father tending his ice hockey bruises, and his father's sternness when he didn't complete his chores, once even stopping him from playing in a league game when he had fallen too far behind in his school work.

What about Chuck's childhood externalized tension, his indefatigable hyperactivity? When we met him at 30, as with all of the participants we had not yet reviewed the childhood record, so we didn't know he had been hyperactive. However Chuck brought this problem up when we asked him to describe his typical mood. "I can't stay sitting down long; even when I was a kid I couldn't stay in one place long." Then his ideas became scattered just like his behavior had as a child. "I like people. I care about them, about things. I'm too accepting like my parents, you know, passive. Sometimes I can get really worked up and kick the hell out of things."

Chuck's biggest regret is dropping out of college but his work in construction suits him fine, even functioning therapeutically for him, "I like being up and about, in and out of doors, in charge of people. My dream is to be a developer like Donald Trump." Then he added very seriously that if we needed any remodeling done in the area, we should call his company for a bid and be sure to mention his name.

He presents himself as tough and tender—he loves his wife, he says, yet demeans her as weak because she talks to her mother daily. This is similar to the way he disparagingly described his mother as "the little woman" to Dr. Brody when he was 18. He is proud that he tells his wife what she can and can't buy, yet also says he couldn't live without her keeping order in the house and cooking for him. He calls himself even-tempered, then describes his fury when supplies don't arrive at construction sites on time. He resented his parents pushing him for better grades in school, then says that he needed to be pushed because his grades fell when his parents backed off. He joins his parents now for dinner monthly.

There is good natured exuberance, warmth and glee in Chuck, as if he would be fun to play and work with. However he made us uneasy at the same time, as if the energy could quickly turn mean, or as if he could suddenly withdraw into self-pitying guardedness. For example, he was so enthusiastic about being interviewed when he received the announcement of the followup that he was the very first participant to respond to the invitation. Then he became the hardest participant to schedule, repeatedly saying that his job was overwhelming him, that he had a cold, or that he needed to rest on Saturdays.

Nonetheless Chuck has done well considering his difficult childhood with his emotionally impersonal and compulsive mother. His gentle, outgoing father's influence has lent balance to his personality. Chuck's hyperactivity seems to have several origins: 1) In the lack of reciprocal interactions with his mother in infancy, which, had they been present, would have given him a more stable basic psychological structuralization, 2) in his need to get his mother's attention, albeit negative attention as he raced about the house, 3) in his opposition to his mother's over-control, 4) as a hypomanic defensive reaction against fears of being passive and vulnerable, and 5) in running from inner feelings such as sadness or lack of confidence.

Gradually as he was growing up Chuck was able to identify with both his mother's and father's support and good values, which kept him from angrily rebelling against them. In doing this he suppressed much of his impulsive restlessness. Still he combats an underlying depression which gives his life a feeling of struggle. He also has a fragile sense of manhood for which he over-compensates in fantasy and in reality by acting tough even though this doesn't really hide his vulnerable self-esteem.

Chuck's earliest memory, which he places at about five years of age, is very poignant. "I was climbing on the second story balcony railing of our house to reach for a red balloon that was drifting away. My mother must have seen me and came up and grabbed me and started yelling at me. I got the balloon anyway," Chuck told us, emphasizing his triumph. This same incident had also impressed the parents so strongly that they told the researchers, and it appears in the record when Chuck was three, highlighting the parents' reactions. The mother had reported how she had panicked when she saw her son on the railing, grabbed him, and started hitting him uncontrollably until the father, hearing the commotion, arrived and restrained her.

Triumph also appears in a recurring ice hockey dream Chuck has had for many years. "It is the last minute of over-time in the Stanley Cup championship. The score is tied. I block a shot on my goal. I'm skating the puck up the ice toward the other goal. The crowd is on its feet cheering and there are a thousand players trying to stop me. I keep going, knocking them aside one by one, then I shoot with all my might. The puck goes in the net as time runs out. We win the game. The crowd erupts; I'm famous; I'm rich. I've brought happiness to thousands of people, but I'm too exhausted to enjoy it."

PART 2

The Question of Diagnosis and Neurobiological Correlates

The lives of the six individuals here are extremely different as is the intensity of their drivenness in childhood, which in some cases may not have reached full present-day criteria for attention deficit hyperactivity disorder. Thus the path to hyperactivity behavior in childhood is varied and the course of life afterward unpredictable. Our group of six represents 8% of the Brody project participants, a figure consistent with the incidence of ADHD in epidemiological community surveys (Amaya-Jackson, et al, 1992). However neither our six subjects, nor children diagnosed today with ADHD have a homogeneous underlying psychopathology in spite of their similar restlessness, inattentiveness, and oppositionality. The syndromic similar behavior of the six children described here and many other individuals diagnosed with ADHD externalizes underlying psychological tension, pain, and conflicts; but the behavior does not of itself reveal their complex, meaningful emotional lives, to which treatment needs access in order to be most effective.

Much of the current literature on pathologically overactive children suggests that hyperactivity's root cause is biological, yet our group of six all had normal prenatal and infant medical histories, unremarkable temperaments in the first six months of life, and normal developmental assessments in infancy, **but** they did have abnormal family psychodynamics and interaction patterns. This suggests that their hyperactivity had a predominantly emotional rather than physical etiology. There is scant research that attempts to distinguish the percentage of children who suffer hyperactivity from emotional causes from those who experience it from organic ones. Neither large scale contemporary surveys of ADHD nor small studies of neurophysiologic function in afflicted children offer detailed examinations of parent-child interaction (Amaya-Jackson, et al., 1992; Hinshaw, et al., 1997, 2000). The older, traditional psychiatric literature provides the richest source of correlations between family dynamics and externalizing behavior (Malone, 1963; Rexford, 1963).

Correlations between **infant-parent** interaction and subsequent hyperactivity are even rarer. The exception is the Minnesota Child Development Study (Carlson, Jacobvitz, and Sroufe, 1995) that has followed 191 children from birth, and most closely approximates the Brody project in its examination of mother-infant interaction, measures of temperament and development in early life, and availability of medical history. By age three 11% of the children in their study were highly distractible, and by elementary school had behavior that fit the criteria for ADHD. The Minnesota findings and incidence are similar to ours: mothers of the children who developed ADHD had been less sensitively responsive, more intrusive, and more over-controlling of their infants and toddlers than a comparison group of mothers. None of the other measures were predictive of ADHD. The slightly higher incidence of clinically significant hyperactivity in the Minnesota sample is probably accounted for by their families coming from a low-income, higher-risk population facing greater stresses than the largely middle-class Brody sample.

The six children we have reported on here are typical of most of the hyperactive children we see in our offices. Only one in approximately ten of the children currently referred to us for excessive movement, inattention and impulsivity seem likely to be motorically driven solely on the basis of central nervous system (CNS) imbalances. When CNS imbalances exist, they may suggest their presence by compromised medical histories such as illnesses or physical trauma during pregnancy or infancy, the presence of physical developmental anomalies, occasionally slight ("soft") neurologic signs of CNS dysfunction, and the absence of explanatory family interaction problems. Additionally, it is possible that in some children a combination of compromised physiology, disturbed family interaction, and stress or crises in the family's circumstances lower the threshold for the contribution of each factor to the appearance of hyperactive behavior.

Specific learning disabilities such as dyslexia (difficulty learning to read) or disgraphia (writing difficulty) also signal central nervous system disturbances. Although there may be a higher incidence of such specific interferences with learning in hyperactive children than normally acting children, most children with learning disabilities are not unusually restless or inattentive, nor are they emotionally troubled, except for the struggles with self-confidence that ensue from their handicap.

None of the six hyperactive children in the project had a specific learning disability, though most of them did not earn as good grades in school nor go as far in their education as their intelligence would have allowed them. If they short-changed themselves in terms of education they did so for emotional not neurological reasons. Nonetheless, they all had some college.

Another factor that may contribute to pathologically over-active behavior is genetics, for genes possibly play a role in shaping whether a child is more likely to externalize or internalize tension and unhappiness. Consider some of the possibilities: It is likely that there are genes connected with psychophysiologic responsiveness which, for example, predispose one child to react strongly to stimuli leading her to grow up externalizing her reactions, and predispose another to suppress and internalize his reactions. Conversely a child who psychophysiologically reacts very strongly could develop extra strong psychological and hormonal restraints, over-correct, and dampen down emotional reactions thus becoming an internalizer.

What of the possibility that genetic inheritance plays a role in determining whether a young child has a cautious nature, that is, a low threshold for fear? Such a ready response to feel apprehension may cause the youngster to retreat when he approaches the edge of a swimming pool in contrast to the child who jumps into the water before she has a chance to think twice. Conversely, it is also possible that a child with a genetically determined low threshold for fear may jump into the water quickly—to get the fear over with before thinking too long about the perceived danger and succumbing to "cold feet." This psychological process represents a counterphobic defense against fear.

Additionally the culture in which a family lives also plays an important role in teaching parents to reinforce certain kinds of conflict management. By way of a broad example, some cultures (and subcultures in larger societies) ask boys to retaliate physically when insulted and girls to not react or to respond manipulatively.

Neither neurochemical science, psychology, nor social science convincingly provide all the explanations for children's behavior. However a classic experiment by the geneticist Ginsburg (1984) sheds light on these issues. In the study a colleague bred a litter of genetically isolated, feral dogs and gave half to Ginsburg and kept half. The breeder's pups were calm, not impulsive, easily trained, and learned new things readily. Ginsburg's half of the litter were impulsive, hyperactive, and couldn't retain their training. Each investigator visited the other's pups and confirmed the behavioral observations. It turned out that the breeder had separated the pups he gave to Ginsburg from their mothers before they had been weaned, and the researchers hypothesized that this was the critical factor in the difference between the two groups.

To confirm, the breeder bred a second litter, and this time gave Ginsburg his half *after* the whole litter had been weaned and separated from the mother. This time both half litters were attentive, well behaved and not impulsive, indicating that separation trauma had been critical. However Ginsburg did not stop there. He returned his attention to his first hyperactive group of pups and treated them with the central nervous system stimulants amphetamine and methylphenidate (Ritalin) often prescribed for hyperactive children. Some of his restless dogs calmed in response to the drugs and some didn't. When returned to obedience training school, those that responded to medication now learned and behaved well. When the medication was stopped, they lost their training. Still following the trail, the researchers sacrificed Ginsburg's half litter of hyperactive dogs and biologically assayed their central nervous systems. They found that the medication responders showed biochemical *variability* in their central nervous systems despite their behavioral similarities. The experiment thus demonstrated that the specific environmental stress of separation from the mother before weaning produced a uniform and specific behavioral picture of hyperactivity, poor learning and impulsivity in a group of dogs, but this group itself was not uniform for they had a different behavioral response to the pharmacologic stimulants and varied biochemical profiles.

Twin studies with human beings correlate (Petrill, et al., 1997) with such animal studies in suggesting that some aspects of psychological and behavioral characteristics are inherited, but it is still uncertain which ones, and how those that are genetically transmitted balance with those characteristics of a child that evolve in interaction with family members, teachers, the child's peer group, and the influence of the culture transmitted in community lore and by the media. The Brody project *did not find* that a baby's physiological or social reactivity in the first six weeks of life predicted response style at six or 12 months of life, a result consistent with other studies that have unsuccessfully attempted to find a correlation between neonatal traits and responsiveness (Carlson, Jacobvitz, and Sroufe, 1995; Sroufe, 1996) later in infancy or toddlerhood.

Research in the field of temperament (Thomas, Chess, and Birch, 1968) points to the stability of characteristics such as irritability, responsiveness, soothability, caution, and curiosity in a child from the end of the first year onward; however, after six weeks of life a baby is already a creature of its environment as well as its inborn nature. In addition there is the havoc which trauma wreaks on development. Ginsburg's experiment with litter mates highlights the role of trauma as well as genetics. They have recast and updated Harlow's (1961) pioneering discovery that profound depressions occurred in chimpanzees who were prematurely separated from their mothers, and that when grown the chimps who had lost their mothers were unable to successfully mate and nurture their own offspring. In the human species, trauma includes a host of adverse events such as separations from mothers and fathers, illness, injuries, sexual molestation, physical abuse, natural disasters, accidents, war, neglect, emotional abuse, and even multiple moves during childhood (which extinguish the support of friends, consistency and predictability).

Any of these experiences will increase a child's quotient of fear, frustration and anger. They will also change, often for life, central and peripheral nervous system functioning, permanently affecting how a person experiences anxiety. The trauma researcher van der Kolk (1996, 2002) refers to this as "the body keeping score," in elucidating the psychobiological abnormalities of people who have suffered extreme adversity: extreme autonomic system responses to stimuli reminiscent of the trauma; altered neurohormonal responses; permanent neuroanatomic changes as well as altered activation of specific areas in the brain; and altered immunologic responses to stresses.

In our study, there were no twins but seven sibling pairs. Farley, one of the externalizing, hyperactive children, has an older brother by one year who also participated in the study. The brother, first-born and the object of more of the father's expectations and frustrations, was even more severely beaten than Farley. Instead of becoming hyperactive in childhood he stubbornly, quietly, and depressively internalized his distress. As an adult he too participates in the family food business but otherwise is different from Farley—he doesn't have anxiety attacks, he is less immature, less able to take responsibility than Farley, and is chronically passive and depressed.

Adverse experiences powerfully teach people what to expect from the world and shape their adaptation to life. Most children who are traumatized encapsulate and suppress their fears, which then continue to disturb the children like a slow-release, life-long-acting bad medicine which causes various degrees of physical symptoms, anxiety, depression, impaired confidence, and withdrawal from activities and relationships. Some take more externalizing pathways, like trying to turn the tables on their fears or tormentors, or trying to be like their tormentors by becoming aggressive themselves. When trauma occurs, the aftermath is damage control. This can occur through attempts to control the body's internal emotional and physiologic environment so as to avoid being aroused in the future, or attempts to control the environment to escape trauma in the future. The course an individual takes (which becomes his characterologic coping style) has a myriad of junctures in which inborn predisposition, the psychological style the parents model, the model society teaches, the influence of siblings, peers, and teachers, and supportive and traumatic experiences all play a role in the path taken.

Common Themes in the Parents and Disturbed Attachment in the Children

There are several critical recurring themes which the families of the children who externalized emotional distress highlight—family qualities and processes which distinguish them from families in chapter one whose children had largely peaceful childhoods and very good outcomes.

Parental Inability to Connect with their Children

The central finding in all six cases was that **the parents were unable to connect with their children as babies, and infant-parent attachment was disturbed.** All six of the mothers had been classified as less effective (Group B) by the original research team in infancy, and five of the six fathers were similarly unfavorable. The problematic mother-child relationships occurred on the level of both microkinesic (second-by-second) and macrokinesic (global) interactions. Once parents failed to connect adequately, they were lost to the children on the deepest levels of emotional security and affection. The outcome of the troubled attachment in these cases was the youngsters' hyperactive behavior—literally and figuratively, a running about rootless. Frequently the parents' trouble connecting was due to **the parents' inabilities to read their children's moods, physical states, impulses and desires.** Taken together the parents in the six cases could not understand the meaning of their babies' behaviors and respond accordingly. As a group **the parents related to their infants as objects rather than subjects**; that is, they had little appreciation of their babies' nascent emotions, intentions and capacities.

After the first year, all of **the parents had adultomorphic expectations of their young children** (they expected more maturity of their young children than was feasible given their age). Frequently **the parents lacked confidence that their children would mature.**

Parental Inability to Play

Further, many of **the parents were unable to play with their babies:** they were too intrusive, too controlling, too inhibited, too disbelieving in the value of play, or in some instances too busy. Parental play with infants is an early form of being-with and thinking-with children. Without play the child misses this connection; if the parent controls "play" it overwhelms and rearranges light-hearted being and thinking together into a didactic, ponderous experience. For the little children who became hyperactive, thinking, feeling pleasure, and acting never coalesced.

Parental Projection and Denial of Feelings

Parental projection of their own feelings and perceptions onto their babies often interfered with parents' accurate reading of their babies. For example, angry parents projected anger onto their babies and imagined their children as malevolent or "bad seeds." Controlling parents saw their children as "manipulative." Some **parents denied feelings in themselves *and* in their children**. They walled themselves from awareness of certain emotions so stringently that they couldn't see them in their youngsters. For example, parents who denied personal sadness or anxiety did not know that their children were upset after separations or after losses; parents who feared being passive themselves were dissatisfied with their children when the children were quiet.

Split between Parental Self-perceptions and Actual Behavior

In several of the families there was a **dichotomy between parents' self-perceptions of their actions and their actual behavior with their babies;** that is, the parents thought and said they acted one way, while in fact they acted the opposite. For example, Dafna's mother said that her baby rejected her food, yet film study showed the mother rejecting her baby's spoon-waving invitation to her to be more involved in the feeding; Dafna's father said when his daughter was six that he was no longer physically punishing her, yet a few minutes later he said he'd recently spanked her.

Parents' Needs Put before their Babies' Needs

A distressing theme was **parents putting their own needs before the babies' needs**. This was often a result of parents' misunderstanding their babies' needs because of the parents' adultomorphic expectations of the child, or because of the parents' needs to undo a trauma from their own past. Thus, one mother ejected her restless toddler from the family dinner table because the child's fidgeting reminded her of her own childhood family where there were no rules and too much chaos.

Corporal Punishment

Corporal punishment was frequent for all six of the externalizing children. There was no indication that spankings benefited the children, and with time the physical punishment became a glue between the parents and children that took the place of normal, affectionate connectedness, a glue that prevented normal separation to unfold. However, the physical discipline did appear to tame the impulsiveness of several children. The taming subdued the outer wildness (as it does when a horse is broken for riding); but the unruliness was driven inward as the years passed, leading the children to feel guilt over their wild feelings, depressions, impaired self-confidence, a fragmented sense of intactness, and unstable moods in youth and adulthood. The spankings—coupled with the children's desires to please their parents—also leashed several of the children emotionally to their parents well into adulthood.

The Mental Representation of Childhood Attachment

What was **the mental representation of childhood attachment to their parents at 30 years** of the six grown hyperactive children? To answer this question we formally assessed them with the Adult Attachment Interview. In the overall group of 76 participants followed from birth to age 30, two-thirds (66%) were classified as Secure (Secure-free/autonomous) as adults. In the group of six who had externalized distress with hyperactivity, only two (33%) were Secure and four (67%) were Insecure in their representation of attachment. In terms of subcategories, of the Insecure cases three were Insecure-enmeshed/entangled with their parents as adults; and one was Insecure-dismissive, that is, he devalued the significance of any attachment. Dafna was Secure with a favorable mental image of her attachment to her parents, but it was in the Secure-earned secure subcategory, indicating that with maturity she had learned over time to realistically balance her parents' shortcomings with affection for the good experiences and support they had provided growing up.

Frank had a straight forward Secure classification, an initially perplexing finding. After further consideration it appeared that his massive need to empty himself of feeling, his need to protect his parents, and his powerful intellect had succeeded in creating a fictionalized view of a reasonably satisfying childhood and equable present. He had "misled" the AAI by responding to it with extreme suppression of anxiety and anger, and gave a false appearance of security through providing positive, socially acceptable responses. As in childhood, he tried to be "a good boy," but at the price of alienation from intimate relationships.

Parents were Concerned and Involved

Ironically, the final theme among the hyperactive children is that **all of the parents were concerned and involved in the lives of their children.** They all had the best interests of their children at heart; they gave what they could; none abandoned a child. Without the parents' basic concern and involvement (in some cases the warmth of one parent compensated for the coldness of the other), the children's disturbances might have been far worse. For example without the parents' involvement and regard, the children might have developed Reactive Attachment Disorders characterized by marked developmental delays, social isolation, or indiscriminate or ambivalent advances towards people. Psychoses or delinquency might also have occurred. In the six hyperactive cases the parents' relational problems were mostly on a subtle or clinical level, and an untrained person, or a too superficial clinician, might not have noticed them.

Chapter 2. Table 2.2 Characteristics of Study Parents of Externalizing Hyperactive Children

1. Difficulty connecting with infants.
2. Difficulty reading babies' moods, physical states, impulses and desires.
3. Tendency to relate to babies as objects rather than as people with emotions, intentions and abilities.
4. Expect children to be more mature than their age.
5. Lack confidence that their children will mature.
6. Difficulty playing with their babies.
7. Tendency to project their feelings onto their babies.
8. Tendency to deny their own feelings.
9. Often deny their children's feelings.
10. Tendency to act opposite of how they say they act with their children.
11. Often place their needs before babies'.
12. Frequently spank.
13. Maintain concern and involvement in their children's lives.

The Transformation of Symptoms

Children adapt, even to extremely difficult circumstances. As Anna Freud (1956) delineated in the mid-twentieth century, psychological growth is the nature of childhood, which sees children establishing psychic structuralization and their personal repertoire of defense mechanisms before adolescence. This occurs through the accretion of experience and in-born potentialities. However a child's capacity to adapt is not unlimited, and at some point trauma or chronic adverse circumstances can breach adaptation. Symptoms will develop and endure, and maladaptive responses will become fixed. In the six hyperactive children we studied, this appeared to have occurred by about six years of age.

In general, the six hyperactive children appeared unremarkable in their first six months of life. They were not stigmatized by difficult temperaments or levels of activity. Disturbances began appearing in the second six months when they showed signs of depression—such as dulled or sad facial expressions, reduced activity, irritability, increasing bodily tension, and trouble calming themselves. By contrast, Dafna by this time was overactive, having been trained to this by her wound-up mother moving her, scolding her, making faces at her, and imposing her own personality on the baby. Thus by the end of the first year of life, the children's experiences with their parents—who were variously over-controlling, emotionally remote, or angry—had begun to take their toll on the children.

The children's second year brought the normal excitement of mastery of movement and new adventures. This excitement became the prototype of a manic defense against depression in several of the children, successfully warding off for a time incipient depression. Locomotion also provided the vehicle for them to both express and relieve their growing unhappiness through action. Their increasing activity discharged their tension and gave them ways to direct aggression. Their tension and anger (and in several, aimless, restless drivenness in the absence of parental responsiveness) boosted normal toddler activity into abnormal hyperactivity, which typically became quite marked in the second year. Anger showed itself in the children's opposition to their parents' wishes, and in their destructiveness, which went far beyond that of normal children.

This set in motion another process that further transformed the youngsters' symptoms, usually between the ages of four and seven. The parents responded to their hyperactivity by redoubling their efforts to control the children with spankings, yelling, and in one case hitting. To avoid punishment, the children suppressed their running and destructiveness, and maintained an appeasing connection with their parents.

In the *New Introductory Lectures on Psychoanalysis* Freud (1933) wrote, "The child has to learn to control its instincts. To grant it complete freedom so that it obeys all its impulses without any restriction is impossible . . . The function of education, therefore, is to inhibit, forbid and suppress . . . But we have learnt from analysis that is this very suppression of instincts that involves the danger of neurotic illness." As Freud taught, neuroticisms began appearing in the six children—in their mental lives, in behavior and in psychosomatic symptoms. For example, there was *exhibitionism* (showing off) and *grandiosity* (boasting) in some of the children. These two qualities were combinations of a *hypomanic defense* with the defense of *identification with the aggressor* (the children were identifying with the controlling and dominating qualities in the parents).

The use of particular defenses also began to define the personality style of the children in ways that endured into adulthood. In *The Ego and the Mechanisms of Defense* Anna Freud (1946) wrote, "Attitudes such as stiffness and rigidity, personal peculiarities such as a fixed smile, contemptuous, ironical, and arrogant behavior—all these are residues of very vigorous defensive processes in the past, which have become dissociated from their original situations (conflicts with instincts and affects) and have developed into permanent character traits."

Most of the children began to use the defense of *reaction formation* against their anger in the form of tenderness and caring for others. This combined *identification with their parents' good, caring qualities* with the defense of *undoing their sense of guilt* that came from being told they were bad by their parents. Reaction formations also functioned in the service of becoming obedient to their parents, even obsequious.

Obsessive-compulsive defenses, symptoms and personality styles appeared in several of the children. These manifested themselves in habits of arranging toys neatly, avoidance of dirt, and counting rituals. The obsessional and compulsive behaviors also served to control inner tension and feelings of guilt through an unconscious mental formula that expressed the idea, "I am not out of control for I am orderly . . . I think . . . I count things . . . I put things in rows . . . I am clean."

As the children approached seven years of age, and subsequently between the ages of seven and 18, their parents *tamed most of their restlessness into compliance* (sometimes over-compliance). However there were still transformations yet to come. Taming the children left most of them *constricted and inhibited.* Their early vitality and exuberance were gone. Many of the children were harnessing their distress into orderliness and behavior that made them acceptable to their parents, but the process impoverished them inside. For several individuals, anxious driven hyperactivity and aggression gave way to *inner emotional depletion,* inner deadness, and outward calm by adulthood.

In others hyperactivity did not mutate into other symptoms, nor did it just go away; rather it continued in disguised or better modulated form. As they grew into teenagers, the children ran about less; but they were still restless, couldn't stay in one place for long, fidgeted, bit their fingernails, let their attention wander, chattered, sometimes stuttered, and occasionally had wild outbursts. Often their restlessness showed in mercurial shifts of facial expression (which appeared like silliness and clowning in young children, and like dramatic expressiveness in adults). Sometimes their restlessness showed in rambling, irrepressible talking.

As parents and schools confronted the young children with the need to suppress their unruliness, affects and anger, their symptoms sometimes transformed into *anxiety.* Anxiety occurred as *phobias* in some of the children and as *panic attacks* later in adulthood. Anxiety also underwent a secondary transformation in several of the participants into *hypochondriacal worries and psychophysiological symptoms.* For example, most of the children were *bedwetters,* some *vomited* when upset, and some felt sick when they entered school. As teenagers and adults several had hypochondriacal preoccupations, stomach distress, and one young man (Frank) experienced a hysterical paralysis. By the time they were 30, there were three principal syndromes among the six early childhood externalizers: Frank, Kandis, and Chuck have obsessive-compulsive personalities; Farley suffers panic attacks; and Kevin experiences dysthymia (minor depression). Dafna has a history of depression, now resolved. Ultimately, the common developmental thread for all of the children who externalized their distress—sons and daughters of troubled infancy attachments—was troubled self-esteem, insecurity and latent depression in adulthood.

Chapter 2. Table 2.3 Signs & Symptoms of Disturbance in 6 Externalizing Children at Age 7

Hyperactivity
Restlessness
Impulsivity
Distractability
Tension
Anxiety
Poor social skills
Low self esteem
Sadness
Immaturity
Enuresis

Chapter 2. Table 2.4 Adult Psychiatric Diagnoses of 6 Children Who Externalized Distress with Hyperactivity

Obsessive-Compulsive Personality Disorder
Minor Depression (Dysthymia)
Anxiety
Panic Attacks
Schizoid Personality Disorder
Anhedonia

Chapter 3

CHILDHOOD DISTRESS INTERNALIZED

All sorrows can be borne if you put them into a story.

Isak Dinesen

UNLIKE THEIR MORE dramatic counterparts who act out their distress in childhood, there is a large group of youngsters who hold their conflicts, unhappiness and tension largely within their minds and bodies. They are not the defiant children, the social butterflies, the constantly moving, the flittingly attentive, the garrulous, or the oft injured of the last chapter. Nor are they among those whose problems and inner conflicts bring them into clashes with teachers, peers and parents. Rather they are the internalizers whose struggle is with themselves, and their most frequent symptoms in childhood are depression, anxiety and fearfulness.

Children, especially young ones, have a hard time finding words for their emotions; while adolescents—who may have the vocabulary—are so driven to be independent of adults that they are typically too reluctant to open their feelings to grownups. But as adults, participants in our project were usually ready and able to speak lucidly of what they had been through in childhood. In the project population of 76 (34 girls and 42 boys), there were 22 (20%)—12 boys and 10 girls—with symptoms that were primarily of an internalizing nature in early childhood, as compared to the 8% described in the previous chapter who had externalizing emotional symptoms in childhood. In this chapter we will learn about three of the internalizers in detail. They show different internalizing mechanisms—marked by different forms of self-struggle, defense mechanisms, and management of feelings of love and anger—that resulted in specific symptoms such as depression, and in specific personality formations such as obsessive-compulsiveness and pathological narcissism. Although the three mostly suffered inwardly in childhood, each one also lashed out at times. Their lives also illustrate processes seen in the whole group of internalizing children and provide a picture of the family experiences that are fertile ground for producing these problems.

Nolan—Self-Disparagement and "A great sad loneliness"

Nolan, an earnest 30 year old, needed little help from us to explicitly describe his family. "My mother internalized her problems, and so do I. My father was so domineering, so tense, so in your face about everything, always demanding this and that. It was like his chant several times a week, 'I need socks, I need shirts, and so on.' As a kid it really upset me, and I held it in. When I got a little older I tried to speak up. I'd tell my mother, 'Do something, say something.' Or I'd remove my soul; totally space out and ignore my father. I had this fantasy that I could change the situation, but of course I couldn't." Reporting this, Nolan's tone was flat, he didn't gesture, rather he rolled his eyes to the ceiling with a faraway gaze, almost a look of piety.

Nolan is so self-contained that his emotions are almost completely suppressed. He says that his wife "never knows what I am feeling because my feelings come out in bits and pieces. Each day when I wake up it's not as if I know what I'm going to do or want to do, but I have to program myself for the day. I sit there on the edge of the bed silently telling myself my schedule. It feels like I'm filling a void by building a scaffold for my life or it would be chaos." Nolan explained that he suffers from a fear of failure and homelessness—truly existential anxieties—while at the same time he goes about the business of his life at least superficially calm, competent and careful. Nolan's capacity for self-containment is a trait in people that often goes along with a fear of letting go of emotions or the body (as in a fear of eating, defecating, breathing, exercising, or being sexual). On the other hand overly self-controlled individuals sometimes also work very hard to let go, as Nolan does with physical exercise, but self-release does not come naturally to them and appears self-conscious and forced. Both too much self-control and forced letting go are hallmarks of people who internalize conflict.

Let's turn now to Nolan's infancy, watch his emotional style take root, and see how accurate his conjecture is about identifying with his mother. When the researchers saw him in the first six weeks of life, he was robust and vital. His developmental testing at six weeks was unusually advanced. Persistent and vigorous, he turned and watched his mother attentively; he was unusually active but not tense; his movements were well put together; and he nestled well when held. But all was not well in his life for Nolan's father—intense, competitive and controlling—couldn't desist from involving himself in all the details of his wife and son's life. Ordinarily we cheer fathers who enjoy playing with their babies, changing their diapers, and helping with feedings when solid foods or bottles are introduced. However Nolan's father was often carried away and allowed few physical and psychological boundaries between himself and the other members of the family. For example, having been in the labor and delivery room with his wife, he doubled over with stomach cramps himself shortly after Nolan was born in a probable primitive emotional identification with his wife.

Still he was a kind man whose over-involvement did not stem from a sadistic desire for power; rather it came from a loving, anxious concern about his child that was insufficiently tempered by patience and thoughtfulness. Furthermore, Nolan's mother herself had a problematic relationship with her baby. At six weeks the observer wrote, "The mother seems warm, alert, attentive, and smiles easily, yet at times she seems quite bewildered, especially when the baby fusses, as if she doesn't know what to do. I can't pinpoint why I had this impression, but I distinctly felt that there were times when the mother considered the child an annoyance to her. At other times her seeming ease with the child gave way to awkwardness and insensitivity in the way she held the child or pulled him up from lying down by pulling on one arm."

The mother and father bickered loudly in front of project staff, the mother ending by submitting to the father, a fractious relationship which Nolan himself described 30 years later. Highly unusual among study families, the father usually came with the mother for project visits, recording them with boyish enthusiasm with his own camera. However not so innocently, he readily reprimanded his wife whenever he thought she was too rough or inattentive to their son. He bossily joked, "I never let my wife touch the camera because it's one of my most precious possessions, but I do let her hold the baby which is the other most valuable thing I own."

At six months Nolan remained robust, handsome, alert, and had started babbling responsively. His mother spoke to him quietly and playfully, yet with sufferance. She was often self-involved, distant, and or inattentive to him. The observer wrote, "The father enjoys the child's company with less reservation than the mother. Her emotions appear to be of two types: On the one hand she is warm and affectionate and good humorously tolerant of the child; on the other hand there is a pervasive cloudiness, passivity or boredom in her behavior." When Nolan was one year old the research team classified the mother in the less competent group on the basis of her uneven empathy and organization, her remoteness and fluctuating over-restriction, and her inhibited affection. More lively, the father at no time ignored his son, but his sensitivity for Nolan suffered because his liveliness frequently made Nolan tense and disorganized the mother in her care for the child.

Around the time of his first birthday the observer noted that Nolan was becoming more bland and moderate in his responses; he ignored his interviewer and was rocking rhythmically in his crib even when others were present. This kind of habitual, stereotypic rocking signifies a child's need to stimulate itself in the absence of adequate responses from its environment. Conversely, repetitive self-stimulation of this kind can also function to calm a child who is being over-excited. Curiously, both parents watched the interviewer unsuccessfully trying to coax a smile from Nolan, and denied that he was somber or withdrawn, saying instead that he was teasing her.

In Nolan's second year, his mother became pregnant with the family's third child. Her preoccupation with the pregnancy drew her further away from Nolan and made her irritable to the point of scolding and slapping him at times. This kind of adverse experience can bend the course of a child's life by making him cautious, or at the least conflicted in the face of his own and other people's aggressive impulses. Later, the mother apologized to her interviewer for her impatience with Nolan, saying sadly that the pregnancy with the third child could not have come at a worse time.

Ironically the pregnancy set in motion another process that was more auspicious. Nolan and his very active older brother turned to each other for companionship, and their growth became psychologically enmeshed in a way that rivaled the mother's and father's enmeshment, of which we will hear more.

At four, little Nolan's symptoms had progressed, and troubled aspects of the parent-child relationship had become entrenched. His tester wrote that he was now a remote, inhibited little boy who often seemed in his own world. Appearing depressed and hungry for affection and contact, he told the tester that he loved her, then leaned on her, and asked her for a kiss. He could work with her systematically on the developmental test toy tasks which he called "my homework"—words that reflected how Nolan's father was anxiously and prematurely acculturating his son into the world of academic performance. Yet, at times Nolan also became so perseveratively fixated in his involvement with an object that he seemed all the more lost in his own world. The habit of rolling his eyes upward and sitting immobile while thinking, which we later noted when he was 30, appeared at this time. His mother reported that Nolan had fallen in love with the vacuum cleaner's noise as an infant, and since then had fixated on anything that made noise and moved. Thus Nolan's early history—with its signs of remoteness, stereotypic self-stimulation, and perseverative fixation on non-human objects—alarmingly suggests autistic features. Happily he also desired people, though sometimes curiously so. For example, he enjoyed helping his parents cook; he still asked his mother to wipe his bottom after bowel movements for fear of dirtying his hands; he could throw a healthy tantrum when his parents disciplined him for hitting his brothers; and to his parents' annoyance he liked crawling into their bed in the early morning.

Increasingly impatient with him, Nolan's parents thought he clung too much, so they spoke condescendingly of him in front of others, and reprimanded him regularly. Because he often whined his father thought that he was "a momma's boy" and his mother likewise wanted him to be more independent. At four and a half they sent him with his brother to an all-day summer camp in spite of his wish to stay home. Twenty-six years later this summer camp experience remained indelibly stamped in his mind. He remembered sobbing and being too scared to mount the school bus step. His mother pushed him up the steps of the bus, pushed the door closed on him, and then he recalled her face receding into the distance as the bus pulled away. All day he was terrified that he would never see his parents or house again, and that evening when the bus dropped him off he was amazed to find himself home again.

In spite of the parents' rude edges, they did provide stability and clear moral and religious principles, values which, on the other hand, they sometimes betrayed in their impatience with their children and each other. By five years of age Nolan's personality was well established. He was timid, cautious, cerebral, and a creature of habit who didn't like things to change. This indeed is how he is as an adult—an obsessive-compulsive young man who carefully follows his routines. He does not show the flares of passion, excitement, upset, and anger of his father and brothers; rather, he dampens his emotions to an extreme.

He resembles his mother, submissive and indistinct. Mother and son favor defense mechanisms such as intellectualization, rationalization, and reaction formation. When they do express a strong feeling or take a strong action, they undo it with qualifications to manage their emotions. The other children and father are more hysterical in style—they over-react, are impulsive, action oriented, emotive, and prone to deny and repress perceptions.

Ironically, in school Nolan's intrapsychic mode of adaptation (his deadened emotional responsiveness) led to strength in learning. For many children their IQ-test scores peak at around five years of age and stabilize at about seven. Nolan's IQ was below average then (at 85 almost borderline retarded), and gradually rose to quite bright (115) by age 18. This was thanks in no small part to the steady stimulation school provided, which diluted the effect of the erratic over-and-under-stimulation at home. When he entered school his biggest difficulty was in his relationship with other children with whom he was passive, apathetic, and apprehensive. He kept his distance from the other children, and sometimes poked or threw sand at them to attract their attention.

He seemed puzzled, worried about broken toys at school, and lacked confidence in physical play. "A sad, lonely, dreamy, distant little boy in need of acceptance by teachers and classmates, but too afraid and awkward to establish effective contact," wrote the school observer. His first grade teacher said, "He is a funny kid, like clay that you push this way and that and it doesn't pop back . . . an absent minded professor."

Gradually in school Nolan learned how to join a group and have fun. He became appreciated for his competence—even though he was slow and methodical—but never showed creative or independent work. His teachers respected his decorous, gentle manner, his knowledge, and his articulate one-to-one conversations. Some children teasingly called him "Mr. Clean" because he liked things to be in order, but others invited him into their games, and he gladly accepted. By the end of second grade he was slowly overcoming the sadness he had shown in kindergarten. Yet underlying self-doubt and worry remained. When he did something wrong, he habitually told his teacher, "I guess I'm not smart."

His childhood psychological tests illuminate his inner life. On the Children's Apperception Test at seven years, Nolan told stories about pictures that depicted lions, tigers, bears, and a mother kangaroo with little ones in her pouch. The story-telling format and the use of animals help children overcome their natural inhibition and defenses against expressing thought and feelings directly, and Nolan's stories provided a grim view of how he experienced his family and himself. In his tales there was little or no sense of affection, safety, gratification or well-being, and much depression. Mother figures were depriving and punishing, though with an admixture of being educational and protective. Nolan's perception of father figures was similar but not as negative. Figures of siblings were described more neutrally, consistent with Nolan's general proclivity to dampen his emotions and expressiveness.

When a child was the protagonist of his stories, the child was ineffectual, alone, angry, guilty, frightened, defiant and babyish. As a projection of his feelings about himself, this was a brutally honest self-depiction, the portrait of an internalizer who refuses to externalize the blame for his unhappiness or misfortune—a person who doesn't inculpate other people or circumstances, and who does not tilt at windmills as many angry, rebellious, anxious, and restless children and adults do. He holds his anger and disappointment within himself, and in doing so doing further compromises himself because he feels guilty and ineffectual for being so truculent.

*   *   *

Consistent with how Nolan's demeanor had seemed set by five years of age, his psychological testing at 18 replicated his testing from childhood. At 18 the psychologist wrote, "Nolan has extreme difficulty in being spontaneous and putting aside self-criticality. He is severely compulsive. The known frightens him and the unknown is even more threatening. He is self-denigrating and gropes for relatedness, and in doing this there are almost conscious (preconscious) bisexual fantasies. To a great extent Nolan denies the great anger he feels, however rage is just below the surface and swells in his associations to murderous, sadistic proportions, especially in relation to his mother. He longs for a release into a pseudo-beatitude devoid of humans, while also longing to be more human, less perfectionistic, less premeditated. Diagnostically he is suffering from a severe obsessive-compulsive neurosis with an ego structure which permits a too easy ego regression to oral and anal sadistic levels."

When Nolan spoke with Dr. Brody at 18, he told her that he no longer felt frightened when his father gets angry with him and that he is able to speak up. Before his father made him feel small. "My dad's a good man, very responsible, good natured but hyper, nervous, bossy; a know it all, ready to jump on you. At least I can talk to my mother. She's a good lady, on the quiet side; but my father tongue ties me." Sylvia Brody concluded that Nolan was unaware of how closely he had identified with his mother, and that his unconscious rage at both his mother and himself were one and the same—anger at his own as well as her passivity and their inability to react. He was also angry that his mother had not been able to understand him and come to his rescue. "He does not seem to feel comfortable in his own skin, and has an enormous need to speak about himself. A great sad loneliness seems to cloud over him."

*   *   *

Nolan's emotional liabilities—his pensiveness, methodicalness, meticulousness, and self-demands—translated into academic strengths that propelled him through an excellent college. Yet he still felt separate from people. Following a breakup with a girlfriend shortly after he finished college, the inner demons with which he had wrestled for so long finally overcame him. For several years he foundered, neither dating nor knowing what to do with his life. He received some financial help from his parents and worked or studied for brief stints. His only real satisfaction was in learning carpentry. During this period he imagined himself alone forever, forever failing at life.

His older brother ultimately rescued him, just as he had given brightness to his life and perhaps saved him from an autistic withdrawal as a toddler. At 26 Nolan went to live with his brother and his wife in Chicago where the brother had become a church minister. They introduced him to a woman in the congregation whom he would later marry. The church also gave Nolan a position maintaining the building and grounds. Though so different from his lively, extroverted brother, Nolan thinks they bonded so closely because they needed each other's support to deal with their parents.

Nolan recalls an early childhood nightmare in which his brother figures. In the dream a teacher gives him an impossible problem to solve. When he can't solve it, the teacher takes him to a haunted house and "dumps" him off. He's terrified because it's night and very dark outside so he can't see where he is. Suddenly he realizes he is standing in front of his own house and goes in. It's dark and empty inside. He thinks he should go to his brother's bedroom but then hears a noise coming from the basement. A voice out of nowhere says don't go down there; it's dangerous. But in slow motion his hand turns the doorknob; he descends slowly and in wonderment he finds brightness and friends down there as if it is a party. At that instant relief floods over him and he wakes up from his dream.

The nightmare—dreamt at a tender young age, probably redreamt many times, and fixed in his mind for a quarter century—is remarkable because it condenses almost all of the important psychological struggles in his life. Nolan said that the image of the teacher giving him an insoluble problem probably represented his domineering father, his often inscrutable mother, and also most of his classroom teachers whom he always felt he was disappointing. We also considered that the image also represented his own harsh inner teacher, that is, his self-critical conscience (superego). In the dream Nolan fails the test and finds himself in a haunted place which probably stands for his haunted, troubled, anxious self. Of course the house also speaks for his family as a whole. The fright he feels when he can't see his house in the darkness at first is likely the traumatic black hole of panic he felt as his mother pushed him away from her onto the summer camp bus at four and a half, and he thought he would never see his parents or home again.

In the dream he then thinks of going to his brother for comfort, but resists the incestuous pull and turns toward the basement where he hears noise in spite of "a voice out of nowhere that says it's dangerous." He is able to rebel against the god-like voice, although in a somewhat passive, disembodied state in which he doesn't take responsibility for his action ("My hand turned the knob."). Still this is enough to banish the nightmare—a classical embodiment of both primitive anxiety and wish fulfillment—for it gives him a glimmer of brightness and the company of friends which he wanted desperately as a child because they helped him be less emotionally entrapped in his family, and could help him psychologically differentiate. This is a drama that Nolan plays out inside himself, in contrast to many other participants who more actively struggled with their families and schools.

The degree of psychological entanglement in Nolan's family is striking. Recall the father's couvade-like stomach cramps the day after his wife gave birth to Nolan. More recently, Nolan's brother had an emergency appendectomy, and Nolan himself became so ill that the surgeons feared that they would have to do exploratory surgery on him as well. These days Nolan is calmer, more fulfilled than in the past, though he still fears what he calls "the abyss." He has never had psychotherapy, and soldiers on. "I guess I'm too stubborn to get therapy," he says. It's this tenacity that gives him strength (as in the dream when he resists the family symbiotic pull toward his brother, and instead turns the knob on the basement door), but it is also the stubbornness that may be his undoing.

Nolan's conflicts have been with himself, his mother and father. However, he has never acted them out or found scapegoats for them. He has been a dutiful son, husband, brother and worker, but to do this he has become extremely compulsive, sacrificed much vitality, and has suffered from severe depressions. Since early childhood, the depressions have come from the helplessness he feels vis-a-vis his frustrations. Recall that these frustrations were his father's over-control and his mother's erratic presence and non-presence. Nonetheless, the parents joined these liabilities with their many good qualities, so that in effect his parents never provided Nolan with a good target upon which to unleash his anger. This is akin to the double-bind described in some families with schizophrenia in years passed (Bateson, Jackson, Haley, and Weakland, 1956; Laing, 1965).

By the time Nolan was in elementary school his depression bifurcated like an angry flow of lava into a second stream which burned, snapped and hissed against him. "I am not smart enough . . . I am not good enough," it and he said. In the true manner of those who internalize their distress, Nolan's mind warred with itself. His suppressed feelings toward his parents were overwhelming his self-esteem, for how could a good child feel such rage. At times his face became mask-like, his movements mechanical, and his emotions numbed. During the worst periods of his life—like a time in his mid-twenties when he sat in his car crying—his inner struggle brought him to a stand-still and the future seemed hopeless.

Ulla—Self-Love

Worlds apart from Nolan was Ulla who spoke with us in the living room of her Los Angeles apartment which was bare except for two director's chairs, a coffee table, books and magazines piled in the corner, and an exercise machine. Ulla was very beautiful in gym shorts and a tank top with lean, muscled arms and legs, and short cropped, curly black hair. Her manner was eager and open, her voice agreeable and calm; and she grinned infectiously, perhaps with exhibitionistic pleasure at some of the more shocking and unusual things she talked about. The ease with which she talked about herself also gave her an air of self-promotion.

Ulla explained with equanimity that her apartment was bare because she and her husband had just separated. She said that their three year marriage had broken down because they had found their values to be different. He had wanted her to be more settled, to be earning more, or if not earning more to start having children. There was a vagueness, which our questions couldn't pierce, to Ulla's description of how she and her husband had gotten together, how they had mistaken each other's values, and drifted apart. Ulla had her regrets but they didn't seem to touch her deeply, and the future looked rosy to her. She said that she had no trouble finding men to date (undoubtedly true), though the danger of AIDS troubled her. She was also applying to the University of California at Los Angeles film school which, she said, would give her the tools to use her intellectual and creative talents, and make a mark in the world. It didn't bother her that she was several credits short of finishing college, and had not stayed with any job for more than two years. She was also blithe about having children, which she said she certainly planned on having, but sometime in the future after graduate school.

Ulla was an enchanting person to interview because of her candor and non-judgementality, her beauty, and her optimism. Affection was in the air for she communicated good feeling and pulled good feelings from her interviewer, but it also gave us pause since it gradually dawned on us in reviewing her interview that Ulla was a very narcissistic, self-involved woman and most of her love was for herself. This self-love was world's apart from Nolan's self-deprecation and self-doubt, yet narcissism is another classic form of internalization of distress. Self-love plays itself out through protecting self-esteem, through enhancing the body, and consequently through the enhanced body's power to seduce the love of others. Narcissism is a marvelous defense mechanism that can create the illusion of beatitude, bring and spread happiness, yet mask a great inner haplessness.

How did Ulla get this way? It is not a pleasant story, though there are compensations in it. She was born into a deeply unhappy marriage which featured nine moves in the first years of her life as her father, a brand manager for a nationwide food company, looked to advance and accepted whatever new assignment the company gave him, chasing the rainbow for a pot of gold. During this period Ulla's mother mostly submerged herself in her husband's ambition though sometimes took caustic revenge on him. Shortly after the last move when Ulla was seven, her parents divorced. In their few contacts with the father, the project staff described him as a cocky, aggressive man with a cold, hard stare who had the notion that fatherhood meant being a good financial provider and thus his place was in his corporate office rather than at home. He interacted little with his daughter and demanded little of her, but this at least meant that the father accepted Ulla as she was without criticism when she was small.

When the project observed the mother feeding Ulla at six weeks, the mother was annoyed at her child. When the baby was gassy and irritable, the mother pounded her back with a force that only increased the child's distress. The observer wrote, "The mother did not seem to really be close to the baby and seemed to enforce a separation of an unnatural kind between them. When the mother remarked that the baby was hungry and put the bottle in its warmer, she sat down and had a cup of coffee herself, letting the baby cry for some 20 minutes. Finally I mentioned that the milk in the bottle was boiling; if I hadn't it was my impression that the mother could have sat there for a good half hour more." In later feedings in the first year, the mother was oddly conscientious in a mechanical way, and the child depressed. There was no emotional connection or communication between mother and child. The mother was limited in her empathy and intrusive.

Reflecting on having children, Ulla's mother said, "It's not such a joyous occupation being a mother. Wouldn't it be marvelous if all the children were healthy and away on their own except when we are out on the street together and people are admiring her." The mother herself was a figure of admiration, glamorous in cocktail dresses for her visits to the project, talking easily and casually, often with an interesting twist. She was flippantly self-aware at times such as when she asked for a cloth to protect her dress, saying, "I know I shouldn't dress this way, but it's my therapy." Ulla's mother had a big, warm, extremely pretty smile which she often beamed at the little girl when the baby was upset. The smile was irresistible and drew the child out of her bad mood, though only temporarily because the mother's manner lacked real intimacy. The smile and her gayness were meant to ease the child out of her distressed mood without really taking note of it, the interviewer wrote.

Ulla was not faring well under these circumstances. In her earliest visits to the project she was irritable and tense. Most startling was her retardation, so much so that at 12 months she had the responses and abilities of a nine month old She was a lumpy, morose baby with dull lightless eyes, who turned away from people and stimulation. She became even more tense when she couldn't see her mother. Like Nolan, she often rocked to-and-fro in her crib when alone, which was too often. Very inhibited and under-developed at one year, she touched toys with a tentative, out-stretched finger rather than grasping them. Her examiner wrote, "She seems hungry for company. It is as if this child is bottling up real anguish and distress in her chronic state. The baby seems most concerned with her own body, making loud groaning and grunting noises to relieve distress, and brings things to her mouth all the time to soothe herself." Amazingly, this observation of the baby at one year forcefully expressing and experiencing herself through her body foretells Ulla's preoccupation with her body as a young woman.

This woeful picture continued well into childhood with descriptions such as this one at three years, "Ulla appears like a frightened, lost soul appealing to her mother for help. It is as if she is holding herself together for fear she will fall apart." At four years, "She can barely separate from her mother. She gets so little personal support for her interests that she must find her solace with toys." Of her stuttering, her mother said, "If I am nice to her, her speech is fine." At five her perseverance on IQ testing was poor and her appeals for help so pronounced that the tester doubted the validity of the score which in fact was average. At six years, she was a passive, sad child who seemed to mirror the tension between her parents.

In kindergarten Ulla was mild, placid, agreeable, and very much in the background. In class she was competent and interested in learning, but on the playground she was much less sure of herself. She was physically awkward, and shied away from the other children. She had established a disturbing relationship with one friend, Betty, who controlled and manipulated Ulla unmercifully. Her long hair, dungarees, sweet facial expression, and boyish clumping gait gave Ulla an oddly neuter gender appearance. The observer described a play sequence in which Ulla couldn't decide whether to carry a velvet purse or wear a fireman's hat. "When Betty grabbed the purse away, Ulla said nothing. Her role in the whole thing was very ambiguous. She was not a mother; and while Betty sometimes treated her like a henpecked father in their fantasy play, Ulla did not really act like a father, nor did she take the role of a child."

* * *

Then came the breakup of the parent's marriage, and Ulla began a gradual transformation that led to the physically striking, cordial, open, aspiring movie maker she is today. Rather than transformation, perhaps the term "make-over" is more accurate, for it both conveys Ulla's present day winsome appearance and the fact that much of her change is only skin deep. Unfortunately the research record fails to chronicle the actual process of her change, for it occurred between her last contact with the project at seven and her return at 18. In contrast to the great majority of the other participants who by seven were small versions of themselves as adults, Ulla's adult personality could scarcely be discerned at seven years. There was little or no prefigurement of her later social relationships, coping style, defense mechanisms, demeanor, skills, and work habits. Probably Ulla's unformed personality at seven years reflects the overall slow development which made her appear retarded in her first year. In turn her immaturity was inextricably linked to the family's chaotic life in which she was often an object to be manipulated or put aside for periods of time.

It is also possible that Ulla's very immaturity—in peer relationships, physical development, self-care, and level of thinking and knowledge relative to her potential—may itself be a precursor of her narcissistic personality disturbance. Slow development leaves a child always in the position of having to play catch-up in relation to other children. Indeed, immature personal and social values appear to linger on in pathologically self-involved people into adulthood and even into mid-life. Witness, for example, that one of Ulla's reasons for wanting to go to film school is to make herself famous. The desire for fame is often part of the defense mechanism of compensation, for fame brings power, attention, approbation, which can do much to compensate for, and bolster poor confidence and self-esteem. Without a solid sense of a core personality, Ulla came alive (as many actors do) by assuming roles and receiving adulation.

Additionally in Ulla's family, fame (and its handmaiden, status) was a brass ring that everyone was taught to chase. Her mother had explained that her own parents had been struggling Eastern European immigrants from a village to New York City who lorded it over the neighborhood when her father rose in the ranks of the borough political establishment. There was also great pride that the mother's sister was a secretary for a well-known theatrical producer. As to her style of dress, Ulla's mother (wryly self-aware and blind at the same time) said, "I dress differently than other women because when I am on the street I can't let the other housewives see me as common."

Sources of Ulla's Narcissism

Thus there are several sources for Ulla's eventual extreme narcissism: 1) The troubled relationship with the mother (neglect and impaired empathy), 2) her slow development, 3) her limited contact with her father, 4) the disruptions in her life caused by many moves which interfered with socialization with peers, and prevented her from having a sense of consistency and predictability in life, 5) the family's desire for attention, fame and money, 6) her lack of confidence and self-esteem (consequences of family experiences), and 7) her identification with her mother's seductiveness.

Nonetheless at seven years, Ulla gave but one sign that a marked change of any kind was taking place—a just emerging snappishness. The wan, forlorn, delicate child was showing anger for the first time, and sometimes resisting going to school. During her developmental testing at seven, her demeanor was mixed—anxious, apathetic, flippant, negative, sly and manipulative. She was even briefly defiant, announcing that she didn't like the work. Ironically her IQ had risen to a bright 116, which the tester thought was still not a true reflection of her ability. Dr. Brody suggested that her improved performance was related to her new aggressiveness turned outward instead of held within, a harbinger of a partial shift from internalization of distress to externalization.

When Ulla was seven, her mother announced to the project, "I've kicked my husband out." After his departure the father increased his already excessive drinking and badly abused alcohol and cannabis for a number of years. As an adult Ulla recalled her father slapping her often when he was drinking during her visits in the ensuing years, and once he pushed her down a flight of stairs. Her mother also frequently spanked her for obstinacy. "My mother's spankings didn't really hurt," Ulla insisted, "because the hanger she used was covered with velvet." Guilty and confused, the father tried to make amends for his anger and absence from the family, so he invited his daughter to join him and his young girlfriend (barely out of her teens) in drinking and smoking marijuana by the time Ulla was in junior high school. As an adult Ulla recalled her tremendous ambivalence about her father during these turbulent years: "He'd be saying 'I'm so sorry for what I did,' pouring drinks and his heart out at the same time. I don't trust him to this day but I love him. A real father is somebody who gives you orders and you rebel against them. My father let me smoke and drink and tried to be a friend. It was really seductive. I wanted him to like me; I wanted to be cool like his girlfriends. He was an athlete in really good shape, and I also wanted to be physically like him, but at the same time I knew he was all fucked up."

In spite of her mixed feelings about her father, Ulla consciously and unconsciously modeled herself on him more and more. In high school she and a group of boyfriends and girlfriends vandalized abandoned houses. Recalling the sound of breaking glass at 30, she said, "It was exciting, like I was Thor or Wonder-woman or something, bringing down bolts of thunder and lightning. Partly I did it to impress other kids, show them that rules were for peons; partly I was just an angry kid." Thus throughout adolescence Ulla made a transition to acting out many of her feelings.

But turning inward of emotions remained inherent in her focus on her body, as if sculpting her appearance could create emotional equilibrium. Paradoxically, as a youth she built up her body while episodically "trashing" the world around her—her dormitory room, other property, and boyfriends. "That's how I was in those days; I never thought about how what I was doing might affect other people . . . In high school I decided I couldn't stand being scrawny anymore. I wanted to be strong like my father; or beautiful like I thought his girlfriends were. So I got into lifting weights. My mother knows about clothes, so I paid attention to her. By my senior year I was into modeling. The attention and money was neat but I was bored as hell. College was mostly parties, dances, bars, meeting people. I loved getting guys to fall for me. I guess some people would say I was loose or didn't respect myself much, but for me sex was more like a sport or athletics; I didn't think much about who the other person was. Also guys were easy prey, like shooting fish in a barrel. I don't think I'm that way now, though it still is nice to be able to walk in somewhere and have people come on to you."

She also told us about the drugs she used from high school to her mid-twenties—speed, marijuana, alcohol, cocaine, and many hallucinogens (which she found "interesting" because it made her "tune in" to her sensations and perceptions). Ulla recounted this matter of factly, without bravado, and with some amazement at the kinds of things she had been through. Her self-commentary at 30 was strikingly in tune with her psychological test report at 18 years which reported, "Her anxieties and poor self-esteem have led her to think and act in unconventional ways as if to show the world that she is not like everybody else. Fantasies of achieving power intrude into her thinking. She is fearful of letting go of her rage, valiantly tries to ward off feelings of dependency and depression, and longs for tenderness and trust. She is intensely self-absorbed, and if she is not already abusing drugs or alcohol, she is at great risk because of her dysphoria, her self-absorption, and need to ward off feelings. She gives a show of sophistication yet in fact is not as mature as most girls her age. Nonetheless there is a core of candor and honesty about her."

When Ulla was 18, Sylvia Brody wrote, "She has been swamped by neglect, probably from both parents, but in different ways. Clearly she is trying to pull herself together, trying to know what to do with her life, but she doesn't know how, where or what to do. Oddly it came up that she most fears losing her mother, and says she sometimes still holds on to an old doll her mother gave her in nursery school. She feels no pleasure visiting her home and her first year of college is boring to her. Her greatest pleasure is dancing and picking out clothes; and her greatest worry is not having people like her so she tries to be careful to not alienate people. She is pleased that she is good looking, and troubled that she regularly disobeys or disappoints her mother. Ulla enjoyed having an audience to talk to about herself, and did it openly, but there was also a confusion in her thinking, a pressure in her speech, as if she had a need to say everything that came out without self-consciousness. It was linked to a wish to understand herself more, though at the same time the pressured speech primed her to escape feeling any emotion. At this time in her life her main felt emotion appears to be anger or excitement that comes out in action. When sadness surfaced in the interview she shied away from it, and reassured herself that she would pull through."

So by Ulla's first year of college, her transformation (the first signs of which we saw at seven) was evident though raw and incomplete. She was working mightily toward a beautiful physique that would draw in admirers and also allow her to admire herself. Both would reassure her that she was an acceptable young woman to her parents, and also that she could protect and take care of herself.

* * *

At 30 years of age, Ulla's childhood sadness was still there, though she gave it a tough spin in such comments as, "When I have children, I'll give them all the love that I can because life is too short for fighting, because the next thing you know, it's lights out." Thus the pain and trauma of her childhood had foreshortened her sense of the future, making her feel that she had to seize the moment before it was too late. The energy she had mobilized in later childhood had stayed with her and kept her sadness at bay. Nowadays Ulla says she has forsworn drugs though she still likes drinking because it makes her merry; she insists she can handle it. She clearly desires people's company, but her sense of men and women is relatively unidimensional in that she values them for how they make her feel rather than seeing them as whole people in their own right. In this sense Ulla's immaturity relative to others her age—first evident in infancy and early childhood—continues to the present as a component of her self-centeredness.

As a grownup Ullla's movement away from her childhood forlornness is firmer and less hard-edged than it had been at 18. Good and bad experiences have tempered her self-certainty; optimism remains, though tinged with the view that life is evanescent. Completing college has been arduous. She initially went astray through partying and was suspended after severely damaging her dormitory room. She returned to school, then left again in her senior year to take up modeling full-time because if offered money, places to travel, and people to meet. However, she tired of being the passive object of photographers, dress designers, hair dressers, and cosmeticians. After giving up modeling, she tried working as a librarian for a television network, and for the last two years she has managed a fitness club. In her recounting, she seems to see herself as fated to have to deal with incompetent people who don't understand her, her skills, or her good qualities, which interferes with her ability to do her job well. This sounds like Ulla is projecting her problems onto others or rationalizing them, but interestingly she caught herself before she went too far down this path, and acknowledged that she had to take some responsibility for her checkered work record. She did this by holding out the hope for a future in film-making as a director, writer or producer, which would yoke her skills and ambitions so that she would be motivated to do well and remain committed no matter what the obstacles.

Her parents gave her a model of life without deep engagement in relationships or work. Her father continues to go from job to job planning the introduction of new brands of breakfast cereal. He has not remarried but has joined Alcoholics Anonymous and stopped drinking. Her mother has never shown Ulla how to engage herself empathically with other people for her contact with her daughter has been characterized by impulsivity and self-interest, although through all the years she has acknowledged her responsibility for her daughter. Now remarried and the manager of an apparel store, Ulla's mother continues to give her daughter financial support and will pay her graduate school tuition.

The leitmotif of Ulla's twenties had been her involvement in physical culture. She has achieved national ranking in women's physical fitness (with the help of illegal steroid drugs, she admitted), and taught aerobics. Clearly her appearance is a great source of gratification. The excitement she gains from it spills over to her sexual life, for when she works out a great deal, she says she often gets very sexually aroused. In her sexual fantasies and dreams, images of beautiful women arouse her as much as those of men. She says that she has never actually been aware of a desire to have sex with a woman. She also adds that sex with men is rarely fully satisfying and she often doesn't have an orgasm.

In trying to understand Ulla's sexual life we remembered the descriptions of the curiously neutral-gendered six year old girl clasping the fireman's hat and velvet purse at the same time. As a girl and teenager, Ulla had a yearning for acceptance by her father, which may have been transmuted into the feeling that had she been a boy she would have been more loved by him. In fact at 30 her most pleasant very early childhood memory is playing with her father. By contrast, Ulla's attachment to her mother (powerfully driven by the mother's enchanting smile) has always been troubled, and because of this she has never completed her psychological separation from her mother. She fantasizes union with a woman as intensely as with a man. Her husband must have suffered from his wife's confusingly formed gender identity. Ultimately, we also speculated that Ulla's sexual excitement after work-outs at the gym, and her visions of beautiful women, reflect her own fixation on herself.

In spite of her problems and inner struggles and conflicts, Ulla feels content with herself these days, for she is banking emotionally and financially on her future success in a career in movies. She no longer worries about herself as she used to do, she assured us and herself at the same time.

Reina—"A complicated kind of love"

Nolan turned his frustrations on himself, denigrating and depressing himself. Ulla transformed herself from the scrawny, weak, unlovable person she felt herself to be into a handsome woman whom she and others could admire. The last person upon whom this chapter focuses is Reina, who found a third way to manage her childhood unhappiness—the path of disassociating herself from distress.

We interviewed Reina in her office at a medical center where she had just finished her residency in neurology and is now an assistant professor involved in genetic research. Business-like in her white laboratory coat and impressively self-possessed, she concentrated intently, smiled gently at pleasant or ironical memories and frowned at bad ones. She also had a slight head-nodding tic from time-to-time. Measuring her words, she said, "When I was young I didn't understand how people related to each other. I would sit in class or stand on the playground watching the kids, not really there, wondering why does so and so do that, how does that person know what to say? How do you know when to laugh, yell, say hi? It was not even like I was in my own skin. I have a strong memory of being on the playground running, but I wasn't really running. The real me was up in the bleachers looking down at my body running around between groups of kids who were kicking balls and playing hopscotch."

"I remember when I was about 20 reading Robert Heinlein's *Stranger in a Strange Land*, thinking that's me, that's what my life is all about. This went on until my mid-twenties when finally I began to feel like I was claiming my body, being here and comfortable with who I was, not having to think through everything but just enjoying my friends."

Then Reina shifted to her parents, "As a child I think I was afraid of my mother. She was so strong and forceful. I was in awe of her and admired her a lot. How good she was in everything. And there was the ongoing pressure for achievement, to do things. There was a sense of emotional distance between us; love, yes, but distance. I was supposed to be the perfect child, the one with excellent grades. There were many fights during those years."

"I recall this science project in about fifth grade. It was one of those group projects where you're supposed to work with the other kids, but the other kids weren't coming through. My mother started getting upset, like I wouldn't get an A or something. She convinced me—actually brainwashed me, there was that little chance that I had to not go along with her—to break away from the group. But these were kids that I liked. You can imagine that they weren't exactly thrilled," Reina laughed slightly at this memory.

"One evening about the same age I came into the kitchen where my parents were after dinner. I was just really sad, like I was a lot then. I said to my mother, 'I just want something to look forward to,' and she's like saying, 'Well you know we're going to visit Uncle Jim and Aunt Nell over Christmas,' and I kept saying, 'No, that's not it! I want something to look forward to.' And she'd go down the list of plans; and I was like, 'Wait a second, those aren't things I'm looking forward to.' So there we were with this sort of lack of understanding between us. I remember when I was very little she said I was awful to have such a messy room. She'd say everything in the room belonged to her, and then take everything off the shelves and make me start over and put them back neatly. We were screaming at each other. She was pretty scary, and then I'd just go limp. Then a little bit later we'd all be sitting in the kitchen and everybody would say, 'I love you.' It was like it took these huge fights to be close."

"I don't want to give you this one picture, because my mother also was exciting. I was only ten but she would let me take the bus to her school where she was the principal, and I'd wait in her office for her to finish up, and admire how important she was. Then we'd go around town running errands together like a team. That was fun."

Reina also told us about her father who was a manager for a building supply company. His mother had died in an automobile accident when he was nine, and his father and stepmother insisted that he "be strong" and bottle up his feelings. Reina said that only a year or so ago, thinking about his retirement and future, her father had gone into therapy and for the first time had begun to mourn his mother and talk about his childhood. Her experience of her father growing up had been very different from that with her mother, "What comes to mind about him is that he was inaccessible. What I mean is that I wanted him to protect me more from my mother and he didn't. But there were these wonderful, long, relaxing Saturday morning drives with him while my mother was at her office catching up on her paperwork. We'd go to the country; it was so beautiful. We'd come to different crossroads and all he'd say was which way should we turn. And I'd say turn right, so he'd turn right, and then I'd say turn left, and he would. We would just meander along based on what I wanted to do."

"At other times I remember a lot of frustration. He didn't talk very much, just didn't respond normally. My father felt a lot of things but didn't say them, while my mother spoke to me but she was always so rational. Or else she and I had these raging fights, and all my father would say was, 'It's just the way your mother is,' or, 'She's working hard,' or, 'She really loves you,' these standard phrases, but he wouldn't ever engage! Though he was loving in other ways. I remember a bowling jacket he had from when he was a teenager with this silky stuff that was so beautiful. He gave it to me to wear. I was just in love with that jacket. I wanted to know what he was like as a kid, and I asked him. He said he didn't know, so all I had of his childhood growing up was this jacket."

"When I was young I was so alone I really hated going to school. Once just when I was starting junior high school, I refused to go and my father started to cry because he was so sad that I was so sad. I mean I was really frustrated by him because he couldn't talk about anything, but I knew he cared about me. We had love in our family, but it was a very complicated kind of love." Reina was crying quietly as she finished telling us about her past.

* * *

What does *a complicated kind of love* look like in action? Hardly gentle. Reina's mother was like a too busy, too brisk Mary Poppins whose charges were entranced by her but could never quite keep up or catch up with her. The mother was tall and angular; she usually wore pants, and no makeup or adornment. She was also generally good humored, genuine, friendly, animated, easy to talk with, thoughtful, and self-assured with grownups. But the researchers noted early on that she was too loud, gruff, excitable, and vigorous with her baby. Often interested in, and enjoying her baby, her investment in being in charge hurt her relationship with Reina. She also had a distressing habit of detaching herself momentarily, impersonally, and without warning from Reina.

When Reina was an infant, Sylvia Brody said, "This is an enormously complex mother-child relationship. The mother both disapproves and reinforces the baby's aggressiveness by engaging aggressively herself with the child, which rewards the baby with attention for struggling. The mother seems to lack the tenderness and warmth associated with mothering, and is somewhat overwhelming. She can be empathic toward her daughter, but gets very bothered by what she sees as the baby's unreasonable crying, and she has no curiosity about what may be beneath it. The baby often appears frightened by the mother."

In spite of the fear the researchers saw in the child (fear which Reina herself recalls feeling), the little girl was not helpless for she was strong and smart. For the first four years of her life she fought back tenaciously against her mother. In infancy she enlisted her mother in battles for control of the bottle, the jar of baby food, and the utensils; and her toddlerhood was a long stretch of apoplectic temper tantrums and regular spankings.

Then shortly after her fourth birthday there was a substantial change. Reina's tantrums largely disappeared and she became subdued and compliant most of the time. This was the beginning of her adaptation through the use of her self-induced hypnotic-like states to dissociate herself from feeling, a form of coping that was predicated on her desire not to lose her mother to their mutual frustration. In taking this course Reina was in many respects mirroring her father, who was emotionally shut down himself, but nonetheless doted silently on his daughter. Not least of the forces affecting Reina were her mother's stormy threats two or three times a year to "pack up and leave" when her impatience with her husband and daughter got the best of her, which cowed the daughter into submission. Describing this at 30, Reina said, "There was an eggshell-like tension in the house. I figured out how to sit quietly and be out of the way, like in a different space. I always felt that if I crossed a boundary I could be rejected."

By nursery school age a staff member wrote, "Reina trailed on her mother's heels like a puppy dog, and waited silently outside the bathroom door while her mother was inside." She seemed sad, depressed, withdrawn, and responded woodenly as if the interviewer was just a provider of test materials, though in fact the testing appeared like a respite for the youngster because she was able to absorb herself in it totally. Socially Reina seemed afraid or unwilling to share any feelings.

Highlights from descriptions of Reina in her first seven years are as follows: In her first weeks of life Reina was "alert, responsive, curious, strong, cuddly, and cranky." At six months she had changed somewhat and was "stern, sullen, and mostly interested in things rather than people." Her mother was very concerned that she was constipated (sometimes a bodily form of internalized tension, or in older children sometimes a tuning out of bodily sensations). At one year her observer wrote, "She is perhaps the most aggressive, independent, and self-assured little girl I have met." Her mother reported that she still suffered from constipation. At three years her determination and defiance dominated her visit to the project. At four, still evolving, she was "spiritless, sat very still, often staring, and her face was affectless as if carved in stone." In kindergarten she was "meekly conforming and able to work quite well independently on assigned tasks, but not able to follow through in unstructured activities." On the playground, "She flows gracefully like quicksilver though she initiates no social contacts. She is looked up to by other children for her intelligence and mature social judgment, and does respond to their overtures, becoming happy when other children approach her. She glows and smiles when others are around her, and seems very conscious that others have feelings and tries to respect them. She is quiet, takes everything in with her eyes."

At six years she was "reticent, tense, and inhibited in her movements, flat emotionally, avoided making eye contact with her interviewer, and gazed off into space in a bemused, preoccupied way. She constantly chewed on her fingers, pulled on her clothes, and has developed a tic or mannerism of hunching her shoulders and nodding her head [still present at 30 years]." In the playroom at the project she moved mechanically as if tuning out the world, though the quality of her concentration and her work was excellent during testing. Her mother said her constipation had gone away but resistance now took the form of reluctance to go to school.

At seven she was "sad, quiet, ungainly, keeps her nose to the grindstone, and works compulsively and expressionlessly. She carefully aligned all the corners when making block designs, and perseveratively insisted on the rightness of several obviously wrong answers during her testing." Socially she was withdrawn from project staff; by contrast, when with her mother she craved her attention, which the mother only gave erratically.

* * *

Reina's growth followed the trajectory that had been apparent in first grade, and at 18 she was still straining toward perfection. This gave her a sophistication that came from her considerable accomplishments in high school. She was also cordial and cheerful, although the strain from the tension of her self-discipline was reflected in her head nodding mannerism. She also suffered from tension headaches and insomnia. When she spoke of her life, there was both optimism and sadness. She was disappointed in her perfectionism which was like a boomerang she couldn't jettison, for if there was a single flaw during the day—as when she didn't feel productive—it corroded her whole day. She was aware of an emotional distance from people, of long-standing loneliness, and held out the hope of being emotionally freer in the future.

Ironically in view of what the project staff knew of her life (and what Reina herself later knew at 30), when she was 18 she said that she had *never* felt dominated by her mother, and fervently wished that she could be as capable as her mother. Dr. Brody wrote that Reina was in fact identifying with her mother's executive skills and her father's quiet caution, channeling her considerable aggression into academic work and achievement, and avoiding emotional involvements outside of her family.

The psychologist who tested her at 18 reported, "This young woman has a depressive neurosis (dysthymia) with an underlying obsessive-compulsive personality. She uses defenses of intellectualization, denial, avoidance, restriction, identification with the aggressor, and reaction formation. Maternal authority is oppressive to her; images of her father arouse phobic-like anxiety; and she experiences the world as deeply threatening and overwhelming. But she has good stamina, humor, resilience and proportion. She meets the sense of threat by constantly trying to impose a fantasy-laden symbolic system and philosophical system on the world to make sense of it."

* * *

In the decade of her twenties Reina continued in this mold, achieving much while also compromising much and paying a price for success that comes from punishing inner pressure and tense self-control. This is in marked contrast to the harmonious successes of Nick and Tatiana in chapter one. Reina had indeed kept her nose to the grindstone and flourished intellectually in medical school while socially she was unsatisfied. In her first year of medical school she had begun living with a classmate, but he lacked her energy and academic commitment, and dropped out of school to take a job as a laboratory technician. "Without his support in medical school I couldn't have made it," Reina said, "His presence around the apartment, his cooking, the little comforts that come from being with someone. But after I graduated I began to have visions that there was not enough to our relationship, that our life would become boring."

Reina doesn't consciously link her ennui with her boyfriend to her ambivalence toward her passive, uncommunicative father; nor does she outwardly guess that she was projecting her own emotional restriction onto what she saw as a potentially barren relationship (that she felt emotionally shut-down herself and thereby took their life together to be empty). She did not seem conscious of how her boyfriend reminded her of her father, but she did know that excitement in her sexual life with her boyfriend came after their occasional arguments. At other times she often experienced pain during sexual intercourse (dyspareunia) with him. In both cases sexual arousal was connected with either emotional or physical pain. Intimacy following an argument felt to her too much like the kitchen table reunions after the storms in her childhood family, and she wanted to distance herself from this pattern. Reina's sexual difficulty (along with her head nodding tic and childhood stomachaches) also illustrates how many people express their internal tension in the psychosomatic language of the body.

After she and her boyfriend separated, Reina turned to psychotherapy, and credits it with helping her manage her loneliness and self-doubts during her post-medical school internship and first year of neurology. Alcohol was another tool she used to stave off insomnia or examination tension. Psychotherapy had also helped her twice before—in fourth grade when her best friend moved and her head nodding tic got so bad for a time that it worried her parents; and in junior high school when she felt so left out by the cliques that she didn't want to go to school.

At 30 years of age Reina says that she is in a good place in her life, perhaps the happiest she has ever been. She loves her work, finds teaching medical students gratifying, and has a few close women friends on the faculty with whom she feels truly relaxed, so that her lifelong loneliness feels gone. Her only real signs currently that all is not well emotionally are her need to return home each day to double check whether she has turned off the bathroom heater and left food for her cat; insomnia; and occasional worry that rivalrous colleagues may be plotting against her for laboratory space and research funds.

She is not presently dating because she first wants to settle into her new teaching responsibilities, but says she plans to go out with men again soon. She has never fallen in love (understandable given her cautious, premeditated approach to life) and hopes fervently that this will happen to her. Neither has she ever been sexually attracted to women. She is one of the few women who at 30 said that they felt no desire for children, though she expressed no aversion to the idea. Insightfully she attributes her lack of a strong wish to have children to her mother's own lack of femininity communicated to her in small ways. "She never became excited when I played with dolls; in fact forbade me to play with Barbies. So I gave it up completely. She never showed me how to use make-up like other girls' moms did. Oddly just yesterday my mother and I had lunch together, and for the first time in our life we went shopping for clothes together. I talked her into getting a dress."

This brought to mind the "Super-child Story," as Reina calls it, which her mother loves to tell. One day in third grade her teacher got lost on a class field trip to the Brooklyn Museum. Reina showed the teacher what trains to take. "If I had it to do over again, I would have directed her to Coney Island. I was always so serious." She wants to shake her seriousness, but it isn't easy. Her choice of profession is a perfect sublimation for her seriousness, energy, anxiety, and what her psychological tester discerned at 18 as her need to find a system or world-view that makes sense of a threatening world. Western medicine provides just such a rational scientific world view. Interestingly, her research focus is on finding genetic markers for behaviors in animals that are linked to their sexual roles. This is an intriguing intellectual search in her contemporary life for something that may have been deadened in her having to do with gender very early on in her own emotional life—what it means to feel like and be like a man or woman.

Conclusion

Even though individuals who internalize distress may suffer quietly, they do not share the same misery. Nolan and Reina consciously experience their unhappiness. Nolan especially reveals this in his need to fill an emotional void and loosen his inner constraints each morning at his bedside by ritualistically rehearsing the hours of the day to come. Reina protects herself somewhat from full awareness of her suffering through her professional sublimations. In her twenties she felt herself "a stranger," but she was not simply alienated from other people; she was also dissociated from her own body and inner feelings. It has taken her many years to "claim" herself, as she described it. Nonetheless her adaptation remains troublesome for although she says that "I became comfortable with who I was," there is a degree to which she has rationalized and accepted her estrangement from herself and others. This is implicit in her stance at 30 that she is "putting off dating" while she settles into her new job.

In adult life Reina is midway between Nolan (who feels the most subjective distress) and Ulla (who suffers little if at all). Reina's choice of research is also very interesting for she is trying to learn about human existence and gender-related experiences by studying microscopic pieces of human material (DNA). On the one hand this is admirable and of significant value to society, on the other hand she experiences life and excitement through pieces of biologic tissue which are kept alive artificially.

Too many of the participants in the study who are having difficulties as grownups saw ambivalence, emptiness, or even dislike in a parent's eyes as infants, and as a consequence their own self-love or narcissism has suffered. Coming from such bitter circumstances, the playwright J.M. Barrie (1947) (whose spirit of immortal youth, Peter Pan, is an ultimate survivor) once remarked that he never saw his reflection in his mother's eyes. On the day of his birth, he said, she didn't have eyes for him but for the new furniture she had just purchased.

The challenge in understanding Ulla is to explain why she feels so well now ("great," as she says) even though her husband has just left her and she has never successfully held down a job for long; and to consider whether feeling great is sufficient in life. Perhaps a useful way of comprehending Ulla is to see her as emotionally "running on empty." Both words are important, for Ulla gives a sense of running (never capable of *being*, always driven to *becoming* something), while paradoxically her inner resources are at or near empty. To compensate she works on her body and replenishes herself with admiration from men and women. She describes escapades of having sex recently without condoms with three different men in one week, and not even knowing their last names. This may be related to her sense of emptiness and the need to literally fill herself up through the act of intercourse.

Complexity of Family Relationships

If there is any single element that characterizes the three cases in this chapter—as well as the whole group of children who internalized distress as youngsters—it is **complexity of family relationships**, the "complicated kind of love," in Reina's words. By contrast, the parents of children who externalized distress tended to have disturbances that were more graphic and discrete, enabling us to enumerate them as a series of problems (chapter two, Table 2.2). The parents of the externalizing, motorically driven children could be divided relatively simply into an over-controlling and under-controlling group, albeit with some overlapping between groups. Hyperactive children of the over-controlling parents were reacting against their parents' intrusiveness, as well as imitating their mothers and fathers. The hyperactive children of the under-controlling parents were growing up in emotional vacuums, not rooted, insecurely attached, having to find their own way, and having to obtain limits for their behavior from their peers, teachers and society.

Of the 22 internalizing children, **seven had Insecure mental representations of childhood attachment to their parents as adults, one was Unclassifiable, and 14 (64%) had Secure AAIs** (three Secure-earned-secure)—a higher percentage of Secure attachments than found in the group of six externalizing children (33%). Of the three cases focused upon in this chapter, Nolan was Insecure-dismissive of attachment, Ulla was Unclassifiable, and Reina was Insecure-enmeshed with her parents. Diagnostically, Nolan and Reina are obsessive-compulsive personalities with histories of significant depressions, and Ulla is a narcissistic personality with a history of substance abuse. As 30 year olds, nine of the 22 individuals (41%) who showed signs and symptoms of internalized distress at seven years have psychiatric diagnoses (Table 3.1). Before the adult diagnoses came the childhood disturbances of the 22 children who internalized distress. Table 3.2 lists their signs as they appeared at age seven.

Chapter 3. Table 3.1 Adult Psychiatric Diagnoses of the Childhood Internalizers

Major Depression
Minor Depression (Dysthymia)
Anxiety Disorders
Somatizing Disorders
Narcissistic Personality Disorder
Obsessive-Compulsive Personality Disorder

Chapter 3. Table 2 Signs and Symptoms of Disturbance In 22 Internalizing Children at Age 7

Depression (sadness)	Fragility
Anxiety	Extreme passivity
Fearfulness	Over-intellectualism
Inhibition	Avoidance of affect
Emotional immaturity	Blandness
Pressured speech	Over-compliance
Obsessiveness	Over-responsiveness
Perfectionism	Low self-esteem
Tension	Motor tics
Social isolation	Motor habits (e.g. rocking)
Withdrawal	Psychophysiologic problems
Lethargy	stomach aches, enuresis, sleep difficulty)

The individuals discussed in the first three chapters created very different kinds of lives through integration of many forces and influences, sometimes with wisdom and ease, sometimes with great pain, always with agility. For the participants in chapter one, relatively smoothly functioning families led to children with *harmonious personalities* in tune with themselves and their worlds. The families in chapter two produced externalizing children who fall into a group that can be described as *reactive characters* and another group we can call *bleak characters* for whom their family life provided very little against which to react. Horowitz (1998), studying the impact of trauma on symptom and personality formation, terms this latter group *deficit characters*. The internalizers of chapter three are largely *conflicted characters*, also referred to as neurotic personalities. In the next two chapters we turn to two other groups in the project: first, those whose early parenting was good and who as adults are having emotional difficulties; second, those whose early care was not favorable, but who are now doing well.

Chapter 4

PROMISE LOST

No telling what shape the troubles would take, how they'd appear, how severe they'd be. Life hung in the balance, no telling what might be.
Mairtin O'Cadhain, Road to Bright City

EACH CHILD'S BIRTH is a new beginning. Through their children, parents can recast their own lives with opportunities they themselves didn't have. They can watch their children grow in ways that are excitingly novel and reassuringly familiar. Anything is possible. To be a parent is to be entranced with one's child's promise. To be a developmental researcher is also to be entranced with children and their possibilities. The original team of researchers in the Brody study gauged each child's promise based on the quality of the care the mother gave her infant. In their minds, the mother-child relationship came first. In the first year, if a mother nurtured with sensitivity and good organization but was not over-controlling, the researchers predicted that the child had the best chance of growing well and successfully.

In many respects these early observers were right in their assumptions in the early years of a child's life, and at age 30 the group outcome data (see Appendix) supports the correctness of some of their predictions into adulthood. Additionally, the case examples from chapter one illustrate most fully how parents' happiness and competence is contagious in its effect and passes on to their offspring. Nonetheless, the group data do not fully support the researchers' initial hypothesis, and in fact points to environmental factors other than early mothering that may have a stronger impact on a child's later well being. In brief, good early parenting does not guarantee good emotional and behavioral outcomes. In this chapter we look at the kinds of things that can go wrong in a child's growth, how damage actually takes place in a child's developing psyche, and how that damage usurps the promise and hopes of infancy. Twenty-six mothers nurtured their babies very favorably in the first year of the study (Group A), and for the most part, the fathers in these families were also effective. However eight of these children (31%) have not done well. As adults, they are struggling in some important respect in their lives. These eight children are also a markedly different group from those in chapters two and three whose mothers (and usually fathers also) were very troubled in critical ways in their childcare from the beginning of their children's lives, and whose children experienced distress from their first months. At age 30 this group with favorable early nurturing (five men, three women) all have lower than average Global Assessment of Functioning (GAF) scores (80 or less). Their scores range from 60-80 (median)—indicating at the least psychiatric symptoms, some difficulty in daily functioning, and dissatisfaction in life. In comparison, the mean GAF score for the entire project is 81.2—absent or minimal stress related symptoms, good functioning, and satisfaction in all areas of life.

This chapter focuses on two of the eight children whose promise, we came to see, was taken from them. In particular we will examine the powerful role of external trauma in undermining one boy's early growth, and how a girl's internalization of complex family influences, seemingly benign on the surface, badly affected her future. Then, with briefer reports, we turn to the lessons of the whole group of eight.

Oscar—When Death is a Part of Childhood

Oscar was the last born in a family with four girls. He was cared for by a mother whom the researchers described as "endearing, sweet, calm, fluid in her movements, with a simple, earthy gentleness." When her baby fussed during early visits, the mother—with the effective parent's ability to maintain affection in the face of frustration—brought Oscar to her shoulder and told him, "You're wonderful, even when you cry." About breast feeding, she commented, "I never realized how close a relationship could be, and I would never want to do it another way." Thoughtful, the mother articulated that the most important experiences in a baby's life were "feelings of closeness to the parents, getting attention, being cuddled, and being read to." Like other exemplary parents, Oscar's mother felt discipline was a priority that could wait until a child began to understand the dangerous actions for which he was being chided, and for this a stern voice would do. She never rushed to toilet train her children.

Also like other especially effective mothers, Oscar's mother was not flawless. On infrequent occasions observers found her too inhibited or self-contained. One wrote, "Sometimes it seems as if something is missing in her. Her affect is almost too quiet, without lights or darks, highs and lows. I did not feel that her reserve was shyness. It rather appeared that some spark of individuality was lacking. Sometimes in the interest of efficiency, when Oscar's sisters intrude, the mother's empathy flags, and she pushes on with her feeding when the baby wants to pause and play." Nevertheless, for his part Oscar was cuddly and lovable. He had a precocious sense of humor and delighted in playing hide-and-seek with his mother and sisters, covering and uncovering his face.

Before she started having children and giving herself full-time to the household, Oscar's mother had been a nursery school teacher. Her husband was a graduate student in theology, and the family scraped by financially on his meager scholarship money, living in a marginally safe Bronx neighborhood. Fortunately, the mother's parents lived nearby and helped with the children, all the more important because Oscar's father spent his days reading, preparing sermons for the church in which he was apprenticing, and working on his graduation dissertation. Although his assistance with the children was very limited, the father loved playing with his son, reading to him and putting him to bed in the evening. After the children were asleep he had to return to his books. The father's interviewers found him friendly, thoughtful, serious, studious, and full of detailed, affectionate stories about his son, and in spite of the limited time he spent with his children they termed him "one of the best fathers."

When he was one year, Oscar was a wiry toddler, generally subdued like his parents, yet readily beaming with smiles when he was enjoying a success or a hug. His physical and cognitive development were at age level in some areas and advanced in others. However more than most children, Oscar needed to be in his mother's lap to manage frustrating test toys. He became unusually irritated when the tester took a block away from him or hid a ball behind a screen. Describing the child and mother's relationship, an observer wrote, "Oscar's mother is quite fond of him and allows him a great deal of initiative, only discouraging him when he is at the point of doing something dangerous or making a bad mess. She spoke to him a great deal and attended to him quickly when he began to fuss, initiating a lot of physical contact with him. I was struck with how much Oscar actually hugged and kissed his mother, and even occasionally bit her neck, shoulder and face. His mother would say 'ouch,' but didn't want to stop his biting because she said she didn't want to discourage his expression of affection in general. Oscar seemed to be somewhat clinging, enjoyed being held by his mother, and spent more time in physical contact with her—actually embracing her—than most babies we have seen."

Some of the subtle imbalances in Oscar's emotions and behavior at one year—his aggressive affection, his tendency to cling, and his proneness to frustration—foretold further imbalances that appeared in his first years of school, where Oscar had trouble in his social judgment, a difficulty his school observer captures in her kindergarten report. "Oscar roamed the classroom staring forlornly at a group of children engaged in happy play, painfully wanting to join them but not knowing how. Trying to get attention he shouted out, 'I'm six years old.' The children ignored him except one boy with whom Oscar occasionally plays who said, 'Oscar, be quiet!' Oscar yelled back, 'You're stupid.' Then the rest of the group scowled at him except one girl who smiled at him sweetly and said, 'You can play with me.' Oscar finally sat down with the other children though he was never fully integrated into the group." Although his academic learning went very well, Oscar's teacher observed that he had trouble separating from adults and was fearful of new things; that he often crabbily insisted on doing things correctly while he also lacked patience and had trouble handling criticism that would have helped him do better. She also noted Oscar's tendency to be aggressive when he tried to socialize with other children.

Oscar's mother's description of him at kindergarten age, differing somewhat from the observer's and teacher's, was also accurate. She emphasized her little boy's good sense of humor, affection, inquisitiveness, and energy. With regard to his trouble mixing with the children at school, the mother said he was at loose ends without his best friend from the year before who had moved away. In these differing descriptions and emphases lies part of Oscar's problem. Though his parents approached child rearing with much understanding and gentle affection, they tended to gloss over or deny their son's difficulties. They neglected to set limits so Oscar never adequately socialized his aggressiveness, nor did they sufficiently nudge him from their nest to ready him for his middle childhood years.

Life's burdens also interfered. The mother's four other children drained the energy she had available for Oscar, perhaps what the infancy observer was noticing when she wrote of the mother that, "some spark of individuality was lacking." The father's divinity school work abstracted him until he finally graduated when Oscar was seven, a cautionary example of the difficulty in being both a graduate student and parent at the same time.

* * *

In retrospect, much that transpired in Oscar's life in the 23 years after his father finished school was presaged in his first seven years. However much that happened was well outside his observers' and most American families' imaginations. After divinity school the parents took a missionary assignment running a school in the shanty-town barrios at the edge of Lima, Peru. For Oscar, this move was from the frying pan into the fire. Although the level of physical danger was no greater in their new home than in the Bronx where they had lived before, as outsiders in Peru, Oscar and his family could no longer benefit from the familiarity, vitality, and tradition that comes from being indigenous to a community. The family was without roots or intimate support, factors which can sometimes compensate for, and give sense to the poverty and rawness of life.

At 30, Oscar described the series of shocks he experienced in Peru with no gilding of exoticism. A thin man speaking seriously, sometimes with animation and sometimes grinning sardonically, he told how when he was eight years old, he and his new friends found a young man's decomposing body while foraging for treasures in the trash dump at the edge of their neighborhood. Some months later he saw a woman acting strangely. A truck came along, and when it was too late for the driver to stop, the woman dashed into the street and died in front of his eyes, a suicide, Oscar thinks. He still has the odor of the truck's diesel fumes in his nostrils. Later, when he was in junior high school, a squadron of police entered the neighborhood looking for revolutionaries and shot to death his sister's boyfriend, who with other teenagers threw rocks at them. Still later, in his senior year in high school, he lost a best friend who was knifed to death in a teenage turf fight.

We asked Oscar how these many deaths had affected him, and if they still affect him now. He said, "It seemed like death was always a part of me because of where I was growing up. But the first time I remember really dealing with it was when my friend was killed in the fight. He and I had started out hating each other in school, beating the shit out of each other at first, and grew to be very close. I wasn't there when he was killed but when I heard about it I didn't believe it, like I didn't react. I just kept thinking of the last time we talked. I had just told him that my family and I were due to return to the United States as soon as the school year was over, that my father had been given another assignment. My friend said he'd save up money to come and visit me. I don't have a memory of much else about his death except that my parents told me that for a long time afterward they'd come into my room at night and find me crying and looking at a class picture of him. When my sister's boyfriend was killed, it was easier to hold onto memories of him because he liked to play music, and that's what I would think about. My sister and I still sometimes listen to tapes we made of him singing."

"I had this strange reaction at my friend's funeral, at the religious ceremony. Actually I call it the anti-religious ceremony because I'm very down on religion, which is weird because I was brought up in such a church oriented famly. I kept looking at his body in the open coffin. I was sure that if I looked hard enough I'd see where the wound was. How has all this affected my adult personality? I experienced so many violent things as a kid, that they kind of numbed me to violence, to death in general. They make me think that is the way life is, that if you care for somebody, you better make time for them and be there for them."

* * *

Today Oscar teaches high school Spanish and English literature in a Quaker school in Boston. He enjoys his students but clashes with the school director over his rules. An iconoclast, Oscar says, "I believe in God but not in the Bible. I love hiking in the country. You can't look at nature's beauty and purpose and perfection—I exclude people from that description—and not believe that some higher power must have created it all. People are the wrench in the system; they fuck it up." In spite of his cynicism, Oscar carries on his parents' legacy of wanting to enrich the lives of other people in spiritual and non-materialistic ways, fine goals in a man of deep character and values. His ambition is to one day start his own school in partnership with the sister (also a teacher) whose boyfriend died.

In some ways, Oscar is indeed fulfilling his earliest childhood promise; yet he is also extremely internally troubled. He has had periods of serious depression, self-doubts, and loneliness. He has severe claustrophobia, which makes him wait up to a half hour for elevators or escalators that are not crowded. He suffers from what are probably psychosomatic symptoms of emotional distress—insomnia, chronic indigestion, and headaches. He is apparently not so desensitized about death and loss as he thinks: he went through a period of heavy alcohol use to numb himself when a girlfriend left him shortly after he graduated from college. Although in retrospect he realizes that he was planning to marry this girlfriend out of a sense of obligation—they had been together for three years—and not because his love for her was strong, he has not been able to have a successful relationship with another woman since. "My problem with relationships is that I get very attached when I like a woman. I think about them all the time. I constantly want to call them to reassure myself and them about the relationship, and I get very jealous. With my girlfriend who broke up with me, I had my whole life planned, and now I'm never sure what love is, never sure what you can count on. It's led me to put up walls. I wish I could be less analytical and more spontaneous with women."

Oscar's difficulty with spontaneity has led him to be very inhibited and conflicted about sexuality. In friendships with women with whom there has been mutual affection, he has abstained from physical intimacy because he fears hurting them—a confusion of normal sexuality with aggression—and instead acts more like a confessor. He feels that he cannot trust relationships to last, and that he or the woman would be too hurt if they were sexually intimate and the friendship cooled.

Although Oscar thinks that his state of confusion over loving, sexual, assertive and aggressive feelings began with his fiance's betrayal, we consider that there are several additional, important sources for his conundrum. It is likely that Oscar's inability to believe that relationships can endure stems from the omnipresence of death while he was growing up. Multiple losses and the violent nature of the deaths he encountered have depleted his capacity to trust and infuse his emotional life so that normal assertiveness, especially his sexual assertiveness, becomes infected with images of violence.

The thrust backward to the source of Oscar's difficulties doesn't stop at the traumatic experiences with death, but reaches all the way back to his earliest childhood, before his family went to Peru. Oscar as a baby was very tuned into the presence or absence of other family members, clinging to his mother. He was angrily frustrated when toys were taken away or disappeared and needed to be in his mother's lap in order to function well during his developmental testing. His attempts to socialize with other children in the first years of school were awkward, his approaches uncertain, tarnished by hitting or yelling. Thus, for Oscar there is a long history of sensitivity both to loss and to separation from people, even sensitivity to losing inanimate objects such as toys. It is likely that each experience of loss was intensified by a prior, complimentary emotional state which progressively distorted his psychological development. Oscar went from acute sensitivity to his mother's presence or absence in infancy, to moodiness and isolation from peers in preschool and early primary school, to encounters with death and losses of companions in later childhood and adolescence. As an adult, he finds relationships painfully uncontrollable and unpredictable.

Today Oscar seems to be suffering from a prolonged grief reaction—chronic posttraumatic stress disorder—following the many shocks he experienced growing up. These traumas themselves found fertile ground for doing their harm in the emotional imbalances that were already present in him before moving to Peru. Yet Oscar remains fond of his parents and connected to them. They all talk once or twice a week by phone, and he visits them every month or two in upstate New York. His father teaches at a seminary, and his mother now runs a nursery school. His description of his parents in childhood is kindly: "They were loving, supportive, available, patient, understanding, close. My father was like a rock. They taught me how to be a good person. They showed me that everything you do affects other people, which is what I live by today." His words are all consistent with the researchers actual impressions of the mother and father. However, in contrast to Securely attached adults in the study, Oscar was not able to recall specific experiences to illustrate the adjectives he attached to his parents. Instead, he cited events that ended badly or ambiguously. For example, there was the time when he was 13, and his parents gave him a big, generous birthday party, but guests accidentally broke a window; times when his mother lost patience with him and painfully dug her fingers into his arm to restrain him; the time his father lost patience with him and his sisters in Peru and telephoned the United States to arrange boarding school for them if they didn't behave (which Oscar only learned much later was a make-believe call). Such contradictions between benign, descriptive adjectives and unpleasant, specific memories left Oscar in the Unclassifiable category with respect to his attachment to his parents. His melange of painful memories and loving adjectives may also be due to the many unresolved losses in his life. Ongoing mourning interferes with his ability to give a more coherent account of himself.

Perhaps the most telling recollection came when Oscar explained why he called his father "close" and "sensitive". Oscar said, "My father never raised a hand to me, but abused me by lecturing to me for hours on end whenever I did something wrong. He would sit me in a chair arguing in detail about how I was wrong, using passages from the Bible to make his point, asking me if I understood his argument completely. He wouldn't stop until I showed I did. To this day, we have long talks with each other. Now we talk about things that worry us. I got him to stop smoking, and he's always sending me inspirational messages about problems I am having in my life."

In Oscar's memories, we recognize decent parents stretched to the limit by their arduous work and five children. We see the father flailing at Oscar (perhaps fearful of not being able to protect his son from danger) with his Jesuitical verbal training rather than with his hand. Listening as clinicians, we also wonder if the father's sermonizing when his son was growing up could have slowed Oscar's psychological separations from his family. The father's brow-beating likely caused Oscar to take anger out on his peers, interfered with his sense of masculine identity, and contributed to his present day paralysis in heterosexual relationships. We also consider the possibility that the father's intellectual and emotional abstraction—his immersion in divinity school and missionary work—might have disturbed his wife's relationship with Oscar as a baby, perhaps the "something missing" in her affect that early observers noted. These paternal and maternal difficulties may have set the stage for Oscar's marked sensitivity to separations and to his ongoing struggles with loneliness.

Oscar's psychological testing when he was 18 supports these intertwining hypotheses. The testing shows Oscar as: 1) highly defended against feelings, 2) moderately emotionally blocked, 3) preoccupied with an image of a youth dying from a knife wound, 4) moderately depressed, and e) having difficulty concentrating. These findings are consistent with post-traumatic residues from encounters with death. His testing also shows him feeling many more conflicts about behaving sexually than do most late adolescents, and uncertainty about whether he admired and identified with male or female role models. Oscar's passivity may be a reaction against the violence and death he encountered in childhood. His sexual conflicts are also in keeping with the passivity into which the father forced Oscar with his sermonizing discipline, and with the possibility that these long father-son encounters may have sexualized the relationship, hindering Oscar's sexual arousal with women. Further, it is possible that Oscar felt intimidated by four older, at times bossy sisters, complicating his response to women, although neither Oscar's psychodiagnostic testing nor his memories point clearly in this direction.

When Sylvia Brody interviewed Oscar just after he graduated from highschool, she didn't know his test findings, nor did she know about his traumatic experiences in Peru because at that stage in his life he suppressed them from consciousness and consequently from his conversation with Dr. Brody. Nonetheless she echoes insightfully the psychologist's report in her summation: "He appears tired and discouraged, as if he had lived through a great deal. On the other hand, he was gentle, entirely friendly and accommodating. But he seems closed off, as if he has lost some capacity for introspection, or is very guarded. There is a tension in him which keeps him from being free and easy. This is a boy who would greatly benefit from psychotherapy. He may yet blossom."

* * *

Sadly, at 30 years of age Oscar has not blossomed yet the potential to flourish remains if he forms the right nurturing relationship. His human figure drawings today suggest intense castration anxiety and a sense of impotence in regard to women. He has resisted psychotherapy all these years because he has read widely in psychology and imagines that he would just compete with a therapist. Here again, as clinicians, we heard echoes of the father-son relationship which makes Oscar feel too vulnerable to chance having a therapist. At the present time, Oscar reports his usual mood as "even." We asked him what his greatest pleasure in life has been in life up to now, and he replied pithily, "I haven't had it yet." He was emphatic that his greatest future pleasure would be having a family and raising happy children. They would keep him from being alone, he said, and being alone is his greatest worry and burden.

Thinking of being alone led him to recall a recurring nightmare he frequently had when he was a child. In the dream, he is holding a big rock and a sledgehammer. Their weight is causing an intense pain to course through his body, but he can't put the rock or hammer down. Only awaking from the nightmare ends the pain and desperation. The last time Oscar had the dream was when he was about twelve, and it ended differently than usual. He dreamt that he carried the rock into the bathroom, where his sister—the one whose boyfriend was shot and with whom he would like to start a school—was washing up. He put half of the rock into the dirty clothes hamper, and half he gave to his sister, telling her that he could no longer carry the whole thing.

As we listened to the dream, we thought of the weight of Oscar's traumatic memories, the demand of his family's moral commitment to the poor, and his loneliness. We also remembered him characterizing his father as "like a rock," which he meant in an admiring way, but which we now understand comes with an unconscious price to pay for he carries the father like the rock in his bad dream. Nowadays, Oscar has a new recurring dream: He saves a man from being run-over by a truck—like the woman he saw killed when he was a child—by restraining him from absent-mindedly stepping into the street. The man turns out to be rich and rewards him with a lot of money which he uses to make life easier for his parents and sisters. Oscar is indeed generous and selfless, a testimony to his upbringing. But that upbringing—marked by his mother's fatigue, his encounters with death, and his father's pressure—has also forcibly limited his emotional freedom.

Olive—The Other Sister

Sometimes it is not trauma or even adversity that changes the shape of a child's life, but happenstance, something so innocent yet momentous as when a sibling appears. It was Olive's fate to be but five months old when her parents conceived their next child, and 14 months when the newborn, Rose, arrived. This new baby immensely complicated Olive's up to then idyllic infancy in completely unpredictable ways that had as much to do with the ensuing bond between Olive and her father, as with Olive's premature, forced loss of intimacy with her mother.

Olive's parents—both offspring of Scandinavian immigrants—had been married since high school, the father working as a wholesale fish seller and the mother on a factory assembly line. Their first two children came early in the marriage and then a decade passed until, to their great surprise, they conceived Olive when the mother was 34, and 14 months later, Rose. With Olive's birth the mother stopped work and the father took on second and third jobs. Rose's birth completed their family and filled their tiny Lower East Side home, an apartment with a communal toilet on the landing and the bathtub in the kitchen.

Olive's mother was sprightly, simply dressed, and had a relaxed air of experience that seemed to say, as her first interviewer put it, "I can take whatever comes my way." Her smile was sweet and open, her voice mellifluous, and she often used her hands to emphasize meaning. Too matter-of-fact for ceremony, she freely accepted offers of coffee and doughnuts from the project (though refused subway fare), and helped herself to cream and sugar. Having grown up in a large family and already raised two children who were well into school, she was a confident and good observer of babies, appreciating their differences and aware of their strengths and weaknesses.

Despite how little time he could spend with them, the father, handsome and fit from two physical jobs, knew more than most about the details of his children's lives. Nonetheless, he appreciated them passively, deferring questions about the children to his wife saying, "Ask her, she's the boss." In turn, she was consistently satisfied with her children's growth. When a problem arose, she dealt with it as a challenge rather than a cause for consternation or anxiety.

Her expressed child-rearing tenets were: 1) Discipline with firmness using talking, the tone of your voice, and depriving children of privileges, 2) spanking is a last resort, 3) wean from the breast by one and a half years and from the bottle by three, 4) toilet train by three, 5) never leave a baby by itself unless there are other people in the next room, 6) never leave a baby overnight except with a family member. While hewing to such basics, both parents were rather permissive with their children, giving them freedom to establish their own rhythms and appetites in life, and to explore their neighborhood and friends' homes. Most of the parents' discipline was directed toward keeping the peace amongst the children.

Here is how the research observers described Olive and her mother in the first year: "Olive's grin melted my heart at once . . . she is lively and strong, with much attentiveness and inner quietness . . . her development is very advanced . . . everything the mother did was almost effortless and the baby seemed entirely contented and well cared for. The mother is sturdy, efficient, and economical in her movements, proud of and satisfied with her child. She has an excellent balance in her ability to anticipate Olive's needs and also to delay gratifying her demands if she has to, or if Olive is being too demanding . . . the mother is delighted by her daughter and plays with her a great deal . . . this is the most vital responsive baby I have seen yet."

At Olive's six month visit, the mother told Dr. Brody that she was pregnant again. She added sheepishly, "It's too soon to be having another child, isn't it?" Not waiting for Dr. Brody's answer, she added positively, "We've been putting off moving. Now we'll really have to." The father took on a third job working Saturdays at an auto-parts store, and the family bought a three bedroom row house in Queens. In addition, the mother enrolled the coming child in the project (see Rose, chapter one, Success Stories). Volunteering the next child for the project had the quality of a propitiatory gesture to make up for feeling guilty for becoming pregnant while Olive was still at her breast. But in truth, the mother also described how she hugely enjoyed coming to the project offices on the Upper East Side of Manhattan, talking to the doctors, and looking at the bright, fashionable store windows en route.

Having both Olive and Rose in the study allowed us to closely compare the two children's growth and learn if the mother may have been right in her concern over having another child so quickly. Like Olive, Rose received exemplary mothering in infancy and thrived similarly. But Rose's arrival meant that Olive was weaned at 14 months—four months before her mother's stated preference—and relegated to her mother's apron strings while Rose took her place at the mother's breast. Additionally, the stress of two pregnancies in quick succession contributed to a severe hypothyroid condition in the mother, greatly reducing her energy over the next two years until it was diagnosed and treated. How these circumstances affected Olive was not quickly apparent; the changes registered slowly in her personality over many years. However, one adaptation that everyone in the family agreed took place was that Olive became her father's favorite. The mother reported, "My husband can be very irritable when he comes home, but he always goes out of his way to spare Olive, maybe because she's his first flesh and blood." The father said somewhat dismissively about Rose, "That one fights me. Olive and I get along better." As a grownup, Rose reports, "My father paid more attention to Olive." Even Olive herself said at 30, "My father always seemed to treat me better than my brother and sisters. Maybe it's because we both have black hair. There's a story about a Laplander in the woodshed way back when in the old country. Everyone else is blond." Thinking as developmentalists, we also considered it likely that the father grasped that little Olive needed his attention when Rose was born. Nonetheless, as the years went by, the father and daughter's relationship by no means remained simple and benign.

The project followed the two sisters in tandem. They would come together for their visits, and while one was filmed playing with her mother the other child was engaged in her testing. By most appearances and measures, the sisters were on parallel, promising courses. In fact, Olive did not even show the usual indicators of troubled development such as separation anxiety from the mother that might come from a too young and quick weaning from the mother as the older daughter of the two. It was Rose, not Olive, who for several years needed her mother in bed with her to fall asleep for several years. The mother reflected, "Olive turns to me if she's not feeling well, but otherwise she's probably bored with me and gets more entertainment from her father and teenage brother and sister."

It was only when Olive was six that her record began to diverge from her sister's. "They are no longer the same baby," an observer noted. On the day of their visit, Olive's tester wrote, "She is capable of being quite competitive, she enjoys herself, and takes delight in winning. She tolerated a day made very demanding by having to wait for Rose very well. But oddly, Rose, though one year younger, seems more emotionally mature. Olive doesn't seem as secure unless she is on top of a situation. Although she claimed her doll was her favorite possession, she appeared to envy Rose's doll. Further, Olive seemed at times to use talk to control situations, and occasionally, impulsively introduced irrelevant topics."

Here we have the first hints that Olive was not as secure or hardy in her self-esteem as her sister and might have been trying to compensate for the insecurity by controlling with speech, though a bit erratically and impulsively. These inauspicious signs were subtle, and her kindergarten observer painted a fine picture of good adjustment: "She is energetic, competent, and well directed. She is well liked, and her classmates who were already at school ran to meet the bus saying they hoped Olive would be on board. She is a helpful, affectionate child, and the one area of concern was that sometimes she seemed to be performing for the teacher to notice her rather than for herself."

At seven years of age, Olive continued to do well, achieving a nearly identical, very bright, IQ score as her sister, impressing her tester with her tenacious performance, concentration and desire to succeed. Olive still strove to make a favorable impression and continued to work to get her teacher's attention. In giving verbal responses to questions, she inhibited herself to short and precise answers and had trouble elaborating, as if she were fearful of saying something wrong. For example, when asked what she liked most about school, she said succinctly, "You learn more things." When asked, "What do you like least?", her answer was, "Nothing." Urged to talk about something that was pleasant but not connected with school, Olive said, "Playing in the backyard with my friends and being with my mother."

When she reunited with her mother at the end of the visit, Olive cuddled into her and "all tension seemed to flow out of the child." The researcher summed up, "Olive is a reserved, shy child with a real capacity to give and share emotionally and intellectually. However, she communicated her feelings more on a non-verbal basis than verbally and seems unrealistically afraid of strangers and apprehensive in new situations, with a dependency on her mother for her sense of security and well being. However, her calm, sweet disposition makes her thoroughly likable and fun to be with. Her persistence in tasks which make her uneasy is admirable. She has not yet recognized her superior abilities or her personal attractiveness, and her confidence in self-expression should increase as she becomes aware of her fine qualities."

It was fascinating to compare the stories that Olive and Rose told about animals on the Children's Apperception Test at seven years. As befits two sisters growing up in the same milieu, the story themes of both children were much alike yet Olive's stories emphasized the protection, food, and nurturing that mother animals provide, and contained more accounts of teasing and defiance than did her sister's. Rose's stories had more anger at father animals and more affection *and* rivalry toward sibling figures. Thus, there were indications that Olive at seven was more concerned with maternal nurturance, had more *inner* anger (indirectly expressed via defiance and teasing) than Rose, and that Rose could directly voice a wider range of feelings, both agreeable and disagreeable, for family members.

According to the mother, both girls were happy and doing well at seven. However, she said that Olive had a tendency to be quieter and moodier than her sister. She felt that Olive could not take teasing or feeling shamed as well as Rose, and gave as an example an experience that had occurred on a hot Sunday afternoon in the backyard with relatives visiting. Olive's bathing suit top kept falling down and finally her father abruptly took it off. Olive cried bloody murder as if she was being attacked, the mother recounted. To be this upset was unusual for Olive, whose bad moods were typically limited to sadness or irritability when she was left out of a game or teased. The mother added, "It's because Rose gets so much of my attention, and Olive feels left out. My husband likes to go to ice-skating on Sunday morning and I don't, so we set it up for Olive to go with her father this year while the rest of us sleep in. Olive loves it, and it may make her feel like she has something special for herself."

* * *

Years passed before Olive returned to the project as a senior in high school, years that were good to the family. There had been no outwardly traumatic events in Olive's life, and the family was prospering relative to their poor beginning. The father had cut back from working three jobs to two, their home was nearly paid for, and the mother was enjoying working outside of the home as a school clerk now that her children were mostly grown. Having grown up in a stable family with concerned parents, Olive was validating the researcher's prognostication at seven years of age that her confidence and expressiveness would increase as she recognized her abilities and attractiveness. Sylvia Brody wrote, "She is a pretty, open, self-assured, talkative teenager who looks somewhat like the popular image of a gypsy with her dark skin and curly hair which she knots in a bandana. She is friendly and now outgoing in comparison to her former childhood reticence. She has many friends and a boyfriend whom she met in the school chorus."

Still, there were areas of concern. "As yet she has no direction nor developed interests. Her academic aspiration is to go to community college, which is below her potential, though this may be my own bias because she actually said she did not want to study in one field nor work in a single career. Although she is open to ideas, my hunch is that that something keeps her from staying with one activity or devoting herself to a career or aspect of it, though she says she has not ruled this out for later in her life. In spite of her liveliness and her apparent good sense and good relations with people, I sense a restless push to experience almost too many things. This may be part of her youth, but I don't think so. It has the quality of an elation, possibly stemming from unconscious guilt about her preferred position with her father. It is true that her good spirits may also reflect the good deal of loving that she receives from her mother, but there is just a little too much need to be active and take pleasure in being 'flaky about my future' as she put it. In summary, Olive is doing well but not living up to her potential. I would not be surprised if at some point in the future she may feel disappointment in herself."

Thus for the first time we hear a clear worry that something is amiss with Olive (too much restlessness, too little ambition), a worry connected to her relationship with her father. The teenager herself tells Dr. Brody, "I could get away with anything with dad, but Rose would get yelled at for the same thing." The favoritism her father showed Olive did not, however, guarantee that she would give her father a favored place in *her* affections, for at 18 she complained about how irritable he could be when he came home tired from his two jobs, or when he drank too many beers with his friends on Friday evenings. She also lamented, "He doesn't communicate much. He doesn't know much about what I do, and we have little to talk about. If Rose and I are having an argument or playing our music too loud, he just screams at us. I ignore him. Rose screams back at him."

Olive's report conveys the unpredictable non-linearity and multidimensionality of family relationships: in spite of saying that she "ignores" her father's yelling, Olive takes his irritability, drinking, and lack of communication to heart, whereas Rose dismisses them as the mark of a hard working, tired, good providing man. In fact Rose's yelling back at her father could well indicate that she is paradoxically more emotionally liberated than enmeshed in her relationship with him. On the surface both girls at 18 were similarly happy, friendly, and decent students with no special academic ambitions. But the two sisters' psychological testing at this time showed that the girls' inner emotional lives were heading in different directions.

Rose's test report described her as "a young woman with an adequate self image, occupied with determining who she is and the kind of person she wants to be, sensitive and aware of the world around her"—all tasks of normal adolescence.

Olive's test findings were different: "Her tension and inner conflict appear to be in her need to establish herself independently, which clashes with her needs for nurturance and wishes to be dependent. At this point in her life Olive is actively though unsuccessfully striving toward independence, especially from a mother figure. Projective stories indicate feelings of timidity, inadequacy, and trouble asserting herself in competitive situations. She has magical thinking that her wishes can change reality, and experiences anxiety in connection with this mode of thought; and has feelings of grandiosity. Both the magical thinking and grandiosity stem from underlying poor confidence and esteem. In spite of her need for a supportive mother figure—and ambivalence toward mother figures as rejecting—there is also some coldness and detachment in Olive's responses. There are unresolved feelings toward the father who is depicted as benign, sympathetic, and ineffectual. Her sexual identity appears shaky, pointing to a rather passive and exaggeratedly feminine style of self-presentation. Her strength is a motivation and capacity to accept challenges, but the challenges to which she aspires may be too grandiose for her level of commitment to enable her to deal with the reality of accomplishing what she wants."

This is not a healthy psychological picture for an 18 year old, leading the psychologist to diagnose her as an Immature Personality. It appears that Olive's untimely loss of her mother's nurturing at 14 months—a consequence of Rose's birth and the mother's subsequent fatigue induced by her thyroid illness—had come home to roost in Olive's unconsciously confused feelings of dependence on, independence from, and rejection by her mother. The mother loomed too powerfully in her unconscious for a youth of this age. Additionally it is likely that Olive's emotional alienation from her mother started even younger than 14 months when the mother began investing herself in the new pregnancy. In Olive's testing the father appears more positively, but the early, strong intimacy with her father, into which circumstances thrust Olive, may have contributed to her accentuated, passive feminine manner.

* * *

After highschool, Olive was undecided about leaving home. She went to community college and lived in a dormitory for a while; left college for work and moved back home for several years; then moved out again and resumed her schooling. Now at 30, after ups and downs with various jobs, she has almost completed training as a physical therapist and is thoroughly enjoying her internship rehabilitating injured children. She has also continued to develop as a thoughtful observer of people and society, having become a much more self-assertive, articulate conversationalist.

By contrast her relationships with men are in shambles. She told us how at 19 she had found the lure of money in her pocket more powerful than her desire for schooling. Like everyone in her family she had become an accomplished ice skater, a Scandinavian tradition and the result of her skating outings with her father. It was very easy for her as a young woman to earn money teaching figure skating to children and to perform in ice shows. She had also been a manufacturer's representative for a line of skating dresses. Like her father and siblings, she didn't hesitate to hold more than one job at a time, enjoying all of her activities. But by her own account, a dark side had been her tendency to clash, and/or get romantically involved, with her male bosses. She also had found herself feeling overly responsible for the success of the ventures in which she was involved, in a way that went well beyond her role or expertise. She would get angry, depressed, and self-righteous when the skating school, a show, or the clothing manufacturer was not doing as well as she thought it should. As clinicians, we recognized in these reactions the grandiosity and magical thinking that the psychologist had noted at 18.

Olive said that three years ago she had recognized the need to focus more and have a "real job." She thought of physical therapy because of the numerous skating injuries she had seen, and the sprained ankles she had had. She pays the cost of her schooling with her several jobs. In this way, she is belying Dr. Brody's fear that she is too restless to commit herself. She credits her persistence (a trait noted by her project childhood observers) in her physical therapy curriculum to a female professor whom she admires, and who has become a friend and mentor. As researchers, we register how Olive has found a woman who can satisfy her dependency and nurturing needs while at the same time facilitating her movement toward independence. Noteworthy also is Olive's report that she occasionally has fantasies of being sexually involved with physically and emotionally strong women She has never had a real life sexual experience with a woman nor does she feel inclined to.

When Olive was graduating from high school, Dr. Brody had wondered if she might not be projecting her own personal investment in higher education onto the young woman when she expressed her reservations about Olive's lack of academic interests and focus. With hindsight, we can say that this might have been the case. In fact, Olive is following family pathways: her older siblings are skaters, and while there is hard work in the blood of this family, there is no intellectual tradition whatsoever.

Her busy, satisfying vocational life notwithstanding, Olive is very unhappy at 30, yearning for a stable relationship with a man and wanting to have children. Yet she keeps shooting herself in the foot by picking the wrong men or sabotaging potentially good relationships. It is her troubled, anguished personal life as a young woman that defines how the promise of her fine, initial parenting and first year has vanished. She has had many fitful, brief encounters with psychotherapy, but now has been working with a female psychologist for the past year and thinks that this time, she may be able to learn how to stop repeating destructive relationship patterns. Olive describes choosing or letting herself be asked out by men who are unavailable because they are married or not interested in a serious relationship. She enunciates that her poor choice of men is linked to her anger at her father because he did not share his thoughts and was seldom home. Olive doesn't know that she must unconsciously resent her father's unavailability because of her parents' fondness for each other, which is similar to her rivalrous resentment of having to share her mother with her sister. In addition to picking unavailable men, Olive says she also chooses men who end up showing a mean streak, and who drink too much or use drugs, both of which she herself has done in the past. She also dates men of other races and religions who are unacceptable to her conservative father, actions which provoke family quarrels that lead her to break off with the boyfriend. She grasps that some aspects of her inability to have a stable relation are connected with her entanglement with her father, but still pursues the unattainable, for her present boyfriend clearly falls into the category of past bad experiences.

When we asked Olive to give descriptive adjectives or phrases for her father, she said, "He was never there . . . kind of indifferent . . . he could be nasty when he wanted or drank too much . . . a smart-ass who makes fun of people . . . unaffectionate, which I know is a kind of contradiction because he gave me more attention than anybody else."

Describing the very same father, her sister said, "Loving, affectionate, caring, close, and a workaholic." Perhaps, Rose's need for closeness with her father was less intense than Olive's, and consequently Rose has much more tolerance for him, whereas Olive feels frustration and unrequited love. Olive's feelings about her father have been so intense that she has apparently unconsciously sexualized her fantasies about him. Perhaps he also has had eroticized feelings for his daughter. Olive's angry, uncontrollable "meltdown" when her father removed the seven-year-old's swimming suit top that wouldn't stay up during a backyard party suggests her sexualization of the experience. In most families, if a parent did this to a seven year old, which is generally before the age of significant modesty, the action has few if any emotional repercussions and is lost to memory. Olive spontaneously cited this experience when she was 30 years old as an illustration of her father's callousness. She said, "He tore the top off me. I was so ashamed," an experience which clearly has echoed in her psyche for 23 years as a kind of sexual assault.

Now in her adult relationships with men that are typically brief and leave her feeling used and self-righteous, Olive is compulsively reliving different aspects of her interpretation of her relationship with her father in ways she understands but can't yet stop (as well as in ways she doesn't fathom).

We compared Olive and Rose's Adult Attachment interviews at 30, and they were consistent with the two women's different ways of emotionally experiencing their childhood. Rose has a Secure AAI, reflecting a benign, solid image of her connection to her parents growing up. By contrast, Olive's AAI shows her to be Insecure in her attachment and in the emotionally enmeshed subcategory. Olive's Insecure-enmeshed rating goes along with her clinical diagnosis of Borderline Personality, given on the basis of her unstable moods, unstable and intense interpersonal relationships marked by extreme idealization and subsequent devaluing of partners, impulsivity, and history of significant substance abuse.

Oscar and Olive illustrate two dissimilar pathways from auspicious beginnings to trouble in early adulthood. In both cases, however, ambivalently-held experiences with fathers played an important role, and fatigue sapped their mothers' energies. In both cases too, the grown children's ability to work productively has been spared, although Oscar is fearful of undertaking graduate studies which would be a logical step for him in his field. Their sexual relationships have been unhappy and unsuccessful. Oscar's life graphically illustrates how external trauma—repeated encounters with death, violence, and the loss of friends—can deplete hope and trust. Olive's history illustrates the convoluted ways in which a child can internalize relatively unremarkable family experiences. It may be tempting to dismiss or rationalize some of the adversities Olive and Oscar encountered—being young children in large families, having fatigued and over-worked parents, having erotically charged, emotionally frustrating relationships with fathers—as commonplace. Yet this rationalization over-simplifies and diminishes the deep, formative impact such experiences can exert on development, undermining and dissipating early promise.

The Group of 8 Whose Outcome Was Not as Good as Expected

Let us survey the other four men and two women in the group of eight whose mothers gave them good care in infancy, but who are now troubled in critical ways as adults. Their Global Assessment of Functioning scores are below the study mean and reflect the presence of mental symptoms. Four of these participants also had fathers who were among the best.

Eddy. The creative director of a small Seattle advertising agency, his life story links a specific early childhood trauma with a specific long-term consequence (Massie and Szajnberg, 1997). Despite being dashing in appearance and happily married, he told us that he is a very moody person, with periods of intense discouragement if not despair, and periods of elation. These moods usually coincide with how well his work and the uncertain fortunes of his firm are going. To combat his mood changes, and to unwind after very long work days, he smokes marijuana almost every evening. To account for Eddy's ups and downs and marijuana use we considered that he may be reacting to the unusual pressures experienced by people who work in a creative field where survival is based on how other people respond to their ideas or art. But, we learned that the explanation is far deeper, lying in Eddy's early childhood psychological structuring. His father also worked creatively as the art director of a prominent magazine, and when the son was small the father told a project interviewer how he doubted his own adequacy, even his masculinity, when the publisher periodically critiqued his performance as wanting. When the magazine was going well and the publisher was satisfied, the father felt on the top of the world.

Children study their parents' emotional habits and learn them well, even if parents try to camouflage them. If children admire their parents, they work at copying them; even when they dislike their parents and try to distance themselves physically and emotionally (counter-identify), children can't avoid identifying with much they see and experience when they are in their formative years. Eddy very much looked up to his father, and learned much of his self-doubting and as well as creativity at his father's knee.

In addition, Eddy's father was one of the few in the project to share early childcare almost equally with the mother. Both parents were intensely devoted to their son and vibrantly active with him, so much so that the sum of their energy may have been over-stimulating for the child. The infancy films of the mother with Eddy were replete with caresses and mutual parent-child excitement. It appears that Eddy may have been "loved too well" and over-excited. If this was the case, as we know it can be from the study of other over-stimulated children (Roiphe and Galenson, 1981), the constantly heightened emotion would likely lead Eddy to have an unstable mental image of his body and a fluid sense of his ego boundaries.

In his professional work, Eddy described for us how he "plays for an audience," needing the exciting, self-defining feedback that comes both from seeing his work in the media and from winning new contracts. He has a sexual fetish that consists of being sexually aroused by women who are blind in one eye or wear an eye patch, which is an external indicator of his body image instability and vulnerability to anxiety. He first became aware of being aroused by the fantasy of one-eyed women at about age six, some two or three years after his parents left him during a ten day vacation with a familiar babysitter who happened to have a patch over one eye during his stay with her. While with the babysitter, Eddy heard her husband ask her, "When will it come out," meaning when will the splinter she had acquired in her eye come out and the patch be taken off. He now sees this in retrospect, but as a child he misunderstood this to mean the eye itself.

Eddy had apparently transferred his very affectionate feelings for his mother, and his anxiety over being separated from his mother, to the babysitter. To this heightened emotional state was added the fearsome image of the babysitter's eye coming out. Such a vision would resonate body damage and castration anxiety in a young child's mind, especially a child with the body image instability he is likely to have had from his unusually physically and emotionally stimulating life with his parents. The whole experience imprinted itself in his mind in a way that was both frightening and filled with sexual tension. Nowadays Eddy feels that his fetish is a harmless psychological anomaly. He sometimes asks his wife to wear an eye patch during sexual relations. This bolsters his excitement and makes intercourse with his wife most satisfying.

Luke. Luke's background is similar to Eddy's in that he was very well loved by his parents; however, their involvement with him as a child was more cerebral and less physical than that of Eddy's parents, and they overstimulated him intellectually. From a very young age, Luke's parents engaged him in detailed discussions about social issues, sex and procreation, including him in the delivery room at four years when his sister was born. As music teachers, the parents began Luke on the violin at the same time he was learning to read.

Luke became a musical prodigy, and by middle school was in a special performing arts curriculum which excluded him from his peers. As a teenager, he never learned to experience spontaneous emotional give and take with friends his own age. As an adult, he is a member of a successful Chicago-based string quartet that spends half the year touring, and when not on the road, he lives alone in a haphazardly furnished pied-a-terre. In high school Luke's psychological testing indicated that his masculine sexual identification was unstable, remindful of Eddy's testing at 18. Today, Luke feels acutely shy and lonely. He is ascetic, intellectual, and obsessional, consequences of his hypertrophied, precocious development of intellectual ability and technical music skills.

Luke has had relationships with women, but says that he never feels he really knows how to interact with them. He has a guarded and mildly superior manner, defensive shields against his inner unease. These qualities may also come from his too great closeness to his parents as they fostered his precocity, so that now, in reaction to their early over-stimulation, he keeps people at arm's length. The interviewer was so troubled by Luke's joylessness that he tried to cheer him up by urging him to take the long view, suggesting that a girlfriend would come in time, but Luke didn't respond. The last comment in the interviewer's field notes was, "I left feeling lousy. Outside it had begun to rain."

Everett. Everett suffered from the unfaithfulness of a father who had affairs and finally left the family when his son was nine years old. Father and son continued to see each other, but the father drank to excess, giving up his work as a pharmacist and setting for a meager existence—hardly the kind of man a boy could look up to. When he was 18, Everett told Sylvia Brody that he was scared of his father's temper when he drank and was training himself to be different. "I never lose my temper . . . I want friends who do nothing to excess," he said. In her summary, Dr. Brody underscored Everett's fear of feelings and his suppressed anger at his father: "I saw no strong sign of any emotion. He is a diffident youth as if he is not quite sure of himself in a world of more fortunate people. He told me that his mother did her best, but that he was often lonely at home after school before she returned home from work. He needed a friend and didn't have one. He also said that his mother's relationships with men after his father left never worked out, and she had lost the optimism and joy she had when we knew her when Everett was young. His mother has given Everett much, but circumstances made her place on him great demands for self-control. In addition, Everett's passivity now seems like an identification with a father figure of dubious power."

As a grownup Everett has remained loyal to his mother, joining her as an accountant in a firm in which she is a senior partner. He is now married and thinking of starting a family, but doubts himself and feels that he may have foreclosed his future by too quickly boxing himself into a career that he is not sure he likes. Resigned, wistful and timid, he gives the impression of being prematurely tired from having worked hard all his life, and from being cut off from passion and anger. He immerses himself in his work and in an isolated life with his wife and mother. He only seems to achieve a broader sense of himself as a human being in his relationship with his wife, though with her he said he still feels tentative. Regular tennis and a satisfying sexual life are his main, and good, outlets.

Nita. The original research team placed Nita's mother in the favorable group because she was warm, empathic, skillfully in control, and organized with her baby. However the mother was also vague and distracted at times, and she sometimes turned over Nita's care to her older daughter. The mother's liabilities could well have been connected to living with the children's father, an extremely rigid and compulsive man. He was so demanding and mean to the children that when Nita was one year old, the mother told her interviewer that she knew her marriage was ill-advised. She obtained family counseling, but it didn't sufficiently ameliorate the father's behavior. Today as an adult, Nita is a disturbingly thin and reserved woman who says that as far back as she can remember her father criticized her, yelled, threw things, kicked her, and pulled her hair in explosions of anger and violence that occurred at least weekly, and twice required trips to the emergency room. This degree of maltreatment was equaled only by Farley's abusive father and Kandis's coldly rejecting mother (chapter 2, Childhood Distress Externalized).

Nita internalized her distress and was depressed and anorexic by the time she was five years old. When she was 20, she made a suicide attempt that almost killed her. Her hospitalization changed things to the extent that she and her parents (still together) renewed family psychotherapy after a hiatus of many years. In an early session, her father made a genuine apology for his behavior, and from then on curtailed his violence and criticisms. Remarkably, Nita forgave her father for his abuse, and they established an amenable grownup relationship.

However, Nita had already been too psychologically damaged to see men clearly, and shortly after this she fell in love with a seductive delinquent. "I had spent my whole life trying to get my father to love me and along comes this man who seemed so different from my father who had used any opportunity to put me down when I was growing up. Every time I began to gain confidence, my dad was there to push me down. I thought my mother was protecting me, but she didn't really." By the time Nita was 25, she had three children, and her husband had disappeared. She lives in a high-rise project in New York, works diligently as a bookkeeper in a grocery store, and gets help with her children from her parents.

Nita is prone to depression, migraine headaches, and panic anxiety when she feels overtaxed at her work. Her children are her happiness, a point which came through clearly as she spoke of them with warmth and sensitivity. A frank lady with much underlying sadness, she nonetheless laughs often, though tensely, in a way that both releases and keeps a lid on the extremes of her feeling. She told us that she cannot imagine or aspire to anything different for herself—be it a husband, education, or work advancement—but does hope to make it possible for her children to have a better life than she has had.

Iris. Iris reminds us of Olive: both have siblings in the project (Iris has a two year younger brother) who are doing well, whereas Olive and Iris are struggling. Iris' father is a doctor, her mother a nurse, and the researchers described the parents as among the most effective in the project. Her brother is now highly successful as a materials procurement manager for a large medical equipment manufacturer. He lives with gusto, enjoys the company of women, and has no doubt that he will settle down in the future. Like her brother and parents, Iris is engaging, articulate, humorous, and attractive. But unlike her brother, she has had false starts in school and work, although now she seems to be settling into her first year in law school. She has never had a happy relationship with a man, which causes her considerable sadness.

Why the divergence between brother and sister? The answer appears to lie in Iris' greater emotional entanglement with her father who, according to Iris and her brother, is loving but volatile in his temper. Both children have fond memories of growing up with their parents, though their remembrances are sullied by recollections of their parents' frequent quarrels. Because of these arguments, Iris by the time she was 12 had begun thinking that her father preferred her over her mother, a thought which still persists. Iris also feels that her parents' fights led her to calm herself by smoking marijuana frequently. Her cannabis use had the unwelcome, unanticipated effect of increasing her tension and compromising her self-esteem because when her parents found out that she was smoking marijuana, they attacked her morals and searched her room regularly.

When Iris was 18, her psychological tester reported, "She is mildly depressed, with a tendency to hide negative, especially angry feelings with passive-aggressiveness or pollyannaish denial. Maternal images are somewhat controlling, and masculine images, though more benign, have a threatening or belittling quality. She told a story of a 14 year old girl who is given a doll and to whom a children's book is being read. The girl pretends to value the doll and be listening to the story, but in actuality the girl is day-dreaming about dating boys. The girl in the story feels others do not take her seriously and react to her as though she isn't grown up. However this appears to be a projection or externalization of self-criticism onto adult figures, because the girl in the story is the one who is pretending to act younger than her age."

Twelve years later at 30, Iris' projective drawings contained signs of significant levels of anxiety and depression, as well as feelings that her world was constricting, depriving, and not to be fully trusted. By contrast, her brother's drawings showed brightness, creativity, and modest anxiety about interpersonal interactions, with some exhibitionistic tendencies, and preoccupation with his virility.

Today, Iris says she feels unattractive—objectively unwarranted—is vaguely worried most days, and has many sad days. She no longer uses marijuana because it had ceased to calm her and made her more depressed. She described how she dates men who *are* available, well educated, kind, but invariably much older than she is, sometimes old enough to be her father. After dating them for a period of months, she backs off from the friendship. With men her own age she says she becomes anxious and insecure. If she understands the oedipal nature of her attraction to older men, or the possibility that competition with, and admiration of her brother contribute to discomfort with men her own age, she did not voice it. However it may be on her future agenda, for she told us that she anticipated the research interview as an opportunity to think about herself and obtain information about how to find a therapist. Iris appears to bear the burden of the parents' quarrels and expectations much more than her brother. She is not easy in her own mind or skin. Her technical diagnosis is dysthymic disorder, a term that comes from Greek and Latin roots meaning that the spirit or mind is troubled or off-center. Her dysthymia is also a depressive and anxiety neurosis because of its etiology in interpersonal and psychic conflict.

Sean. When Sean was very young he developed rheumatoid arthritis which caused recurring crises of crippling pain in his joints. In his mid teens, as his immune system matured and as newer medications became available, his condition subsided, but before this improvement he had to attend school on crutches or in a wheelchair several times a year. During Sean's childhood, his loving and largely competent parents, the research project staff, pediatricians, and teachers all admired his ability to cope: he was a good student, gamely upbeat, and sociable. However Sean had been hiding emotional agony and shame, which he only revealed when he met with Dr. Brody as a senior in high-school, *after* the new medication was successfully treating his condition.

He told her how in grade school and junior high school, when he was on crutches or in a wheelchair, and sometimes simply on days when he was unable to join the boys in playground sports, he was regularly teased, shoved from behind, or called names like "queer." The worst abuse occurred on the school bus, where there was no supervising adult. Lonely, with only one close friend, he had wished so much to fit in with other kids that he had never told his parents about the teasing. His inability to go to his parents for help may also have been exacerbated by their impatience and the spanking they reported using to try keep order among their four children. Without protection, Sean's self-consciousness about his condition, and the harassment he was enduring, profoundly shaped his personality.

At 18, he explained to Dr. Brody how much he wanted to find a career in which he would stand out and make a social contribution. He felt that being known for something would make him more acceptable. His emotions about his illness that had just recently become relatively asymptomatic were raw. He spoke of feeling unworthy and inadequate as a child. His parents' support had given him the bravery to struggle, but oddly not the courage to admit weakness and emotional pain. He had come to live by such mottos as, "A body without mental strength is nothing . . . my handicap is only physical . . . the only real fear is fear of not succeeding." He added, "My parents are very good. They have been concerned with my physical problem, and it is good that they haven't tried to do too much for me, except in obvious ways, because it made me become stronger."

Sylvia Brody wrote about him as a youth, "He tries making himself strong by bearing pain and suffering. There seems to be an intense need to deny that the pain and the handicap have brought him great unhappiness and longing which can never be fulfilled. He turns things around, ennobles his experience as if it has done more for him than being normal in the first place. I suppose there is a good deal of whistling in the dark that goes on in this boy. It is of course far better for him than self pity or surrender to passivity. He is on the whole what one might call a really good fellow, with very civilized attitudes, a great wish to do well with people, and to contribute something that will please them and make himself admired and loved. He has been fortunate in having successful parents to emulate, who encourage him nicely. Sean has developed well."

Years later when we met Sean as an adult, he was tall, muscular and handsome, with no sign of disability. If we had not been alerted to his childhood physical handicap, we would not have had any inkling about it, for his emotional pain is no longer raw and obvious. The former disability has been fully assimilated into his personality and adaptation to life. His past struggles, in fact, seem no longer even obvious or alive to Sean because he has largely completed the process of defending himself against the unhappiness his condition caused him by counter-phobic and self-compensating means. For example, his passion is the dangerous sport of hang-gliding which gives him the illusion of being able to soar like a bird. Although he explained briefly that "my medical condition in the past used to make it hard for me to get about," he made no connection between that condition and the sense of freedom that comes from hang-gliding. Rather he talked with obsessive appreciation about glider design, competitions, and the importance of wind strength, direction, and altitude.

Sean works as a television weatherman, a job which also links him to the wind: winds hold him aloft when he hang-glides, and wind and rain are the staples of his reporting. Not a scientist by nature, Sean says he comes to his job with only junior college courses in meteorology and communication, as well as a strong desire to be "on the air," loving to be seen and heard on people's TV screens. He is facile with words, handsome, and indefatigably, though blandly, smiling. Up close, there is sadness in his eyes, perhaps invisible on the screen.

So far he says that he has only "cracked small Eastern markets" such as Rochester, New York and Worcester, Massachusetts, explaining that his field is very competitive. To boost his ratings—and also because, "I like to think on my feet and feel a connection with my audience"—he has attempted to intersperse weather reporting with call-ins from viewers and commentary about community events. Unfortunately, he told us that he has a penchant for putting his foot in his mouth, because his irreverent style angers some viewers. Twice he has not had his contract renewed because of bad judgment, but he is trying to learn from his mistakes.

His social life with women is equally unfulfilled. From his descriptions, it appears that women reject him because he lacks an aspect of empathy and social judgment. He must be avoiding deeper levels of intimacy for fear of being hurt emotionally as he was so often in childhood. His most reliable social pleasure is getting drunk with colleagues from work a couple of times a month. His psychological testing at 30 gives further insight into his troubles. The psychologist wrote, "He relies on obsessive-compulsive defenses to manage anxieties and conflicts. He is concerned about presenting an acceptable social front that appears to mask underlying paranoia and frustration about his environment. He further manages by seeking satisfaction in action and in fantasy. He is likely quite sensitive, and prone to seeing others as hostile when he is uncomfortable. He shows schizoid and narcissistic traits. Overall his emotional development is immature as are his relationships with people."

A lesson to draw from Sean's life is the extremely destructive effect that teasing can have on the development of handicapped children. Children who are different by dint of a physical incapacity often discomfort their peers who lash out at them for making them—the physically intact—feel vulnerable. Only school administrators, teachers, and parents can curtail such hazing; and parents need to remain alert to their child's strong need for acceptance to counter rejection by others and the self-dislike they may have because of their disability.

Conclusion

There are broader lessons from the eight participants whose years have not gone as well as the researchers predicted after their good start to life. The children's promise has been taken away by two over-arching phenomena: for four of the eight (a Trauma/Adversity group), the blunt blows of trauma and adverse life circumstances diminished their potential; the other four (a Family Influence group) primarily internalized complex, at times virtually in-apparent family processes which led to psychological disturbances. Tables 4.1, 4.2 and 4.3 summarize these findings.

Chapter 4. Table 4.1 Children with Favorable Mothering but Troubled Outcomes due to Trauma or Adversity

	CHILDHOOD		ADULTHOOD			
Case	Quality of Parenting	Trauma or Adversity	Problem, GAF*	Strengths	Adult Attachment (AAI)	Maturity of Defenses**
Oscar	Favorable Mothering and Fathering	Witnessed deaths, loss of friends, parents' fatigue	Lonely, . anxious, Post-Traumatic Stress Disorder, GAF 60	Caring, strong values, hard worker	Insecure	Mental Inhibitions, Disavowal (Level 6,4)
Everett	Favorable Mothering, Poor Fathering	Divorce, father's absence and decline	Doubts self, emotionally restricted, GAF 80	Competent, reliable, contentedly married	Insecure (Dismissive)	Disavowal, Minor Image Distorting (Level 4,5)
Nita	Favorable Mothering, Abusive Fathering	Physically abusive father	Depression, Anxiety, migraine headaches, GAF 61	Devoted parent, hard worker, forgiving, humor	Secure (Earned-secure)	Minor image Distorting (Level 5)
Sean	Favorable Mothering and Fathering	Crippling illness, badly teased	Lonely, schizoid & narcissistic traits, work problems, GAF 60	Keeps trying, cooperative, pleasant	Insecure (Dismissive)	Disavowal, Minor Image Distorting (Level 4,3)

- Median Global Assessment of Functioning (GAF) for all project participants = 81.2 (No or minimal symptoms,good functioning, satisfaction.)
- ** Mean defense level for all project participants = High Adaptive/Mental Inhibitions (Level 7,6)

Chapter 4. Table 4.2 Children with Favorable Parenting but Troubled Outcomes due to Internalization of Complex Family Influences

	CHILDHOOD		ADULTHOOD			
Case	Quality of Parenting	Trauma or Adversity	Problem, GAF*	Strengths	Adult Attachment (AAI)	Maturity of Defenses**
Olive	Favorable Mothering, Adequate Fathering	Sister born when 14 months, father always working	Troubled relations with men, mood swings, Borderline, GAF 54	Lively, expressive, hard worker, ambitious	Insecure (Enmeshed)	Mental Inhibitions, Action (Level 6,2)
Eddy	Favorable Mothering and Fathering	Parents over-stimulating	Mood swings, heavy marijuana use, GAF 80	Creative, ambitious, happily married	Secure	Mental Inhibitions, (Level 6)
Luke	Favorable Mothering and Fathering	Parents over-stimulating, isolated from peers	Lonely, obsessional, mistrustful, GAF 80	Successful musician	Insecure (Dismissive)	Mental Inhibitions. (Level 6,)
Iris	Favorable Mothering and Fathering	Quarreling parents	Lonely, poor self-image, depressive, GAF 75	Humor, engaging, enjoys work	Secure	Mental Inhibitions, (Level 6.)
* Median Global Assessment of Functioning (GAF) for all project participants = 81 .2 (No or minimal symptoms, good functioning, satisfaction.) ** Mean defense level for all project participants = High Adaptive/Mental Inhibitions (Level 7,6)						

Chapter 4. Table 4.3 Destructive Influences in Lives of Children with Favorable Mothering: Children Who Did Not Live Up to Their Promise

INTERNALIZATION OF COMPLEX FAMILY INFLUENCES
Siblings born too soon
Parental fatigue
Father unavailable/unsupportive
Parents quarreling
Child loved "too well" (i.e. overly doting/overly involved parents)
TRAUMA
Divorce
Abusive father
Witnessing violence
Death of friends
Isolation from peers
Physical handicap & being teased

Conceptualizing in terms of direct cause and effect does not do justice to these lives, giving short shrift to the complexity of inner emotional processes. In fact, most of the men and women whose promise was disturbed have considerable strengths in various aspects of their personalities. These strengths are linked to identification with positive qualities in their parents, and to the good ways in which one or both parents raised them. Thus, all eight are willing and able to work gainfully, and six don't simply take home a paycheck but obtain considerable pleasure and personal meaning in their work (Oscar, Sean, Olive, Eddy, Luke and Iris). Three are able to love well (two their spouses, and one her children), and the rate of marriage and parenthood in the group of eight is similar to that of all the participants in the project. Six (Oscar, Everett, Sean, Olive, Eddy and Iris) know how to take time out from their work to play and relax, an essential part of life.

We would anticipate that trauma and psychologically confusing family enmeshments would each threaten the long-term sense of security children have in their attachment to their parents, and this expectation is borne out. In the Family Influence group, two of four had Secure attachments, and in the Trauma/Adversity group, only one of four was Secure, and that was an Earned—secure attachment. Thus, only three of the eight were Secure (38%), as opposed to Secure attachments in 64.5 % of all participants in the project. The Insecure mental representations of attachment to their parents of these eight individuals—reflective of apprehensive emotional working models of relationships and life in general—correlated with having more psychiatric symptoms than most project participants as indicated by their lower GAF scores. In addition, the Trauma/Adversity group used more immature psychological defenses to manage inner conflicts and external stress (Minor Image Distorting—devaluation, idealization, omnipotence; and Disavowal—denial, projection, rationalization) than most of the participants in the study. The Family Influence group was spared this immaturity with defense mechanisms at the same level as the overall group of 76 (Mental Inhibitions—displacement, dissociation, intellectualization, isolation of affect, reaction formation, repression, and undoing); (see Appendix for details).

It is likely that the Trauma/Adversity group didn't fare quite as well as the Family Influence group because the children who experienced traumatic or adverse circumstances generally **also** internalized complex family influences. For example, some of Oscar's depression stems not only from his encounters with death, but also from his mother's lack of sparkle—a sign of her burdens—and from his father's sermonizing Oscar into passivity. Additionally, had Oscar's parents understood his sensitivity, they may have sacrificed their missionary ideals and lived in a safer community. Likewise, Sean's parents may have been insufficiently attuned to his need for buffering against teasing and self-denigration. Furthermore, the demanding, threatening circumstances faced by the Trauma/Adversity children usually affected their parents as well, often compromising the parents' functioning. Sometimes the destructive events that families encountered came when their children were scarcely out of infancy, sometimes later in childhood. Thus, the children frequently had to cope with their particular traumas and challenges as well as with their parents' increasing frustration and diminishing responsiveness and ability to express affection. Conversely, sometimes adversity led to complex family relationships. For example, if Olive's mother had not become ill and weak with thyroid disease, Olive might have escaped her neurosis-inducing relationship with her father.

Turning attention from the inner landscape of psychological developmental compromises, these children with checkered histories also draw our attention to a global landscape of insensitivity and violence. We think especially of Oscar, but also Nita with her abusive father, Sean taunted in school, and Everett whose father left the family and declined into alcoholism. Oscar's life in many respects is the story of children too numerous to count all over the world, children who grow up with their emotional futures foreclosed because their parents have to work too hard and are too tired to give their children the time they need to sustain their early promise. Furthermore, Oscar's encounters with human bodies, witnessing death, and losing his friends to violent deaths as a child and teenager—anathema to middle—and upper-class America—is more the rule than the exception for children in the many warring parts of the world. Violence and loss is also not uncommon in economically marginalized communities in the United States where many families live at or below the poverty line; where many youth have little hope of finding work that will provide a living wage while also being personally meaningful and enhancing to their community; and where disparities in wealth and opportunity between their lives and the rest of society angrily gnaw at them.

We also think of the children too numerous to count in other parts of the world who have become refugees and mourners of family members and friends because of the actions of men with guns and bombs. It is easy to label these children survivors once warfare ceases, and to imagine them ready to construct or reconstruct their lives, which some may indeed do. But like Oscar, some capacity for pleasure and optimism has forever been taken from them, and psychosomatic symptoms and anxiety often typically impair their physical strength. Their future friendships and intimate relationships will be strained or distorted by the aggression they have internalized.

Had Oscar received intensive psychotherapy following his experiences with death and loss (therapy cognizant of his pre-existing dependency on his mother, anger at his parents for not protecting his well-being because of their needs, and guilt over not pleasing his father) his life would likely be more auspicious. On the world-wide stage, however, the number of traumatized children is simply too great to contemplate providing remedial psychotherapy. There the goal must be prevention of trauma to maintain the promise in children's lives. To that end needful parents should receive support through respite from work and decent childcare; and children should be protected by taking the weapons out of the hands of men who would be violent or use war to advance their agendas.

Returning to the study's eight whose potential has been truncated, they nevertheless have strengths and accomplishments as adults. Sadly, several do not see or trust these virtues in themselves. They have constricted their emotions and inhibited their activities and relationships, with the consequence that they are either lonely or doubt their future in their work and their ability to change. Still, we expect that some will find ways we can't foretell to undo misfortune and reclaim their early hope. By contrast, the next chapter is about the nine women and men in the project who have had the good fortune to do better than the researchers predicted they would in their infancy.

Chapter 5

EXPECTATION EXCEEDED

You can play with me, you can hold my hand
We can skip down to the pretzel man
You can wear my mommy's shoes, wear my daddy's hat
You can even laugh at me, but don't you push me down,
Woody Guthrie, "Don't You Push Me Down"

HOW ARE SOME children able to lift themselves above adversity and say "no" to being pushed down? In our study, there were nine men and women who had this capacity. They began life with mothers and fathers whose parenting was less than favorable (Group B) in the eyes of the researchers. Their outcome was not predicted to be good. However, at 30 years of age these children, now adults, have lives that are going very well. How this shift came about is the subject of this chapter.

We study the lives of two participants closely, and the other seven briefly. The seven women and two men who did better than expected—these children of Group B mothers and fathers—represent 18% of the 50 children whose parenting was considered unfavorable in infancy. Now as adults, they have Global Assessment of Functioning scores at the highest level (91 or above), indicating that they have "no symptoms . . . superior functioning . . . and that life's problems never seem to get out of hand." The essence of their success reveals something of the elixir of a healthy emotional life.

Other researchers have sought for this *élan vital* both by examining how children who faced different kinds of adversity rose to the top of their group, and by describing the skills that helped children in non-traumatic or normal circumstances outstrip their peers. The prototypical studies are Werner's (Werner and Smith, 1992) birth to adulthood survey of economically disadvantaged children on the rural Hawaiian island of Kauai; Anthony and Cohler's (1987) overview of longitudinal studies of children whose mothers were schizophrenic or severely depressed; and Murphy and Moriarty's (1976) examination of children growing up in seemingly normal families in a small Midwestern American town.

In both Werner's and Anthony and Cohler's studies, approximately 15% of children did well in spite of adversity, similar to the 18% figure in our project. Werner termed the children who were able to break the circle of poverty "resilient" and found two common threads in their lives: good physical health in spite of limited medical care, and a personal vivacity or openness that made them attractive to people outside their family such as teachers, so that non-family relationships added richness to their lives. Anthony and Cohler used the phrase "vulnerable but invincible" to describe the schizophrenic mothers' children who did well. One key to their success was an ability to sense when their parent was going through a period of exacerbated psychosis and giving the mother a wide berth during that time. When the mothers were better, the children reconnected with them. These same children, similar to the resilient children of economically deprived families, also learned to turn to others—such as the father, or neighbors, teachers, and family friends—for support and guidance.

Anthony and Cohler also learned that the high-achieving offspring of schizophrenic mothers were not truly invulnerable, that they paid a price for their struggles. As adults, these children tended to be "thing oriented," not comfortable with emotions and interpersonal interactions. Their spontaneity was limited, and they gravitated to scientific or technological professions rather than those involving human contact. These high achievers often grappled with "survivor guilt" for having done better than their parents or siblings, guilt which branded them with a chronic, anxious sense of responsibility for their families. Anthony and Cohler found that the course of children of severely, chronically depressed mothers was far more pessimistic, for these children had almost uniformly dismal outcomes.

Neither resilience nor invincibility but "coping mechanisms or skills" were the qualities that Murphy and Moriarty unearthed in the children of normative Midwestern families who did best over time. Whereas defenses are primarily intrapsychic mechanisms for dealing with intrapsychic conflict, the coping mechanisms Murphy and Moriarty addressed are intrapsychically based external behaviors or actions that master external conflicts or problems. These coping behaviors made it possible for some children to handle external challenges better than others. The children who coped best shared at least some of the following eight characteristics: 1) positive peer relationships, 2) humor, 3) physical soundness, 4) reflection (as opposed to impulsivity), 5) goal orientation, 6) good control over feelings, 7) ability to comfort or soothe themselves, and 8) creativity.

These major studies of resilience and coping have been instrumental in helping social scientists grasp the many factors involved when some children do well in the face of adversity, and to understand that the children's successes often come with psychological scars. However the studies' conclusions also show a circular process at work. That is, a child with good relationships with peers will feel accepted, supported, validated, and in turn will be able to make more friends who will further augment his or her confidence and esteem. One could say the same about most of the other qualities for they mutually reinforce each other.

What the investigations haven't shown is how the circle begins. Why is a particular child able to turn to others, be attractive to others, become goal oriented or creative? The mystery of the "why" stems from the limitation of most research that uses measures of outcome and adaptation in life which are phenomenological. These studies scan the surface of a person's existence—his or her behavior, expressed feelings, and felt symptoms. The Global Assessment of Functioning Scale also suffers this limitation, and so remains simply a screening tool of adjustment.

With these thoughts in mind, our discussion of the nine participants who exceeded expectations concentrates, as do preceding chapters, on the internal "why and how" by which some people overcome adversity. We follow the inner lives of these men and women—their conscious and unconscious identifications with parents, their laying down of defense styles, and the internal emotional compromises (mostly hidden from measurement and everyday view) which the participants have been forced to make in order to succeed in the face of very difficult family experiences.

Danny: "I'm very resilient."

When we called Danny to schedule his interview, he insisted that we meet at his new restaurant, Danilo's, in the wine country north of San Francisco. There was excitement and pride in his voice, and he clearly wanted to show us what he was doing. On our arrival he took us into an old stone building converted into a 40 seat dining room. He pointed out the framed restaurant reviews on the wall and introduced us to his wife, who appeared elegant and reserved. "She runs the dining room, and I take care of the food," he explained. She excused herself to return to her chores, and Danny led us into the garden, beyond which grapevines fanned out in neat rows toward hills in the distance. Like an impresario, he toured us through neatly planted herbs and described a special dish he was planning for the next day.

We started the interview and quickly learned that Danny's mother had died when he was 20, almost certainly a suicide. He talked about her death with amazing poise, like a consummate professional interviewee, looking us in the eye, holding an expression, and not betraying emotions he didn't care to reveal. In fact, he told us that he does occasionally appear on television and teach cooking courses. His mood was happy, forceful, reflective, and he shed no tears talking about his mother.

The interviewer asked him how he was able to keep going after his mother's death, and he said, "I'm very resilient." His words were uncoached, and we wondered how he would explain his resiliency. Danny went on: "I'm a very optimistic person. That was what my mother liked in me, and after she died, I wasn't going to let her down. Those qualities came from my father."

He described his father and mother with strong, perhaps hyperbolic adjectives and fluent gestures. Sometimes he leaned forward to engage; sometimes he leaned back in his chair, his arms broadly extended on the armrests, receptively awaiting the next question; always he was ready to chuckle at his experiences, albeit often with touches of sarcasm. He turned his attention first to his mother, "My mother was loving, affectionate, warm, caring, comforting, completely enjoyable, very genuine. I always felt safe with her, as if she was the most wonderful thing, and my brother and I were the center of her world. This is why I'm such a secure person today."

"She had toys in her office for my brother and me whenever we would visit. She was a doctor, a very generous person, always ready to help others and volunteer time working in poor people's clinics. There was no bullshit about her. She could talk directly to me. I remember when I was 13, and my first girlfriend broke up with me. I was so upset. She sat me down and said, 'You're a wonderful person, and you will have many girls in love with you. One day you'll wonder why you were even interested in her."

At this point, Danny's interviewer thought to himself that he was hearing a vivid, polished account of the roots of emotional security from a man who appeared secure and successful, but something didn't ring true. After all, he had just a moment earlier said that his mother probably committed suicide. A person doesn't kill herself out of the blue.

Danny switched to his father: "We always have been very close. I'm a carbon copy of him, emotionally and physically. We're both big people, though he's always had this bear-like full beard. It's always been a good relationship, but we're so much alike that our relationship gets volatile because we see things in each other that piss us off about ourselves. We're really friends now and make a point of getting together at least twice a month. He drives up from the university where he teaches drama, or I drive into the city. I've felt incredibly close to both parents."

"My brother Carlo is 3 years younger than I am, and he's much more like my mother—elegant, quiet. My dad and I are like the same person—we talk alike, we like the same things. I loved being with him as a kid because I thought he was the handsomest father and one of the smartest people I've ever met. He showed me you don't have to look or act a certain way to be taken seriously."

At this point, Danny's account of his father and their relationship seemed more real than that of his mother. Their vivacious affection and conflict made more sense than the contradictory report of a mother who was "warm" yet able to abandon her family by taking her life. It seemed likely that Danny did, as he said, get his resilience from an identification with his father.

We asked him about his mother's death. He said, "I think she waited until she thought my brother and I didn't need her anymore. It was the year after I finished my sophomore year of college and Carlo had just finished his junior year in high school. We were home and she seemed her usual self, working very hard. In retrospect, she had said something unusual to me the week before. She said if anything happens to me you and your brother won't have to worry about money for your education. I just let it pass at the time. My father told me later that she was under a lot of stress because a large research grant had been turned down, and that meant that she'd have to let go lab assistants she needed and who depended on her for their jobs. This had happened to her a couple of times, that things at the hospital seemed to be falling apart."

"After she died my father told me that when I was in junior high school she had spent several weeks in the hospital because she was feeling suicidal, but she had always kept this side hidden from us. I guess I just accepted the story that she was in the hospital because she needed a rest. The mother I knew was super-responsible; perhaps that's what killed her. My father said she had told him that she had a chemical imbalance in her brain, and she couldn't bear to let us see her unable to get out of bed in the morning." Danny said all this in an utterly rational tone, betraying feeling only when he briefly contorted his face into a painful expression as if to illustrate his mother's distress. The apparent absence of anger or sadness in Danny ultimately led us to wonder whether he might be somewhat impersonal or detached, despite his obvious capacity for joie de vivre.

Danny continued his story. "It happened up at Lake Tahoe. My mother and father had gone up to our cabin at the lake on a Friday night and when he woke up she was gone. The police found our canoe drifting way out in the lake, and later her body. There was no life preserver, which was unlike her—she always had it on board. It looks like she planned to jump in the water, and she knew that in early June she would pass out from hypothermia in a few minutes."

We asked him how he took her death. "I was in shock. I got in my car after the funeral and drove north up the coast all the way to Canada. I couldn't deal with it. I thought if I stayed I'd lose my mind. It took three weeks, and I don't remember a single thing about the trip, a single thing I saw. I just recall thinking about my mother every day. I couldn't believe I'd never see her again. My brother couldn't deal with it either. He had a nervous breakdown later that year. He's okay now and working on a graduate degree in biology, but he's more sensitive than I am."

How has his mother's death affected Danny over time? He explained, "I'm smart, resourceful, and healthy. I never expected not to support myself." Although reassuring us *and* himself that his mother's death had not impaired his ability to cope, Danny was skirting any feelings of pain, anger, or anxiety. He simply wasn't going to deal publicly—or maybe even privately—with the loss of his mother, just as he had fled San Francisco as soon as the funeral was over.

To clarify his family experience, Danny said, "My parents had this 25 year wondrous marriage, and I remember having this idyllic childhood. Although my wife and I have a beautiful relationship that goes back six years, I wasn't sure I wanted to get married because I didn't think I could ever be sure she was the right one the way my parents were so right for each other. My mom and dad were madly in love but they were both very strong personalities, and it must have gotten hard for them to get along at times. They separated twice, once when I was in fourth grade and once when I was in eighth grade. Each time it was for a few months. It was a shock, but it was okay. We still had our mother and father, just they weren't together. Maybe those times they separated were times my mother was depressed or manic or something. She would continue her work, getting more research ideas than anyone could possibly expect to be able to pursue or get funding for. I think all of a sudden she'd realized that and she'd crash. But she never stopped carrying out her family obligations."

At this point in studying this interview, we considered that Danny must cope through denial of conflicted feelings and sadness. If true, did he also deny the actual reality of his parents' actions and was his "idyllic childhood" a fantasy? Whatever the case, his defenses seemed to work for him. His restaurant and marriage were not mirages. As long as denial helped him adapt to life in a productive, satisfying way, it was not pathological. We were eager to explore Danny's early research record and films to compare his adult depiction of his family with the project's documentation. If Danny's sense of reality were faulty, stress or derailed ambitions might one day topple him like a house of cards in a breeze, bringing on symptoms like his mother's.

The interviewer continued by asking Danny why he thought his parents acted the way they did. He answered forcefully, "I don't think a chemical imbalance was the source of my mother's problems, though if she had held on a little longer she would probably still be alive now with all the new antidepressants there are today. I know from my father and the hints my mother dropped that her parents were incredibly cold. She was an only child, and they never told her they loved her, just pushed her to achieve things, and when she did it was her accomplishments they said they loved. I think my mother ended up always trying to get people to love her. With us, my mother set out to be completely different from the way her parents had been with her, to be very supportive of us as human beings, which she was."

"My father's life was completely different. He came from a large family of growers, right here in the valley. He's told me that when he was a kid, people were always bouncing off each other, and you had to yell to get attention. He says that's why he went into drama. He once told me that his mother was so hard to get close to, and had so little education and little idea about how he felt about anything, that he would have given his right arm to have a mother like mine for ten minutes."

* * *

Some months after Danny's interview, we opened his record and watched the films of him and his mother, looking to see if his recollections were based on fact or fantasy. The answer was somewhere in between. He had given us a largely true story, but there were so many details and subplots that neither he—nor any child—could have known all of them. Consequently his story was partly an unwitting fiction.

To begin with, the films showed that Danny's mother treated him in a reasonably competent way, though very blandly. She had empathy, gave structure, and paid good attention, but her emotional tone was always sober. She rarely smiled, played, or took pleasure in physical contact with Danny during the feedings in the first year; although nutrition was adequate, their relationship was not joyful. Nor was it obviously depressed, for the mother's strength was her calmness, sureness, and attentiveness, which kept the baby peaceful. The researchers offered such adjectives for her as "somewhat detached . . . a certain coolness . . . a kind of patrician aloofness."

At three months, the following description appears: "It is typical for this baby's feedings to be slow and measured, for the mother is remote. She encourages no reciprocal activity; no ebb and flow of tension is present during the entire feeding. Although the mother draws him in toward herself at the end, her manner is static and inhibited." At six months, an interviewer wrote, "The mother's combination of both positiveness and uncertainty pervades her personality—she has confidence in her desire to do well with her child, but isn't sure if her best is good enough. Success in connection with achieving recognition is important to her." When Danny was three years old, the interviewer wrote, "The mother says that she and her husband work to show the child that he can really talk about problems and express anger. As a child, this was not acceptable to the mother's parents, and she says her emotions stayed inside and caused damage. Her words were, 'Even if I'm not around as much as I should be, Danny knows how I feel. I didn't have a mother I could lean on or even snuggle against because she was not there or interested in me. When I criticize myself as a mother I'm talking about my own mother and her constant physical complaints about ulcers and heart attacks, which made me feel guilty.'"

The mother reported that she was in psychotherapy because her parents had been such poor models that caring for a baby was hard for her, and she was torn between her commitment to Danny and work. She knew that her parents' rejecting behavior toward her was the root of her problems and was thankful that her son was easier to be with than she could have imagined. Without her husband's easygoing nature and the fun he had with Danny, she didn't know how she would manage. As we read of the mother's conflicts, we understood with the advantage of hindsight that her detached coolness was the congener of a hidden, brutal self-censor that made her constantly measure her maternal and professional adequacy, and prevented her from spontaneously enjoying herself with her son.

With respect to Danny's father, the early project reports were also ambivalent. Sometimes during his interviews, or when he was seen at home, he was hearty, warm, enthusiastic about his son and the project, and full of details about the family's life. At other times, his cordiality was forced and his cooperation minimal. In spite of his devotion to his children, the father, like the mother, was invested in high profile social and academic activities. It sometimes seemed to the researchers that the only reason the parents were participating in the project was that they felt it added to their status. Ambitious for themselves and their children, they even persuaded Dr. Brody to forward a letter to an exclusive grammar school on Danny's behalf.

Two vignettes of Danny with his father convey the variability of their relationship. When Danny was two years old the interviewer wrote, "During my visit to the home, the father was exhibitionistically competing with the mother for my attention, but when he was playing with his son he was loving and gentle. At times he overreacted to Danny and over-excited him with rough and tumble play, but the genuineness of his feelings predominated, and he seemed very sensitive to even the most subtle communications from the child. Danny himself is very responsive to his father and greatly enjoys being with him."

Another view of the father appears at three, "He gave the appearance of being quite positive with Danny but it seemed superficial, even cold and distant or bored and annoyed at times when the child made demands on him. The father has so many inner agendas that it is hard to know which father will appear on a given day—the fun loving or the didactic father. He is not a restful person to be with; his emotionality is excessive so that one feels it necessary to respond to him a great deal of the time. In repose the father sometimes appears a little sad, and when he was tuned into me or Danny the intensity of his contact was at times over-absorbing."

Shedding some light on his chameleon quality, the father said, "My own parents were masked people. Everything was kept a big secret or hidden. They wouldn't give a straight answer to anything from the time of day to why somebody was acting a certain way. My father was aggressive with a mask of sweetness, and my mother was afraid to take a stand on anything. The home was chaos. In self-defense I became a very willful child as far back as I can remember."

* * *

Notwithstanding his statement at 30 that his childhood was idyllic, Danny had difficulty growing up with parents who created cross-currents of energy that ebbed and flowed around him. The research record followed both good and bad periods. For example, when Danny was one year old, his tester said: "He is bright, coy, and a compact bundle of pleasure. He has a nice balance between expansiveness and withdrawal, much more on the expansive side, with no negativism whatsoever. A thoroughly easy child to be with." He also had a quiet side that resembled his mother's reserve and could be alone longer without fussing than most babies. Sometimes his parents came upon him humming to himself—a habit he may have internalized from the live-in housekeeper who herself often sang while taking care of Danny. As soon as he saw his parents, Danny would emerge from his reverie, reach to be picked up, and start clowning.

Danny put his energy into socializing; his physical development lagged. At one year of age, his testing showed that his body movements were inhibited, his performance with test objects poor, and his demand for physical comfort excessive. Despite these difficulties, the mother's interviewer reported, "It is easy to see how his parents find him very easy and pleasing. His unusual social responsiveness gives the mother relief and the father excitement. I can imagine Danny growing up to be quite outgoing, effervescent, and always on the go. Given her anxiety about leaving her son when she is at work, the mother is doing extremely well, using all of her ability to make her son happy, and probably will maintain peace with herself by allowing Danny to identify with her husband's sociability and her own competence." This report is prescient about Danny's adult friendliness and energy, but sadly wrong about the mother. She apparently never achieved peace with herself except perhaps in death.

Danny walked late at 16 months, and the researchers hypothesized that he was being kept a baby longer than necessary through the countervailing forces of his mother's emotional detachment, his father's excitement, and the housekeeper's readiness to pick him up and do everything for him.

At three years old in nursery school, Danny's mood was worried, guarded, and a bit sullen. The observer did not feel that Danny enjoyed his contacts with other children: "He seems buffeted about and unable to make his wishes known. Sometimes he is confused and wistful, dependent on adult recognition." By four years of age, as his coping style took shape Danny was working his way out of the buffeting emotional cross currents in which he lived. That year when he visited the project, he was relaxed and happy; he worked diligently and controlled his anxiety during the testing with three maneuvers: talking very busily; using denial (saying that he had succeeded when he couldn't figure something out); and using aggression to slap away test toys that offended him. His tester concluded, "He is no longer the submissive or resistant child of last year with his mother's neutral expression. Now there is more animation, restlessness, silliness, and controlling behavior. He appeared to enjoy the testing, but I didn't feel warmth or a close rapport with this child who seemed tense and both over-controlled and impulsive."

By five in school, Danny had an appealing personal quality, enjoying his skills and ability to organize his energies and work alone. His problems came from his capriciousness with peers. At times he was friendly and helpful, then would become rude and condescending. He clung to toys he brought from home and whined to teachers in a way that suggested the insecurity of a child who isn't often heard at home and wants to be listened to. He was at his best in structured school activities. His teacher said, "He can be the ablest of diplomats and rudest of companions. He has all the wherewithal to be a fine boy but some inner discomfort prevents him from using his abilities fully." The research observer concurred, "There is something unresolved in his attitudes toward others. He seems to use haughtiness as a defense against unmet needs for affection. He strikes one as a rather temperamental, narcissistic child, and although he would be loathe to admit it, he is quite dependent. His air of sophistication and self-possession seems unreal, unstable, and masking an inner uncertainty."

As Danny's childhood progressed, the reports continued to be a mosaic of contradictions, very unlike those of the vast majority of participants which showed families establishing stable patterns and children consistent behaviors. Some interviewers found the mother agreeable, psychologically insightful, dedicated to her family, contemplative, and emotionally accessible. Others commented on her inability to enjoy her children, her reticence, and her depressive tone. Some found the father dynamic, full of details, happily in tune with Danny and supportive of him. Others commented on his narcissism, dissolute self-indulgence, and patronizing manner.

When the parents met with Dr. Brody when Danny was five, they talked about their pleasurable family vacations, their satisfaction with how well Danny was growing up, and his humor, which they felt well compensated for his stubbornness and strong opinions. Then they bickered about what the father felt was the mother's lax discipline, and what she felt was her husband's impatience. Interestingly, the parents did broach the subject of the school's worry that Danny sometimes seemed immature relative to other children. However the parents asserted that the problem lay with the teacher's immaturity and rigidity. When Dr. Brody gently attempted to counter their impulse to externalize Danny's difficulty onto the school by adding that since the project had observed something similar, it might be worth thinking about, the parents would have nothing of it. Dr. Brody wrote, "My attempts touched no responsive chord. The parents had no ear for anything that might suggest a critical comment. They quickly ended the conversation."

A year later, at six years of age, Danny had advanced in significant ways. "At the project he glowed with bright-eyed enthusiasm, vitality and alertness, and was polite and cooperative." His mood strikingly paralleled his father's ebullience that year, while his mother was as she usually was—disciplined and low in affect. At school, he was competent and often satisfied, but he was also "a child in conflict, tending to boss and control other children and have trouble conforming to groups." The project had its last preteenage contact with Danny at age seven, and once again the family did an about face, as both parents were so evasive that it was almost impossible to schedule their appointments. Danny must have picked up their attitude. He was resistant during his visit, established little rapport, and performed poorly on testing. "Still, given his opposition, his facial expressions didn't convey any sadness or anger. He smiled at times, keeping up the appearance he must have felt was in order, and at other times he was bland. He remained so detached from the testing tasks that there was little chance for glimpses into the inner workings of his mind."

* * *

By flashing backward from Danny the restaurateur to baby Danny and slowly playing his life forward, we watched him evolve. He didn't have an easy time making sense of his parents' differences—his mother's detachment and suppressed anguish, his father's erratic camaraderie. However, by age seven, it appeared that Danny was identifying with his mother's self-discipline as he became academically competent at school, and with his father's socially engaging, lively manner. Nonetheless, Danny was not out of the woods. Inner anxiety showed in his restlessness; he relied too heavily on the family defense of denial, which served his father better than his mother; and in relationships he seemed to lack warmth, an outgrowth of his mother's coolness and his father's exaggerated bonhomie.

When Danny was eight his mother finished her medical training in New York, and the parents obtained positions in San Francisco, allowing them to return to their roots. After 10 more years, shortly before leaving home for college, Danny flew to New York City for his 18 year followup. By then, he was tall, chunky, deep voiced, and dressed in a hodgepodge of jeans, hiking boots and a Greek over-shirt. His appearance combined with his blithe, rambling speech brought his father to Dr. Brody's mind. Danny told her about the exclusive schools he had attended, praising his teachers and lambasting the rituals, which he found silly. He talked of many friends, yet said the last two years of high school had been hard because most of his friends had left for college, including a girlfriend who planned to be a doctor. The most fun he had in his teenage years had been summer vacations, working in his uncle's vineyard. When Dr. Brody asked him what kinds of things had made him unhappy, he immediately told about his mother's hospitalization for a depression when he was in junior high school, and about one of her earlier crises during which the parents had separated for several months. He added, "Everybody in my family is self-centered, high-strung, ambitious, smart, determined, in good and bad ways. I'm like dad, fun-loving. Mom's like my brother, reserved, sensitive. There's lots of loving even if we're all very different, because we're all the same at the same time."

In her notes, Dr. Brody commented, "I should say that the family is probably very cohesive in a negative way. There seems to be deep attachment on the part of all to something no one profits-by enough." She asked Danny if there was anything in particular he would like to change about himself or other people. He said that he would like to be less impatient and wished his mother were happier but didn't know what would make her happier. He also wished there was less poverty and meanness in the world, and in the future, he would like to do something with his life that would make people happier, but he had no idea what that might be.

Sylvia Brody's last thoughts were pessimistic, "Because of my keen interest in all that he was saying it was only after he left, and again after I dictated what I have, that I realized how profoundly disturbed he is. I am ready to suspect that he has the seeds of his mother's manic-depression. He was almost overly dedicated to the interview, to talking about himself and his family, and his reports were suffused with denials and confusing statements. He made many all or nothing statements such as, 'Everybody makes me happy . . . or I'm irritated by nothing . . . I regret nothing I've done.' There was certainly evidence of a thinking disorder a number of times, enough to make me think he may have a borderline personality. He made so conspicuous an effort to laugh things off, at the same time saying he liked challenges, yet he has avoided challenging himself academically. A false over-confidence was apparent most of the time. The need to denigrate people and situations was disturbing and left me with the impression that he is profoundly fearful of placing trust in any people other than his family and close friends. Everyone in the family, although said to have certain faults, is presented with a rosy glow. The boy's intelligence is good, but there seems to be so much confusion emotionally and cognitively that I should think the future does not look very good. In sum I could describe him as being histrionic and narcissistic, constantly making an effort to hold down anxiety, which is itself a kind of running away from reality." Dr. Brody's concern is alarming, and we have learned from her predictions about most of the other participants that she is an extremely perspicacious and accurate clinician.

However, Danny's case is very different from the others in the study. The reports from various interviewers, testers, and observers over the years have been highly variable. In fact, the psychologist who tested Danny at 18 gave a more optimistic accounting than Dr. Brody, even though it was not altogether different: "He had an unpretentious, mature appearance compared to many his age, and described many interests in a lively if somewhat scattered conversation. He made use of a sardonic, self-observant humor when he felt defensive about his abilities, which for the most part was appealing and allowed him to think about himself and worked well. A degree of emotional lability seemed to characterize Danny, and his associations, though never bizarre, could be quite random-seeming and loose. At times this seemed almost cultivated as if it gave him pleasure to shock in an 'artsy' style. There was great variability in his performance from systematic and organized to impressionistic, vague, and obsessively self-doubting. Danny is imaginative, lively, responsive, and at times quite creative; however he also seems at times vulnerable to his impulses and affects. He can draw well on his intellectual defenses to maintain needed distance from feelings. The world he paints of people and their interactions is mixed—there are many appropriate, nurturing, even tender interactions containing concern, playfulness, and the capacity for mundane experience and sadness."

"However there is a darker, more complicated, less well-controlled side to his fantasy life with sexuality as threatening and violent, occasional sadistic impulses, and competitiveness with his sibling, peers, and parents. There is especially conflict with his identification with his father that is mixed in tone with yearnings for closeness and an idealized father-son interaction. Women are seen as appealing and frightening, and he alternately idealizes and depreciates them. Overall, Danny is dealing with the range of teenage turmoil and sexual and identity issues, coming to them with a mixed array of defensive abilities in the context of a generally histrionic personality structure characterized by excitability, over-reactivity, attention-seeking and self-dramatization. However it is likely that he brings to his activities real creative potential. It seems difficult at this point to differentiate the sensitivity and creativity of an artistic adolescent appropriately struggling, from the disorganization of a more borderline personality organization. His considerable conflict about sexual and other identificatory processes and much capacity for anger may be part of a working through of age-appropriate tasks in the context of a vibrant, sensitive, but basically strong personality. I think if and when his capacities, interests, and emotional life come together, he can be a powerhouse."

* * *

Now 12 years later, we see Danny at a restaurant which no one less than a creative powerhouse could have fashioned. Perhaps Sylvia Brody, in her pessimistic analysis when Danny was a teenager, missed his fundamental identification with his father; although the father is histrionic, he is also imaginative, professionally successful, a diligent worker, and devoted to his children. It is also possible that Danny's mother's death after his second year in college freed him from her unhappiness and family conflict and allowed him to throw himself into following his father's lead. Looking even further back for sources of Danny's success, we found it also likely that when he was an infant and toddler, his housekeeper—the one whose singing he imitated—compensated for his mother's flat emotional tone. The housekeeper remains with the family, still working for the father today.

After his mother's death, Danny did not return to college but went to work instead as an apprentice in a famous, innovative restaurant, pursuing an ambition he had secretly harbored for some time, but which, he said, might have displeased his mother. The work filled his need for camaraderie, drama, recognition, and creativity; and from there it was off to the American Culinary Academy, where he met his wife-to-be who was a fellow student. Danny said that "she brings order to my life," but that she also has a penchant for demanding too much perfection. In the operation of the dining room, she gets "down on herself," so that Danny has to try to get her to relax and lighten her moods—a role the father had with Danny's mother.

In his enjoyment of good wine and food and by providing the building for the restaurant, Danny's uncle has been a mentor to him. Danny says his biggest problem nowadays is his impatience, the same flaw he saw in himself at 18, which made it extremely difficult for him to court investors for the additional money needed for the project. "That was the only time I've questioned my own worth, when I didn't know if we could actually raise the money. Cooking is the fun and easy part. I never follow rules, and think I can do more than I know how to do. Maybe that's also a strength. That's why I cook such interesting things. I get along with everybody who works here as long as they let me be the boss and don't start competing with me. I can make an exception for my wife. She's the boss of the dining room, even though that's hard for me sometimes."

Danny said his greatest sadness was wishing his mother were alive to see what he is doing, but he feels lucky to be who he is, and that his mother taught him a great deal about how to be a human being. As far as his greatest pleasure in life, he said, "I don't know; I've had so many." This response led to a very early memory of his mother and father presenting him with a birthday cake when he was two or three. "Running a restaurant is like giving a birthday party everyday."

At the end of his interview, Danny offered to host a grand party at his restaurant—a kind of "This Is Your Life Gathering," complete with television cameras, for all the participants in the Brody project. The interviewer explained to him that this would be very difficult because the project had promised to protect the participants' confidentiality, including their identity. Hearing this Danny became quiet and withdrew emotionally as if he had been unfairly rebuffed. This reaction at 30 is remindful of how his parents coldly withdrew when Sylvia Brody tried to discuss Danny's troubles at seven with schoolmates. Her phrase, "They wouldn't hear anything of it," comes to mind. Thus, in spite of Danny's present day adult satisfaction, success, and resilience, it is still possible that "the darker side" of his personality may emerge later, as Sylvia Brody fears, if the restaurant doesn't do well, if his wife turns out to be too much like his mother, or if future outlets for his restlessness, creativity, exhibitionism, and ambition dry up.

Our last task in constructing Danny's psychobiography was reviewing his Adult Attachment classification. He turned out to be straight-forwardly Secure with respect to his representation of attachment to his parents in childhood, despite having parents whose relationship with him was troubled by their own problems and lapses. Even as a child, he seemed to have made peace with what they could and could not offer him. What made Danny feel good about his parents was more important to him than what was wrong with them.

Reba: "It hurts you more to hate . . . "

Reba's story is more prosaic than Danny's. There isn't the tragedy of losing a parent, nor the confusion of shifting attitudes set against the background of a seductively dramatic life-style. Nor is there the difficulty of deciphering whether recollections are fact or defensive fiction. Instead, we learn of a child's long, steady, successful struggle to build a highly functional and happy personality against the odds of her parents' less than favorable behavior when she was young. Indeed, Reba's ability to assimilate supportive influences and compartmentalize or dismiss unfavorable ones is far more typical of the group of nine who overcame adversity than Danny's more chaotic and extreme experience.

When Reba was six weeks, old the researchers described her mother feeding her: "The baby is held away from the mother's body and gropes with her open fingers for something to touch. The mother, though aware of the child's discomfort, offers no warmth or reassurance, and remains silent and distant. She scrutinizes the baby evidently not realizing that the little girl might be soothed by hearing her mother's voice. The child starts hiccupping and the mother gives her no attention. Holding Reba at her shoulder the mother waits without giving her child any smiles or expressing any other emotion. She only responds to those needs that the baby makes obvious by crying."

At the end of the first year, Dr. Brody summarized, "The mother is unable to offer adequate stimulation. Her empathy is restricted, her control insecure and efficiency uneven. When her infant's needs are obvious she may not respond. Love for her child is there but the mother is detached and uncurious about her relationship to the baby. Withdrawn, Reba's mother protects herself by routine, rarely plays spontaneously with the baby, and her relationship to Reba is impoverished."

With regard to the father, his interviewers typically found him serious and lacking animation. He was cordial but not warm or friendly. When he spoke of Reba, there was a feeling of distance and impersonality in his matter-of-fact descriptions, as if she was more of a specimen than a treasured child. In fact, the researchers were concerned that Reba was not fully wanted, given the parents' busy lives and the presence of an older brother and sister already in the family. The parents' participation in the project appeared part of their methodical, serious approach to life, coupled with a desire for data about Reba's growth that would facilitate their care of her.

In spite of her intellectual interest in child development, the mother came to the project with strongly held convictions about child-rearing: 1) Babies can be left alone from their first days, 2) by six months children are "control freaks;" therefore, it is important that they not be the center of attention, 3) start disciplining early by not picking-up the child if she cries, 4) "Hit the child where it hurts." The mother recalled that her own mother was a "rigid ball of fire" and spanked her too much, but Reba's mother didn't hesitate to spank Reba's behind when the toddler tested the mother's limits. The project staff found the mother to be self-important and very controlled. At the end of the first year, when Dr. Brody attempted to help the parents think more about what might cause their child to act in a certain way and to think less in good or bad dichotomies, she was unsuccessful.

The parents' rigid regimen took its toll on Reba. As an infant, she was constipated. Against the pediatrician's objections, the mother—by her own account frustrated at not being able to be at her law office as much as she wanted—inserted anal suppositories twice a day into Reba to prod her into regular bowel movements. It appeared that the mother's view of children as "power happy" was a projection onto the baby of her own need to be in charge. Additionally, like Danny, Reba was slow to walk, and the researchers wondered if she was receiving sufficient pleasurable stimulation from her parents.

As Reba approached her first birthday, an upper respiratory infection developed into asthma, which became a chronic illness. As the months and years passed, allergies and colds triggered asthma attacks that were frequently very severe, involving multiple medications, several emergency room visits each year, and avoidance of pets and many foods. When she became a teenager, her condition started to improve, so that by the time she went away to college her asthmatic attacks were less severe and down to two or three times a year.

The child's asthma brings into focus several important issues regarding the interconnection between psychological stress and bodily symptoms, issues which have been a longstanding interest to psychoanalytically oriented investigators. Franz Alexander (1968), a pioneer in the study of psychosomatics, postulated that when the soma and the psyche become connected in early childhood conditions such as asthma, skin, and gastrointestinal disorders, three conditions operate: 1) a genetic specificity for a particular end organ (e.g. the bronchial system); 2) an increase in life stress prior to the onset of the condition; and 3) an enduring emotional conflict such as a need to be physically held and an inability to experience holding, as in eczema, or a desire to cry and the need to inhibit crying as in cases of asthma.

Nathan Szajnberg and coworkers (1993), Krall and Szajnberg (1995), and Szajnberg and Waters (in preparation) elaborated aspects of Alexander's work in finding that for a group of teenagers with irritable bowel disorder a severe life stress had occurred in the year before the onset of the disease. Puberty was the time of greatest risk for the appearance of symptoms; and there was a familial, possibly genetic pattern to the disease. Additionally, Szajnberg found that the mother's own attachment to her parents correlated with her child's condition: 90% of the mothers of children developing irritable bowel syndrome had an Insecure mental representation of attachment to their own parents on the Adult Attachment Interview. Mrazek and colleagues (1991, 1999) in an investigation of asthma administered the AAI to a series of mothers who suffered from asthma themselves and were expecting a child. Mothers who were Insecure were significantly more likely to have children who developed asthma than were the mothers who had a Secure attachment to their parents. The investigations into both illnesses illustrate how genetic predisposition and maternal caregiving interact in regulating the expression of psychophysiologic conditions.

* * *

Chronically wheezing, physically weak, underdeveloped, and slow to walk, Reba graduated from infancy and toddlerhood into childhood. At this point, however, things began to turn in her favor. She had always been a very visually alert child who eagerly responded to social contact with people, and as she grew her older brother and sister captivated her. Additionally, like Danny, she began singing to herself by the time she was four. Such singing is a self-soothing lullaby. It is also a way in which children use the sounds they make to *hold themselves*. Alternatively viewed, some young children use their humming like a security blanket or stuffed animal. Winnicott (1951) referred to these as *transitional objects* or *transitional phenomena*—the blankets, toys and sounds represent and create the illusion of mothering at the same time that they smooth the young child's process of psychological individuation and physical separation from the mother's orbit.

It is exceedingly unlikely that small children sing to themselves without some happiness and gratification to tap into. Reba's happiness was with her father. In her third year as she became a walker, runner, and little girl, she and her father came alive for each other. Years later as a 30 year old, she spoke about adoring her father as a child, and how he was the favorite uncle of all of the children in the extended family. On weekends, he would gather Reba, her brother and sister, and their cousins into his station wagon. They would go on trips to the beach in the summer and to movies in the winter, Reba's father unstintingly paying for everybody's treats. The early researchers never had the opportunity to see the father in this role; however, he told them that he had been happy and indulged as a child—unlike Reba's mother's childhood—and that he wanted his children to have as much fun as he had, and to raise them without spankings.

Another extremely significant event occurred when Reba started school. She recalled as an adult how she felt she "had arrived" the fall she was old enough to walk to school with her brother and sister. They were treasured mornings, and she remembers her siblings telling her one day, "We love mommy, but she isn't the best mommy. She can be very selfish." From then on this message became the coordinate by which Reba set her emotional sails. Hearing this statement about her mother—and feeling supported by her brother and sister recognizing her mother's selfishness—spared Reba years of confusion, anger, and guilt, feelings that have hobbled many other children who blame themselves for unhappiness in their family. Although her older brother and sister liberated Reba, they themselves struggled to understand their mother on their own. Now, as adults, they are not doing nearly so well as Reba. Her brother has had problems with substance abuse and a failed marriage, and her sister has had a long history of treatment for depression.

As the years progressed, the researchers' impressions of the family changed very little. The house seemed to be run in a business-like manner with clock-work routine. For example, when Reba was six, an observer described a play session: "The mother was humorlessly intellectualizing; and despite efforts to the contrary, she lacks warmth and spontaneity. She talked with Reba a good deal but she was unsmiling and stern. Eye contact between mother and daughter was rare, and physical contact non-existent. The mother's comments were directive, for although Reba generally placed the pieces in the dollhouse, her mother told her where. The mother would say, 'Shall we put some children on the bench,' and Reba immediately did so. Although the mother was quick to direct, she was slow to satisfy her child's curiosity for when Reba asked her mother to suggest a name for one of the dolls, her mother said, 'What do you think it's called,' like a teacher giving an assignment and maintaining control of the interaction. The mother was somewhat haughty and only once complimented Reba after the child solicited the compliment by asking her mother how the classroom arrangement looked. The mother said, 'Very nice,' then immediately qualified her praise by instructing the child, 'Don't forget to put the teacher in the classroom,' illustrating her inability to stop teaching and to play.

The father continued to elicit lukewarm reviews from the researchers because of an ostentatious pushiness that was increasing hand in hand with his growing success as a financial planner. However, there were also good signs, for seen with Reba, the father was tender and solicitous, as if her frail appearance stimulated his protectiveness. The researchers also recognized how the father's show-offishness and bossiness translated well into having fun with his children by taking them places and buying things for them, activities that were completely congruent with Reba's adult memories of fun with her father.

Perhaps most important, **both parents liked and accepted Reba** in their own ways, and, not incidentally, they liked each other. Separately, the parents described their daughter in nearly identical terms—usually happy, competent for her age, enjoying life, and not difficult. They added that she tended to cry too much when she didn't get her way, which they attributed to the attention she was used to getting as the baby of the family. They accepted her asthma matter-of-factly as a chore to be managed. They tolerantly described Reba at seven as "a gentle maverick . . . cautious . . . doesn't like to be pushed into doing things . . . a worrier . . . happy . . . sensible and responsible . . . attention-seeking . . . a pretty good sport . . . sociable . . . likes to lead with other children . . . fashion conscious . . . likes to fix her mother's hair . . . easy to live with . . . not particularly flexible."

Reba's promising kindergarten behavior justified her parents' contentment. The school observer wrote, "Her delicate, little bit of a girl appearance belies her many strengths. They include enjoyment of her skills, an ability to work alone and organize her energies, humor, and an interest in learning. In addition she is an unusually alert and efficient child [qualities both parents have—brackets ours], and uses school to her advantage [both parents were ambitious]. She also possesses initiative and if something is not clear or doesn't suit her taste for exactness, she takes the responsibility for gaining the additional information she needs. She strikes one as a very capable, self-contained child who is not easily thrown. She sets high standards for herself, although they are at the same time realistic goals . . . As might be expected of a child who demands a great deal of herself, Reba is also rather demanding of other people and is inclined to be a little superior in her attitude toward other children. It is just that this child is quite familiar with all of the classroom rules, follows them consciously, and expects others to do the same. Thus she is sometimes preachy toward other children. For example in one incident Reba sharply called to the attention of two children their mistaken use of crayons instead of pencils for a task, and in another instance when a boy told Reba that she had taken his place in line, she indignantly and self-righteously retorted, 'But you got out of line.'

"When interactions did not center about matters of this sort, Reba was noticeably less forward, and, in fact, a little timid and unsure with peers, though in general she had a friendly disposition toward her classmates and they to her. Basically happy and confident in school, she approaches the entire situation in a serious frame of mind and, again, is tuned to the practical and organizational aspects of her activity [like her parents]. Some hints of perfectionism were present that served her well in getting and acting on information. Rare in a child her age, she seemed to have leadership potential [like her parents], and she is looked up to by her classmates. At the end of the school day her teacher remarked to me, 'Reba is a dreamboat.'"

When she visited the project at five, the psychologist found her inner life more complex. First reserved, then excited, Reba became agitated by difficult performance test items, saying, "I'll never get this. Aw shucks, this is hard. For Pete's sake, how do you get this kooky thing to work?" She then slapped the puzzle pieces aggressively onto the table and whined, "I wish my mommy was here to help me. Why do you have to give me such hard ones? Don't expect me to do this in a rush." Nonetheless, despite fatigue and tension Reba forced herself to stay attentive and did all that was asked of her, even to the point of being over-compliant.

Her Children's Apperception Test stories about animals were lengthy and imaginative; disturbingly, most of the stories were violent. Thus in one story, the protagonist animal broke his legs; in another, the mouse died; in a third the monkey was cut in half and eaten. Those stories that didn't have violent themes concerned themselves with abandonment—a mother going out without telling her children where or why, or a mother telling a baby animal to leave home because the mother didn't like him any more. The tester's overall impression was that Reba was a very bright child who performed exceedingly well. However, it was as if she needed to assure herself of attention, to comfort herself as she had with self-soothing singing. Reba's driven-ness reminded the researchers of the mother, and her intense concentration was like her father's. The reports described a tense, excited little girl—euphoric one moment and desperate another—and predicted that in the future she might have difficulty if faced with severe challenges. The tester concluded, "Reba is a delightful companion, a brilliant conversationalist for her age, intellectually curious, and even had a lot of curiosity about me as a person. Despite her high good judgment, there were two disturbing things in her social behavior: The first was that her attention to me was excessive so that when we were not actually involved in tasks, she had a hard time amusing herself, and chattered endlessly as if there was underlying anxiety about letting go of me and a need to preserve close physical contact with me. The second was her tendency to compliance for she never acted without receiving directions from me, and when she did comply it was all too quickly [the ingredients of a "dreamboat" student]. She did not need her mother's presence as much as she did mine. In fact she didn't want to be reunited with her mother after the meeting but wanted to stay and play with me."

* * *

For the next 11 years, Reba persevered, and when she came for her interview at the end of high school, she was a composed, cooperative, healthy-appearing young woman, dressed in coordinated colors with small, matching adornments. Once again, her psychological testing indicated that considerable intensity of feeling and emotional conflict simmered beneath her composure and carefully constructed outfit. Her inner youthful turmoil was remindful of Danny, as both she and he were emerging from childhoods that had been far from easy. Both Reba and Danny's testing showed aggressive thoughts and feelings frequently boiling to the surface and disrupting their thinking, with thought processes at times insufficiently grounded in the test pictures. Reba's responses contained imagery that suggested that she felt unconsciously sexually competitive with, and victimized by a mother who found flaws and dictated to her.

Reba's imagery of interactions with other people were tinged with sadism, violence, and hostility. She resolved the stories she told on the test in a discouraged way: protagonists watched voyeuristically rather than becoming active participants and problem solvers; her characters lapsed into dejected passivity or they conveyed cuteness as if to say *look at me and like me because I am pretty*. These stories suggest much about how Reba experienced herself as an 18-year-old. Nonetheless, her actual accomplishments and social manner were more successful, just as they had been when she was seven. She had been an excellent student in high school, with satisfying friendships and extracurricular activities. She had even been class president one year—fulfilling her kindergarten observer's prediction of leadership ability—and had become an avid soccer player in spite of her early childhood frailty and asthma.

At 18, Reba generously described both of her parents as warm and affectionate, volunteering that she was so close to her father that she still liked to sit in his lap when the spirit moved her. Trying to broaden the picture of her mother, Reba said, "She is a career woman and gets a kick out of being in a field with mostly men." Sucking in her breath, she added, "If you'll pardon my language my mother has a bitch streak in her. She snaps at you for no reason. But she has big shoulders and supports you. She is easy to confide in and doesn't judge people." Reba's dissatisfactions with herself at this time in her life were her procrastination, her tendency to hold grudges if things went badly in a friendship, and her hesitation to do things unless with friends.

Dr. Brody was struck by how much Reba wanted to paint people rosily and how she worked to suppress negative thoughts about people, feelings that she nevertheless eventually brought out because she also valued being open. She found Reba was a thoughtful late adolescent, capable of tenderness and empathy, but emotional restriction and tension limited the depth of her feelings. Similar to Danny at 18, it was as if Reba felt herself on stage and needed to speak well of her existence and family. Reba's description of her mother as "warm and affectionate" jarred Dr. Brody, who recalled very well how the mother had acted anything but this way in her daughter's early years.

* * *

Not only were Reba's 18 year old descriptions of her parents, especially her mother, disjoined from the researchers' observations, but there was also an apparent discrepancy between Reba's competent adjustment throughout her school years and the picture of her chaotic inner life in repeated psychological testing. This same disjunction between inner and outer occurred with Danny. The psychological test pictures of powerful, disturbing internal conflicts and passions were more in keeping with the researchers' knowledge of the families and their predictions for the two participants than with Danny and Reba's actual successes, illustrating the fluidity of psychic structures of adolescents with potential for emotional difficulties but who fall short of psychopathology.

The discrepancy between problematic unconscious emotional life and effective outer behavior may be explained to a great extent by the inherent drive all children have (described by Winnicott [1962] in *The Maturational Processes and the Facilitating Environment*) to overcome external obstacles and make the best life possible for themselves. To do this, children model their behavior after what seems pleasing and successful to them in their parents, siblings, teachers and friends. At the same time, children can't escape characteristics of their parents which stir their emotions violently. It is this turbulence that psychological testing visualizes. Even when they find their parents reprehensible, children are still drawn to imitate them. Parents are omnipresent teachers and role models in the early years of life. Sometimes there are tempering influences which are life-saving, and Reba and Danny found just such influences in their siblings and extended families.

As we have seen earlier in the lives of other participants, the first 18 years are especially formative. The young person's personality (psychological defenses and manner of handling conflicts, feelings, and impulses) has emerged by about seven years of age and their identity (the sense of who they are in relationship to other people, schoolwork, and tasks) toward the end of adolescence. In their twenties, the participants consolidated themselves, a process they facilitated by physically and emotionally distancing themselves from their parents, developing intimacy with a partner, and mastering work skills. Reba illustrates the process: Readily understanding that her interest came from her father's work, she went away to college thinking she would go to graduate school in economics and then work in banking. But academics never took sufficient hold for her to go on to graduate school, so after college she went directly into the workforce, lured by the glamour of Manhattan and a Wall Street stock brokerage's offer of on-the-job training. Reba continued there for three years with reasonable success, but found the competitiveness and lax ethics distasteful. Reba was especially disappointed by how little control she could exercise—clients came and went, her secretary was disrespectful, and the firm did not fulfill their promise to assign her new accounts equitably.

However, during those three years she fell in love with "a wonderful man ... the man of my dreams ... he's all I could ever hope for ... we share the same dreams, sports, taste in movies and books, the same sense of humor." Her husband to be was eight years older than she and on a fast track to success at the firm. Shortly after beginning to date him, she left the brokerage firm and went to work for her father—commuting against the traffic from Manhattan to Connecticut—thinking that she would learn more and have more control. But a strange thing happened when she started working for her father. She began to find faults with him for the first time in her life. Many of the same things that had troubled the researchers about Reba's father early in her life—his impatience, his glossing over what he didn't want to see, his impersonality, self-importance, and bossiness—Reba now experienced in his behavior in the office. Frustration from the reality of having to work with him now displaced her former "unconditional love" for him.

De-idealizing her father went along with loosening her emotional ties to him, and facilitated a transferring of her idealization to her boyfriend and falling in love with him. As her brother and sister had demystified her mother for her as a school girl, perhaps Reba sensed an unconscious need to experience her father also in a clearer light in order to be free to make a life with a new man—an understanding that may have stimulated her decision to transfer to her father's office. Admired by her father (a boon to any daughter's development), he soon made her his office manager, but as Reba found out, "The trouble was that my father didn't know how to delegate enough authority to me, or to anyone for that matter, to allow the job to get done right."

Reba married her boyfriend when she was 25, had a daughter when she was 26, and gave up work to "have fun with my children at least until they finish grade school." She had a son a year ago, and we filmed her feeding and playing with him. Many families transmit their problematic behaviors and attitudes from one generation to the next, but this handing over is not obligatory, and Reba shows that a daughter can act differently with her children than her mother did with her. In fact, Reba was the exact opposite of her mother. Feeding her son his first taste of cauliflower, she saw him hesitate. She paused, took a piece and tasted it herself with comic relish. Then, like a French chef, she pursed her fingers to her lips, kissed them, and exclaimed in a great show of excitement that the cauliflower was the best food ever. Her entranced son picked up a piece of the vegetable, ate it, and tried to make the same gesture. Their joyful, well-paced, and emotionally attuned interaction was a microcosm of the rest of their play together.

Listening further to Reba as an adult sheds more light on her long, arduous traverse from a physically frail infant with disquieting parents, through a childhood and adolescence in which her outward conformity and accomplishment belied severe underlying emotional conflicts, to an adulthood replete with satisfaction and an exemplary relationship with her children. She explained, "When I was growing up my mother was respectful, tutoring like a teacher, and absolutely loving—I mean, I knew that about her—but she didn't show it. She wasn't the kind who was warm and kissed me. And she was disappointing, like the times she was supposed to pick me up and forgot because she was too busy. One night when I was about eight I had to wait for an hour all alone in the dark after my piano lesson. The building was locked up and I was scared. It took me a long time to come to grips with her selfishness, and make my peace with it. I've told you how my brother and sister explained it to me. And my uncle—her brother—once told me, 'It hurts you more to hate someone than it hurts them. There are positive things in everyone.' He's a real nice man who taught me a lot about life. He made me feel special because I think as the youngest child in the family I got his attention since he didn't have kids of his own. I could have grown up angry at my mother, but people helped me understand that the things she did were not because I was doing something wrong. I learned to stay away when she was in a bad mood. It was also easier being the youngest because it gave me more freedom from being controlled by my mother than my sister and brother had. I turned out more optimistic than they because I was more independent, more removed from my parents."

Reba's earliest memory in life struck the same note of fear and abandonment as her memory of being stood up by her mother after her piano lesson. When she was three or four years old, she was shopping with her mother and got separated from her. Reba thought she saw her mother and grabbed her leg, but when the lady turned and looked down at her, it wasn't her mother. Ironically, the night before she met with us for her interview, she had a nightmare that highlights her fear of separation from loved ones. She dreamt of losing her baby, but the baby, perhaps a representation of herself, had a phone number on him, and in the dream a woman calls her up to return the child. It is likely that anticipating talking about her ambivalent relationship with her mother in the interview the next day precipitated the dream and brought to the cusp of awareness buried feelings from childhood.

Reba went on, "All the while I was growing up I thought if I pleased my mother a little more, you know acted a little better, did a little better in school, she wouldn't be selfish. I was a kiss-ass in school to get the highest grades. I knew who the right people were and how to play them. I was catty to my friends and made sure I was always in the group that would cast me in the best light. But it was futile because my mother had no idea that anything was wrong with how she treated us. What has changed now is that I've learned to accept that. Now that I'm a mother I see her problem in spades, how self-centered, how rigid she is; and realize how differently I act with my own children. I mean, I have friends whose parents baby-sit for them all the time and help them out, but my mother would never think of baby-sitting for me. She's too busy, too self-absorbed; her schedule's too important. It wasn't like one day I woke up and said, 'I can't expect different from her.' It was an evolutionary process. Nowadays I love my life with my children—there are surprises every day and I'm in charge of each day. The worst part is loneliness for adult company. My mother says I'm unfulfilled. I disagree. I'm fulfilled, but some day I'm sure I will return to school or work. At least my father is proud of me."

Although Reba's voice was composed talking about her mother, there was sadness in her eyes. When she reminisced about her father, the sadness evaporated and her eyes sparkled. "He held my hand out of affection. My mother did it out of function, you know, to get me somewhere. My father was fun, warm, and also a teacher to me. My brother and sister and I decided he was the most brilliant and capable person we knew, and should be elected President of the United States. When I went to work for him in my twenties it was hard to see that he was only human. Maybe making mistakes is also a qualification for being President."

In spite of both Reba's misgivings about her mother and her bad experiences with her, the mother's regard for her daughter was considerable, and Reba, like Danny, had a Secure mental representation of her attachment to her parents in childhood.

At 30 years of age, for the first time in her life, Reba's psychological projective tests finally gave a picture of stability that was consistent with her external happiness and competence. There was no longer the dyssynchrony that had occurred at younger ages between the testing view of her inner life and her outward behavior. Now the psychologist reported, "She has adequate ego strength and internal resources. She is open to her environment and has the capacity for mature interpersonal relations. She may compartmentalize when under stress or overwhelmed, and feel overly anxious at these times. She appears to have good internalized representations of herself and others. Her drawing of the opposite sex indicates some sexual conflicts or anxieties. Her primary defenses are denial and reaction formations of altruistic good will against underlying anger." Reba's asthma is largely in the past, which she attributes to her contentment, for she believes her asthma was an artifact of former upset feelings and stress. She concluded, "Being a real person, becoming a person is a hard job. I still work at it. I ask myself, 'Are you listening to yourself? Can I understand myself? Can I work at changing?'"

Surveying the Lives of the Other Seven Who Exceeded Expectations

Dafna. In chapter two Dafna was one of the children who externalized her childhood unhappiness with hyperactivity. Her mother had been overactive with her from birth, and her father had suffered intermittent episodes of binge drinking in connection with his severe moods swings. He plunged the family into repeated crises, but Dafna's mother, blessed with the gift of humor and optimism, kept the family going until the father got back on his feet. The family confusion took a toll on Dafna, pushing her in her youth into substance abuse and a bad marriage to a man like her father. However, three phenomena righted her in her mid to late twenties: her underlying identification with her mother's competence and upbeat courage asserted itself; psychotherapy helped her overcome guilt and separate from her first husband; and her second husband's maturity and support gave her stability.

Today, Dafna and her husband manage a store and are expecting their first child. She enjoys a sense of calm that she had never felt when she was younger, yet remains animated and expressive. She speaks articulately about how her life only relatively recently ceased being a roller coaster ride, and that her former, constant apprehension of a storm brewing has passed. She maintains a good relationship with both her father and mother, and had an Secure-earned-secure mental representation of her sense of attachment to them in childhood.

Lorna. Whatever judgment one makes about the value of conformity, the pressure to adopt family, peer, and community standards is a powerful developmental force. Conformity is what most characterized Lorna's emotional growth and adaptation as a child, and, indeed, her successful life now. She is a contented and well remunerated mechanical engineer, planning soon to start a family with her husband, also an engineer. But 25 to 30 odd years ago, the researchers had significant misgivings about Lorna's future. At six months an observer wrote, "Lorna's attentive mother says that her baby has little interest in food, but rather than help the baby sit more comfortably or relax, she hurries on with the feeding, and produces excessive discomfort in the child. When this happens, the mother becomes increasingly formal and constrained. She says she feels the baby doesn't need to be played with, and consequently misses Lorna's gestures and glances toward the bottle and away from it when she wants diversion.

Allowing the baby to handle the bottle might reduce both mother and child's tension, and increase their pleasure in the feeding. The mother allows no rest and no time out for a social interlude."

At 15 months, Dr. Brody's impressions were, "Overtly the mother is friendly, confident and concerned for her daughter's well being. However her interest is to the surface of her child's life, though she may not realize this. Although considering herself competent, she is actually little giving, quite formal with the baby, and unfeeling rather than harsh. Her own personality seems to be severely constricted. She needs to set up situations in her way, and thus becomes demanding toward Lorna, expecting her to accommodate to her needs. She is quite concerned about spoiling her child and expresses neither sympathy nor resentment to her, treating her rather over-objectively, over matter-of-factly. She makes many conventional statements about a child's need for love and affection but actually is much more concerned with the baby's physical state and physical development. She stresses the need for early discipline, training, and the adaptation of the infant to the parents' way of life. She shows little capacity for enjoyment of mothering, and places a high value on a child's self-sufficiency, which leads her to expect her child to adapt without the mother taking special pains to provide comfort or gratification. The mother is not aware of inner anxiety, nor is she aware that she withholds affection from her infant. She is indeed quite concerned about being 'a good mother,' and does not seem to understand that her emotional freedom lags far behind her intellectual concern." Dr. Brody's complex thoughts and observations recurred in the reports of other observers over many years.

Lorna's father was a home-remodeling contractor, and apiece with the mother in his organization, attentiveness, and reasoned concern for his daughter, but in his manner even more brisk and emotionally detached from the child. Lorna worked hard to be the child her parents wanted and to fit in with their clear, consistent expectations that were, fortunately, not egregious in terms of the actual number of chores. To accommodate her parents, however, she dampened down her own emotionality and became a painfully shy schoolgirl. As a student, she worked diligently and successfully, enjoying her skills, but without a spark or gaiety. As one observer put it, "She is wary of people and emotionally distant, she has adopted her mother's style."

When she was 18, Lorna's psychological testing indicated no severe emotional disturbance, but a lack of spontaneity. "She sees herself like a little animal in hiding, feeling alone, looking out to find friends. It seems that she is afraid of showing strong feeling and tries to maintain a stoical veneer, perhaps the way she perceives her mother. Her constraint is hard on her for she felt much better the few times she let her guard down and expressed feelings." Interestingly her testing showed sexual identity conflicts and confusion as indicated by her drawing a male figure first, and by her tendency to see percepts that are typically seen as anatomically male as female, and vice versa.

With the advantage of hindsight and a reading of the full record, we can link the 18 year report of Lorna's sexual identity confusion with observations—made when she was seven—that Lorna took the role of the father when she played with dolls. Additionally, we speculate that the absence of emotional vitality, warmth, and spontaneity in the mother-daughter relationship led her to turn to her father as a role model.

Dr. Brody said about her at 18, "She is not used to being introspective and it may be she is used to looking at others more than herself. She is not in my opinion a thinker, and is not particularly resourceful or creative. I have the feeling that she couldn't show much more than what is conventional because she was covering a good deal of tension about her life at home and anger and concern about her rebellious younger sister. I had no feeling of her response to me as a person, and no feeling of deep aspirations though she may do well in being a good student and achieving what she wishes. I see her possibly fitting into a responsible role in any profession she chooses."

Over the next several years, Lorna did break out of her mouse hole, so to speak, and became more spontaneous by force of will and necessity. She told us at 30 that by the end of high school, she couldn't stand her shyness anymore and vowed to start afresh in college by being open and spending time with people. Her determination paid off, and she formed a circle of friends with like-minded, studious habits. Their scrupulousness did not prevent them from gathering two or three nights a week for beers when the library closed, but unlike her friends—and unlike 90% of the project participants—Lorna refrained from experimenting with marijuana. She had boyfriends in college who were her first sexual partners, and then met her husband-to-be in an engineering class. She said that her choice of profession seemed natural, "because I have a very organized mind and was always good at solving math and physics problems." Lorna does not consciously link being a mechanical engineer with an appreciation for her father and his work as a contractor, a trade which demands similar problem solving skills.

Today, Lorna is an intense woman who dresses plainly in bluejeans and a blouse, with no jewelry or makeup. She sat for her interview self-protectively, with her hands clasped or arms folded in front of her. Still, she laughed frequently and gaily at amusing thoughts and to relieve tension. She often searched her mind before speaking, and gave childhood memories that were almost uniformly good. For instance, she said her mother was "fun . . . exciting . . . understanding . . . supportive . . . and tough about things I was supposed to do." Recalling her mother's toughness brought forth a sharp laugh. She said that her father was "fun . . . exciting . . . embarrassing . . . smart . . . and available." We asked how he was embarrassing, and she explained, "He was always outgoing, telling jokes, teasing me in front of people." She punctuated this also with her gay, quick laugh. "He wasn't straight and buttoned down like my friends' fathers. I loved going to his shop. His secretary would give me blueprints to draw on, and I was so impressed because everybody was always asking him questions about things and he always had the answer. He always showed up at my softball games unlike the other kids' fathers."

If we omit the parents' unfavorable qualities such as briskness, matter-of-factness, and detachment from attention to their daughter's feelings, in many ways Lorna has led a charmed life. There have been no traumas in her life. Her parents got along well together, and she grew up well provided for in the same safe, suburban community from the time she was four years old. This kind of continuity, predictability, security, and freedom from trauma surely had a protective effect and helped her compensate for her underlying insecurities. When the time was ripe in college, she could dare to try new ways of relating to people. "I came out of myself, and people really liked me. Nobody ever could figure out why I was so insecure about myself, let alone me. My parents just wanted me to be the best person I could be, but I always had the feeling they expected more of me than I could do, especially that I could never satisfy my mother. Now we're really friends, and talk several times a week."

Lorna and her husband live in a spacious house with a distant view of Long Island Sound, materially, personally, and professionally successful. Dr. Brody anticipated the likelihood of such an adjustment when Lorna was 18, but she was also right in calling attention to Lorna's conventionality and absence of creativity—a state which persists. Lorna reads only best-selling romances and mysteries; her favorite television programs are evening soap operas. She feels her greatest strength is working hard and solving problems, and her self-assessed weakness is "feeling that I could do a better job if only I had more time, but my manager says my work always turns out okay."

Lorna has a certain emotional constraint or "pulling in of her personality" recognized by Anthony and Cohler (1987) in many vulnerable but successful children. She is not introspective in the sense of examining or observing her emotional state or mental processes, and has never experienced psychiatric symptoms in her adult life. Her earliest memory is going fishing with her grandparents and cousins, something she did often when she was small. "They divided us up into girls versus boys, and whomever caught the most fish got the banana split at the Dairy Queen. It was fun." Her greatest satisfaction in life has been meeting her husband "who is more laid back than I am. When we go out I ask him if we're dressed right and he always says, 'You're just fine.'" Their sexual relationship is active and satisfying, yet in the best of all possible worlds she wishes she could be freer and less inhibited sexually. She says, "I don't really fantasize during sex, and I have always worried that I might get pregnant before it was time to have a child."

Lorna believes her greatest future pleasure will be having happy, confident children. She doesn't want them to have to endure her earlier insecurities. But this wish dovetails with her greatest worry, which is that she might not be able to conceive children, though she says there is no rational reason to be concerned about this. We, on the other hand, feel that there is a rational explanation for her worry, but the reason is an unconscious one. The lack of spontaneity and warmth between her mother and her when she was a baby; taking the role of father in fantasy play as a child; signs of sexual identity ambiguity on her 18 year psychological test; and now thriving in a male-oriented profession: Lorna's modest anxiety about being able to have children is likely the surface manifestation of continuing gender identity and gender role blurring. Her choice of a sexual partner, however, appears firmly heterosexual. When Lorna does have children, it is unlikely that she will be as free and warm as Reba is with hers, but will more likely replicate her mother's mechanical style of care-taking, at least as long as she remains unaware of the inner workings of her psyche.

Donald. Themes from Lorna's life echo in Donald's. For example, Donald also has an unconscious blurring of his gender identity, in his case because of great closeness to his mother and limited contact with his father when he was growing up. Similarly to Lorna, his adulthood is marked by close and cautious conformity to the ethical values of his parents, who themselves hew closely to the conservative standards of their religious community. Donald's acceptance of his parents' model is a source of his health and strength for it provides him with good standards of behavior and a clear role in life. On the other hand the degree to which he follows their footsteps also restricts his personality: Donald is both circumspect in his thinking and behavior and limited in his fantasy life. He functions extremely well without any emotional symptoms in the roles he has chosen—director of sales for an eminent golf equipment manufacturer, gentle and loving son, mentor to his younger sisters, and squire of eligible young women to society events.

Early life vignettes of Donald and his parents illustrate why the researchers were concerned for him, and why they originally placed him in the group of children whose parenting was less than optimum. When Donald was a baby, a project observer described his mother feeding him: "Her impatience with his poor appetite becomes apparent. The baby resists his cereal and would like to play with his spoon. She pulls it away and instead hurries to clean his hand. He chews at her finger but this amuses her only momentarily and she turns to the bottle, feeding in a determined way. Her entire attention is focused on the bottle. Each time the mother and infant were observed, the feeding began with an appearance of quietness but soon became restless. As the baby grew more and more uncomfortable, the mother seemed more and more impervious to his distress."

In general, the mother's interviewers found her friendly, tensely gay, eager, and very invested in social decorum and good behavior. Careful scheduling of the family's life was paramount; as a researcher observed, "Routine is her primary emotional defense, and she finds it hard to tolerate any ambiguity in her child. She inhibits all feelings in herself and behavior in the baby that doesn't fit into her picture of virtue." Fortunately, the mother liked Donald very much and said that he was "an easy and regular baby." Indeed, the mother insisted, "The very first time I saw him I knew he would be precious and lovable." She treated her baby son sweetly like a "good doll" in a manner that was superficially loving in a stereotyped way. When he didn't obey her instructions after two warnings, she quickly and firmly corrected him.

As a couple, the mother and father were in concert regarding Donald, and truly proud and respectful of each other. The mother's domain was the home, and the father, though devoted to his family, was a skilled executive who spent virtually a third of the year at factory sites around the country. When he did come home, it was usually 15 minutes before his son's bedtime, and on weekends with a briefcase of papers to attend to. One interviewer said, "The father is robust with an appraising gaze and a hard-hitting manner. He guards his feelings, and I felt too intimidated by his impatience to pursue some portions of the interview." Of himself, the father said, "My strength is giving my children standards for themselves," and of Donald he said, "He is a joy, no bother at all."

At one year little Donald's adaptation to his family was taking shape: he was somewhat listless with a slack muscle tone and an unvaried facial expression. By the time he was in grade school, his adaptation was more complete and, in many ways, pleasing. At school he was relaxed, confident, and friendly with his schoolmates. He worked seriously in class and enjoyed his playtime. His teacher said that he was cautious and obedient, "a mature, even-tempered youngster, pretty much of a conformist." When playing with his mother as a seven year old, he acquiesced to her didactic manner and seemed dependent, but with his interviewer, his affability was such that she, like the school teacher, found him "grownup." Thus by seven, Donald was becoming the child his parents had hoped for. The trade-off was, as his psychological tester reported, that a "process of inhibition seems to be going on in the child."

When Sylvia Brody met with Donald in his eighteenth year, the inhibitory process was crystallized. She wrote, "Donald is a restricted, quiet, unassuming young man. He is too still physically as if lacking inner vitality, rarely smiles, and is mostly solemn and thoughtful. He seems to have surrendered initiative, though he has good sense, practical skills, and a real integrity with abiding faith in the moral virtues his parents and church taught him." About himself, the late teen said, "My parents think I'm a very nice kid to have. They're not ashamed of me. I'm presentable, warm, sincere, maybe a bit lazy."

Dr. Brody asked him if his parents had given him enough support and provided enough information, including sexual information, while he was growing up. He answered with a striking memory. He said that when he was about eight years old an older boy told him how grownups have sexual intercourse. Donald was disbelieving and asked his mother if it was true. She appeared flustered, and said it was true. Donald recalled being so upset that he yelled back, "You and daddy shouldn't have! You shouldn't have," and cried despairingly until his father came home and calmed him. "I had somehow gotten it in my mind that sex was bad." This event had also struck his parents, for they themselves had reported it when their boy was seven.

Twelve years later, Donald was a handsomely dressed, gentle mannered, 30-year-old, and in an executive business position his mother's family connections had made possible. In his interview, the same upsetting sexual event came up again, but with a twist. His interviewer asked him to begin by talking about what his parents had been like growing up. To answer, Donald offered his earliest memory in life, which he dated to about three years of age. He was lying on the couch with his head in his mother's lap, and recalls fishing in her purse for her car keys which he "accidentally" dropped under the couch. As a result, his mother couldn't drive to the airport to pick up his father. After this snapshot-like preface of his family life, Donald fondly described his mother as "giving . . . understanding . . . always there . . . proper . . . occasionally frustrating."

By contrast he said his father was "distant . . . funny . . . generous . . . [and] intimidating because he was so successful and so disciplined . . . a formidable foe because he could get so impatient with my relative lack of discipline." Then Donald's mental associations leaped to his childhood despair over learning about the facts of life. "I guess I had gotten it in my mind that sex was disgusting but my parents knew how to calm me when I got upset," he said, and he told the same story over again of being told about intercourse by the neighborhood boy and his mother confirming it, to his despair.

We speculate that this memory lingers and resurfaces at such widely spaced intervals due to Donald's unusual closeness to his mother, an intimacy that existed despite her need for order and limited spontaneity. His father's austere personality and long absences alienated Donald from him. Donald may have been so close to his mother that he experienced his father as a formidable competitor for his mother's affections, and when small couldn't tolerate the discovery that father and mother had a sexual life from which he was excluded. Going into her purse as a little boy was partly sexual exploration, just as losing her car keys was a psychologically determined attempt to keep the father away. In his 30 year interview, Donald retrieved the memory of his head in his mother's lap and losing the keys first in relation to thinking of his parents as comforting, placing the lost keys at three years. He retrieved the memory of his conscious discovery of sex in relation to thinking of his father as a foe, placing that experience at eight years. His associations convey how mental and emotional life are an amalgam of present day stimulation, remembered and forgotten past experiences, and conscious and unconscious thoughts and feelings.

As an adult, Donald is like his mother—decorous, soft spoken, cautious, and not ambitious for highly skilled professional attainment. He is satisfied that during his twenties he had long relationships with first one woman and then a second. These liaisons ended by mutual agreement, and he remains friendly with both women. He has no doubt that he will marry and have a family when he meets a woman who shares his mother's social and family values. As he says, "I had a very happy childhood. I learned to be a good person and have a positive outlook on life, and I want to marry a woman with whom I can make that possible for my own children." Donald is the epitome of temperate balance; he has arrived at this state by identifying strongly with his family's principles and never rebelling. Settled into a religious community and its practices, his parents were very strong models, and would have brooked no rebellion. Fortunately they, and the extended family, offered Donald enough liveliness, warmth, and generosity so that he avoided the anger and depression that can come from acquiescing to strong family controls. He had no need for rebellion. Donald's great pleasure these days is singing in his church's choir, an activity which allows him to feel and express deep, strong feelings. It remains to be seen whether he will meet a woman who matches the standard his mother represents, and if he will allow himself to become sufficiently involved to marry.

Lainy. A haircutter and stylist in a popular Greenwich Village salon, Lainy broadcasts her skills with her appearance. Her hair is purple and spiked; impossibly large hoops hang from her ears; and her ankle-length caftan matches her hair. When her interviewer couldn't refrain from saying that he found her hair striking, Lainy replied brightly that if he were to return next week it would probably be a new color and style. Conformity, balance, temperance, the developmental adaptations that serve Donald and Lorna, are certainly not central to Lainy's personality. Indeed, she said that her parents have trouble accepting her because they want her to be more conventional like themselves. Lainy said she is happy with herself. She likes her work and her clients—who sometimes become friends; her computer programmer husband is her "sweetie-pie;" and her year-old son is "God's gift to me." In spite of marked tension with her parents, she feels they remain friends. The family gets together almost weekly.

Lainy's mother, a nurse, and her father, a hospital administrator, raised their children materially secure and free from trauma, but the original researchers felt that something was missing in the parent-child relationship. Both parents seemed relatively mechanical and closed off from showing deep or tender feelings toward Lainy. For example, the observer reported, "At six months the mother rarely holds the baby during feeding. By shifting the baby's face away from her she hinders their visual communication, and when the baby tries to catch sight of her mother's face and becomes tense, the mother remains indifferent. Even when they face each other, the mother seeks no expressive interaction. She attends to the technical aspects of feeding, with no sign of emotion." At 12 months, Lainy, who formerly was curious and vital, was somber and listless, poking at or refusing her food during the observed feeding. Her mother said that this indifference was typical, and that she didn't have the patience to encourage her daughter to eat. While she occasionally looked at and spoke encouragingly to Lainy, the mother was mostly perfunctory and formal. "Although the mother's demeanor with her child is friendly, it is constricted."

In person, the mother was unusually self-certain, self-satisfied, superior or archly dismissive of any possible worries. Amongst parents in the project, she was striking in her insistence that everything was all right, and in her refusal to acknowledge any unhappiness or need for assistance in any regard. The researchers were even less sanguine about the father, finding him "shallow, narcissistic and materialistic, with little capacity for warmth with his children. Both parents have perhaps not taken Lainy seriously enough and have treated her as a pretty doll with whom to have fun. The father especially favors flirtation as his way of expressing affection, and does not feel Lainy needs to aspire to do things as well as her older brother, and in fact discourages her more serious curiosity by not acknowledging it."

Lainy copied her mother's self-assured manner and responded to her father's flirtation; by the age of six and seven, she had regained the vitality that had flagged at the end of infancy. At her project visits, she was confident and ebullient, though she had a tendency to withdraw from difficult test items and brag, a trait which marred her performance. So great was her cheeriness that her interviewer wondered if it was a facade, especially in view of her mother's sharpness with her. At school, her teacher was pleased with Lainy's adjustment, noting that she was cooperative and popular with her classmates. Her observer noted how much Lainy enjoyed her classroom skills, her ability to work alone or in a group, and her humor. "Her most noticeable quality is her harmony with others. She moves with grace in relation to others and possesses an unusual amount of tact for a child her age."

Ironically, when Lainy was 18, she appeared less mature. Her psychological tester wondered, "Is her blandness and lack of reflection the result of an untroubled life or denial of unpleasantness? Some of her responses suggest that she is quite lacking in empathy for others in situations that are unstructured and unfamiliar." This last observation dovetailed remarkably with Dr. Brody's comments about Lainy, "She made a striking appearance with a great mane of red hair hanging loose. She was cordial, intelligent and thoughtful, but her presence was tarnished by an apparent need to be constantly gracious and positive. She was constantly sure of herself, laughing throughout the meeting though sometimes in a way that was entirely unrelated to what she was saying, and acknowledged no faults in herself or parents unless pressed strongly. Despite her seeming warmth and interest, I had the feeling that at any moment she could close off and turn away. This happened at the beginning when she greeted me warmly and then turned to her book and seemed far away. What she did was reasonable had she not similarly broken contact with me several times later during the interview."

Dr. Brody is describing in personal, experiential terms what the psychologist had picked up from Lainy's flawed responses to novel pictorial designs, and labeled as empathic failures in unstructured and unfamiliar settings. Lainy's trouble responding in situations which are ambiguous to her, or in which she is unsure, may be distantly descended from having a mother who did not give her sufficient cues, and who didn't engage strongly with her emotionally or expressively when Lainey was small.

Twelve years later when Lainy was 30, her interviewer said, "She is a delightful woman, joyful, warm, modest in her needs and aspirations. She seems fulfilled and buoyant. She is insightful in her thinking about people and herself, and brings creativity to her work. Her good humor and somewhat pressured speech were infectious, but after a time I began to tire from the constant upbeat mood. I wondered if it was defensive." He asked her if anything makes her feel sad or down. Lainy replied, "No. My friends ask me where I plug in. I just have my energy. I don't have many words for sadness. I had a happy childhood. I learned to have a positive outlook, to believe in myself that I can get over problems, and not to blame others for things that happen."

She described her parents growing up as patient and loving, added ambivalently that they were goal-oriented, and ultimately acknowledged feeling that they weren't satisfied with her when she was a child, comparing her unfavorably to her bookworm brother, because she liked to play rather than study. Lainy's earliest memory may relate to this strain over not being as grownup as her parents wanted her to be. "It was my fourth birthday party. I loved my party dress and then I peed in it. My mother had to change me and I was so ashamed. But it was not a real trauma because I was just four." Does her insistence that it wasn't traumatic mean just that, or, that there is an underlying, uncontrolled sadness; or, that she is indeed effectively suppressing sadness with her mantra of positive thinking? A recurring dream from childhood shows Lainy flying high above her troubles by identifying with a powerful fantasy hero. "I used to dream that I was super-girl's younger sister. I'd swing from ropes and do fun things like leap tall buildings, in living color."

Should we call the grownup Lainy, with all of her energy, excitement, and paucity of "words for sadness" (similar to her mother) a hypomanic personality, which may have a pejorative connotation? Or should we admire her for her vitality and indefatigable exuberance? Trying to differentiate strength from what may be problematic in Lainy may be impossible, but to a certain extent assessment depends both on the defense mechanisms she uses and whether her sense of reality is intact. Lainy seems to have forged her personality through identifying with her mother's self-certainty, while channeling her anger and frustration with her parents into rebellion against their conservatism through her appearance and choice of profession. Though Lainy's dress and hairdo may seem outlandish, she nonetheless carefully orchestrates her appearance. One of Lainy's principal defenses, as shown in her 30 year psychological testing, is the archetypal hypomanic tool of denial. On the other hand her other defenses are at the High Adaptive level (mature and effective) and include humor, self-assertion, self-observation, sublimation (of her desire to stand out) into her work as a stylist, conscious suppression of disturbing thoughts and feelings, and reaction formation against angry feelings with kindness and generosity. She does not show pathological defenses associated with mania such as omnipotent fantasies of control, identification with people from whom she can borrow power, and projection of a sense of badness about herself onto others. People who use these manic defenses tenuously hold on to their freedom from depression, guilt, and anxiety by sacrificing a fullness of personality and appreciation of others' motives and feelings, as well as by compromising their sense of reality.

Nonetheless, just as her work as a beautician creates evanescent surface effects, Lainy's adult testing suggests some fragility and superficiality in her adjustment. The psychologist, who knew nothing of Lainy's background, wrote of her figure drawings, "They indicate feelings of inadequacy, insecurity and shyness. Although she attempts to present herself as emotionally open and receptive, there is interpersonal tension. Her figures are small and diminished, which appears to be in reaction to her conflicts regarding her exhibitionistic desires. She also has some obsessional traits which may be in response to troubling internal processes."

It is very possible that Lainy will go through life never missing a beat and never suffer depressive symptoms. Hypomanic people often accomplish prodigious amounts of work and bring great happiness to others, but they often are like tightly stretched drums whose tone lacks depth, resonance, and flexibility. They can be repetitive and stereotyped in their interpersonal relationships and keep much hidden beneath the surface.

Lainy told us that her relationship with her young son is the most important thing in her life, and we filmed them together. With her son, she was mildly to moderately overstimulating. She missed opportunities to enter into the baby's curiosity, to support his initiatives, and to play with him. Lainy gave no sign that she was warding off hostility, impatience, or depression with her child, but passivity, quiet play, and talk were too small a part of the mother and child's repertoire. Thus, Lainy is rather like her own mother and father were with her in her limited emotional engagement with her child and inattention to his curiosity. This following of their pattern is much in contrast to Reba who has created a much richer relationship with her child than she experienced when she was young.

Carole. Her parents were impatient and childlike. Not introspective, they neither observed nor responded to the more muted emotions of their four children. In many respects, Carole's mother's was similar to the mothers of Lainy, Lorna, and Donald—phlegmatic, full of platitudes about child rearing, relatively confident, concerned, and not unkindly. A difference was that Carole's family's economic circumstances were far more stressed than most of the study families, and Carole watched them struggling to make it into the middle class. During Carole's preadolescence, the parents lost their modest home after the father was laid off from his work as a machinist and had to endure two years of unemployment.

When Carole was very small, the mother used her to keep her company at night during the father's evening shift, and later, as more children were born at almost yearly intervals, parentified Carole into sharing with the childcare. Self-absorbed and over-burdened, the mother often reacted to what she thought Carole thought or felt, rather than ascertaining what was really on her daughter's mind. The mother had no investment in fostering her daughter's creativity or imagination. When she did solicit Carole's ideas occasionally, the mother most often ignored them anyway or tried to convince the child otherwise. Once during a home interview with the mother, Carole started teasing her younger sister. The mother excused herself to stop the teasing. Carole fled and the mother gave chase, yelling, "You miserable child, that's what you are, a miserable child." Carole screamed back, "Don't hit me, don't hit me."

As a schoolchild, Carole was dutiful, friendly, liked by classmates, and in many ways overly responsible for her age. She often took this maturity to extremes by trying to boss other children, her voice echoing her mother who filled the house with many family rules in an effort to keep order. Schoolmates teased Carole liberally for her being preachy, but she bounced back, undeterred. When she was in first grade, Carole said she wanted to be President of the United States so she could "be the boss of things." Graduating from high-school, her goal was to be a lawyer because she felt it would give her the tools "to help society return to strong constitutional principles in which power would revert to the people," words she said she borrowed from President Reagan, whom she admired. Not a stranger to leadership, Carole had run her church's youth group, taught Sunday school, held an after-school job throughout high school, and maintained a B+ average.

Her psychological report at this time read, "Carole is somewhat grandiose and exhibitionistic, which covers over anxiety regarding underlying feelings of inferiority and inadequacy. Her self-importance allows her to express hostility toward authority figures in socially acceptable, reformist ways. She appears fiercely competitive, though at the same time gave responses on her projective tests that indicated strong underlying trends toward dependency and passivity." When we reviewed Carole's record, it was clear that her hidden dependency and passivity were well explained by her frustrations in gaining attention and support in her large family, and by the pressure of earning money to support herself from a very young age. During her 18 year interview, Carole also revealed for the first time that when she was 11, an adult male neighbor had lured her into his home and sexually fondled her before she ran away. She reflected that she had been vulnerable to this seduction because of her disappointment in her father after he lost his job, and felt the experience left her with anger "but no other trauma," in her words. On the other hand, Dr. Brody thought the molestation had engendered in Carole conflicts and self-doubts over her femininity, which explained some of her personality mix of blustery assertiveness and flirtatiousness.

At 18, Carole abjured drugs and alcohol, saying she was "high on life." Twelve years later at 30, she was still "high on life," still abstinent of drugs and alcohol, still outgoing and engaging. Slightly masculine appearing because of her robust figure and forceful movements, Carole was busy and productive. Her internal emotional conflicts from earlier years remained, but she kept them in balance with her defenses and compensatory achievements. For example, at the state university she attended near home, she had switched from prelaw to education because of her impatience with studying and her need to start earning a salary as soon as possible. For some years, she has taught junior high school in her home town, particularly enjoying giving her students "the leadership they need at this mixed-up time in their lives." Active in the teacher's union, she has just been elected representative from her district to the state council. She is also working on a master's degree in business in night school.

Three years ago, Carole married a fellow teacher several years younger than herself; at her interview, she reported proudly, "He is an alcoholic, but hasn't had a drop to drink since we got together. I make sure he goes to AA regularly." When asked how her husband felt about her overseeing his attendance at AA, she said, "He's very appreciative. He tells me he owes everything to me." Carole described a very exciting sexual fantasy she indulges in with her husband. She encourages him to tie her up and pretend to "ravish" her. The excitement of this sexual practice is not mysterious given how hard she has striven since childhood, how much she avoided passivity, and how hard she worked to keep the reins on her brothers and sister growing up, and her sexual molestation at 11. By letting her husband tie her up, she allows herself to express, experience, and master passivity *in a controlled way*, the sense of emotional helplessness she has fought off all her life, and the physical helplessness she resisted when she was 11.

Carole has a Secure mental representation of her attachment to her parents. Her principal defense mechanisms are altruism, reaction formation, and self-assertion, the latter connected to the mechanism of identification with the aggressor (her mother, in some respects, and the man who molested her). Carole also uses the mechanism of devaluation of others in order to see herself as more estimable and to find people to aid who need her helping energies. She disavows from awareness feelings about herself such as self-doubt and emotional neediness, and projects these feelings onto people she assists, such as her students and husband. But this process may lead her to have an overly rigid, law and order, right and wrong, me and them value system.

All told, Carole likes herself very much, and for good reasons: she works hard, is loyal, and optimistic. She regulates her self-esteem through a strong identification with her mother's assertiveness, by receiving approval from her parents for her success in work, and by having a husband who idealizes her. Her overall adaptation follows the pattern of several of the other children of less than optimum parents who are now doing well—she is *a hypomanic achiever,* which compensates for inner doubt, and *conforms* to her parents' rules and fondest expectations.

Deborah. Debbie's case is an anomaly in that her mother had a focal difficulty feeding her baby but was otherwise an exemplary parent. Since competence in feeding was the strongest determinant in deciding in which parenting group to place the mothers, the original research team classified Deborah's mother in the less favorable parenting cohort. The ease, empathy, efficiency, and pleasure with which mothers nursed and fed their babies did indeed mirror the mothers' overall relationship with their babies in 74 of the 76 families. Besides Deborah, the only other anomalous case in which feeding was disjunctive with the rest of a mother's behavior was one in which a mother was seriously depressed. That mother fed her infant tenderly and effectively, and was classified as parenting favorably, but her chronic depression hampered her in her other activities with her child, and the child has not done well over the years.

Of Deborah's mother, the observers said at six months, "The child was in subacute distress with gas and irritability much of the time during feeding, and the mother held off giving comfort and juice to relax the child . . . In general this is an animated, sociable, confident mother. She is spontaneous, vivacious, and smiles frequently. She carries her child adeptly and gently, and talks softly and encouragingly to her. She takes great pleasure in, and has much pride for her baby." At 12 months they wrote, "The mother's handling of the child's fussiness when hungry was insensitive, but she handles her fondly at other times and clearly loves her child very much."

When Sylvia Brody met with the parents to report on Deborah's development after the first year of life, they were unique among project families in bringing their two older daughters, eleven and six, with Deborah to the meeting. For this family, raising the baby was a happy family project. Dr. Brody wrote, "Deborah is a very expressive child, easy to like, jolly, laughing, more able to express pleasure than almost any baby I have seen her age. She was always responsive to little games initiated by her mother. The father is intelligent, articulate, with much feeling for his children. The mother is energetic and ready to show emotion for her children who themselves are all amenable and friendly. The mother is genuinely related to them, and easy for me to talk with." Given such an auspicious debut, Deborah's childhood continued apace. Over the years, project staff, her parents, schoolteachers, and her friends enjoyed her emotional expansiveness, competence, cooperativeness, and forthright expression of thoughts and wishes. Although the father at one year impressed his interviewers favorably, over the long-term they found him fairly restricted in his feelings and behavior with his daughter and insensitive to the details of her life. It was her femininity that beguiled him.

This was a family that emphasized moral rectitude and conscientiousness, so that when problems arose, the mother usually took the position that they were her responsibility. She examined herself critically to see what she may have done wrong and asked herself what she could do to make things better. On the other hand, the father tended to become over-silent and withdrawn in response to difficulties.

When she came for her 18 year interview, Debbie greeted Dr. Brody with an embrace—a show of affection and poise that set her apart from the other 18 year olds. She was happy, accomplished, and had clearly internalized her parents' emotional styles and moral compunctions. She hesitated to speak badly of others, preferring to paint them rosily and talk more of her own not-so-severe faults. When Dr. Brody asked her whom she admired most in the world, Deborah said her mother because of "her compassion and willingness to help others. My mother notices the little things that make people feel good. She sees beauty in the smallest things." Deborah's unalloyed admiration for her mother was connected with more dependency than is typical for her age, and also to a tendency toward denial and altruism to avoid anxiety. Deborah was a less than fully realized youth, and, in fact, chose to go to community college and live at home rather than go away to school.

By 30, Deborah had gained her independence and had left home for graduate school in political science, a field related to her father's. When she was 24 and attending a professional convention, she was first attracted to the young man she later married when she saw him and her father in deep conversation over a journal article. For a moment while they talked, the young man rested his arm on Deborah's father's shoulder in a tender, convivial way. This protective, amicable gesture predisposed Deborah to like the young man when her father introduced him and to fall in love with the man later.

Deborah's closeness to her family—including her choice of a career that crosses over between her father's in political science and her mother's in social welfare—facilitated her being in the right place at the right time to be introduced to her future husband by her father. Lest it seem that the husband is a copy of her parents and that Deborah remains insufficiently individuated from her family, it is noteworthy that her husband is at the left of the political spectrum and her parents on the right. Deborah is in the middle.

At 30 Debbie remains thoughtful, outgoing, and confident. She has a staff position in the Department of Education in Washington, D.C.; her husband is in the Department of Commerce. They regularly travel to New York to be with her parents and sisters. Deborah has matured considerably over the past 12 years and now can speak up directly about what she likes or dislikes in people. Fear of others' disapproval no longer holds her back as much, though other people people's opinions of her remain a mild worry. Like her mother, angry or aggressive thoughts disquiet Deborah. Striking in her psychological testing at 30 was her drawing of a man and woman on the same page *holding hands* instead of, as instructed, on different pieces of paper—an unusual response to the task. On the one hand, her drawing suggests that Deborah still has conflicts over individuating and separating from loved ones, and that she may emotionally merge with them. On the other hand, her pictorial depiction speaks to her affection and empathy for people, a quality that comes through in her behavior as it does in her mother's.

Roxanne. One of nine children in the study whose parents divorced before the children completed high school, Roxanne struggled with the consequences of her parents' bad marriage all of her growing years. The compensation for her efforts is that she is a content, productive adult. The oldest of three sisters, Roxanne was born shortly after her mother graduated from college, while her father was in law school. At first, the mother was excited with her role as a fulltime housewife and mother—acting animated, warm, empathic, and attentive to Roxanne. In the first three months of life, the baby, whose development was extremely advanced, was an energetic, responsive infant with a mobile, expressive face.

However, by the second half of the child's first year, the mother was grasping what marriage to her husband would be like. He arrived home from the library or meetings nightly at about ten p.m. and was away most Saturdays, hours that didn't change when he joined a law firm. For most of her childhood Roxanne only saw her father every three or four days since she typically was asleep before he came home and not yet awake when he left in the morning. She said at 30, "I knew he was there only because I knew the sound of his car on the gravel driveway. I never saw him." The father lamented his long hours and blamed perfectionism for his drivenness in his work, a pace which contributed to his getting high blood pressure at a young age. However there may have been more than work to the time he spent away from home, because he also propositioned one of the women who interviewed him for the project.

Roxanne's mother lapsed into a chronic, resentful, lonely depression which she tried to combat with denial, superficial cheerfulness, and having two more children. When Roxanne was six months old, the observer wrote, "The mother's eyes are heavy and sad, and there is no longer anything vibrant in her although she tries to mask this with her loquacious friendliness. She often spoke with endearing words to the baby but at the same time she wasn't really there emotionally." Roxanne lost her vigor in the succeeding months, became increasingly irritable, and needed her mother's presence to function adequately on her testing. At one year, the mother was ". . . excessively permissive and gave no real direction to her child. Though fond and gentle, she didn't seem to enjoy holding Roxanne until the very end of the visit when the little girl fell asleep on her shoulder."

As the child grew older, her mother became increasingly cursory with her, especially as the other children were born. When the children's rambunctiousness wore the mother out, she resorted to such denial-ridden explanations for their behavior as attributing it to low blood sugar and at other times to high blood sugar from candy. The father remained remote with "nil insight about his daughter," as one interviewer put it.

By school age, Roxanne was shy though manipulatively friendly to get her own way and attention. She hated her academically high-pressured school. Although her intelligence was at least average, and she tried hard, she fell to the bottom of her class. Her teacher observed, "Her performance is hampered by her fear of being wrong. She needs a buildup of confidence." At seven years, her evaluator wrote, "Socially and emotionally Roxanne seems to be developing into a cold individual, withdrawing from the outside world. Her tension stifles her ability." When the parents asked Dr. Brody for advice, she told them that the school might be too demanding for a child struggling with over-inhibition and self-esteem problems, but the mother kept her in the school, swayed by the fact that Roxanne had a circle of friends and didn't want to leave.

Ironically, in view of the tense, if not bitter, home climate, when her interviewer asked Roxanne in her seventh year who her favorite person was, she said, "I have two. My mother and my father." At home at least, she could speak up forcefully, yell and cry over frustrations, and tell her parents, "I'm not going to have any kids. I don't ever want to be a mommy and do all the work." She frequently argued with her parents, and they retorted with room restrictions and grounding, a process that did help Roxanne learn to accept compromises.

Finally her parents divorced when she was in eighth grade. After the divorce, the father spent at least a day a week with Roxanne, time which she enjoyed and could count on. The mother returned to school, obtained a graduate degree in library science, and found satisfying employment. In her senior year in high-school, Roxanne was in many ways similar to herself in childhood—comely and largely cooperative with non-family members, yet still tense, anxious, and self-doubting. Roxanne remained "tied in knots," as she put it, over taking tests and doing homework, and her grades were mediocre. More positively, she felt much less shy and could speak up—even yell—at friends when she wanted. However this flowering of assertiveness also revealed underlying anger and aggression which her former shyness had suppressed. Roxanne's anger in turn led to shoplifting and highway speed violations, for which she was arrested. Dr. Brody's impression was, "She has a certain amount of thoughtfulness about herself, though she denies rebellious feelings and shows no thoughtfulness about society. She is superficially cheerful, though hungry for affection. She lacks inner direction and is comfortable only with friends, especially her boyfriend."

Roxanne reminds us of Ulla in chapter three, a child of divorce who internalized distress in early childhood and later acted out her impulses with youthful delinquency. But Roxanne's parents were far less disturbed than Ulla's. Ulla's mother was narcissistic and erratic, and her father was not only a heavy abuser of drugs and alcohol but physically abusive as well. Both of Roxanne's parents became better role models after the divorce, and as a youth, Roxanne had the opportunity to continue her emotional development rather than find it prematurely foreclosed by ongoing adversity. In essence, in youth she experienced a gradual emotional liberation. Some years later, Roxanne recalled, "I can't believe how I changed when I arrived at college. For so many years all I had been doing was yelling at my mother or not speaking to her at all. And then the first thing I did when I got my own phone in my dormitory room was call her up to talk with her. We've been doing that several times a week ever since." These words are music to the ears of any parent who has struggled through difficult teenage years with a child.

Roxanne continued, "I've forgiven my father for how he ignored us all those years. As a child I didn't know how unhappy my parents were. When my mother told me they were getting divorced, I was really shocked. But I can see now she tried to hang on as long as she did for our sake." As a grown woman, Roxanne is forthright, sincere, energetic, and enjoying life. She married her second boyfriend in college, and though she never became an academic achiever, she did take a degree in fashion marketing and now has a management position in a suburban department store. Roxanne also works hard to broker peace between her parents and her youngest sister who is rebelliously rejecting her parents' values. On various scales, Roxanne uses a range of psychological defense mechanisms. She relies considerably on suppression and self-assertion which are High Adaptive, mature defenses. On the other hand, she also uses less mature defenses at the levels of Mental Inhibitions, Minor Image Distortions, and Disavowal to avoid awareness of internal emotional conflicts: reaction formations against unacceptable impulses, repression, intellectualization, over-idealization of people, and projection. Her charitable feelings towards her father spare her from the guilt and anxiety that would come from anger at him. At the same time, she recognizes that as a grownup she is still trying to impress him and get positive responses from him to overcome the feeling of having been ignored by him in childhood.

Roxanne has made sure her husband is cut from different cloth than her father. A chemist with a pharmaceutical manufacturer, he is home daily at an early hour for dinner, adores their three year old daughter, and readily helps with the childcare. Roxanne played blocks with her daughter as part of her followup. she had a tendency to momentarily drift off and concluded the play before her daughter had finished building and playing out her story. Nonetheless, Roxanne's general interaction with her daughter was pleasing, and she was far more present with her daughter than her lonely and depressed mother had been with her.

In spite of her good adult adjustment and her generally successful emotional working through of both her painful childhood and the parents' divorce, Roxanne has not escaped their effects. The psychologist reading her adult tests reported, "Her responses suggest immaturity and emotional impoverishment, perhaps because of limited emotional resources or limited cognitive resources, or both. Because her internal resources are underdeveloped, if her environment does not give her sufficient satisfaction she may be prone to turn to fantasy. Her responses were somewhat naive and reflected a simplistic view of people. Her refusal to go beyond stick figures in her drawings also suggests oppositional or impulsive tendencies."

Roxanne has an Insecure-dismissive mental representation of her attachment to her parents. This representation emerged in two ways: beyond saying that she still tries to impress her father, Roxanne cannot articulate further *how* her father's early rejection affects her today. She leaps instead to her solution of forgiving him, albeit a much more emotionally useful solution than holding a grudge. Second, when her husband and child go off without her, she worries that they may die in a car accident. Her inchoate fear of something terrible happening grows out of her insecure relationship with her absent father, frustrated mother, and the divorce, rendering happiness in her own family as an adult untrustworthy. The feeling that contentment and security may be ephemeral may prevent Roxanne from deepening her relationship with her daughter as fully as might otherwise be possible, as her truncated play with her child briefly demonstrated.

Conclusion

In spite of their tenuous beginnings, the seven women and two men in this chapter obtained sufficient sustenance and direction to find contentment in their personal lives, satisfaction and effectiveness in their vocations, and freedom from psychiatric symptoms. At the beginning of the chapter, we speculated that studying this group who overcame adversity might reveal an elixir of successful development. To a certain extent it has. Table 5.1 (Children with Trougled Parenting Who are Doing Well) summarizes findings which point to several sources of the group's strength. For example, although their parents were problematic models, the women and men in the study recognized specific, favorable qualities in them with which to identify. Their parents offered such strengths as a productive work ethic and energy; in several families, the parents modeled self-confidence even though it was sometimes a blind self-certainty, lacking thoughtfulness; and in some families, a parent offered enthusiasm and generosity. In spite of their limitations that prevented optimum empathy and interaction with their children, all of the parents were committed to their children. In this group of nine families, no parent abused a child or dropped out of their lives. By contrast, in the overall study **every** child who suffered abuse, severe neglect, or rejection succumbed to marked symptomatic impairment as an adult.

Chapter 5. Table 5.1 Children with Troubled Parenting Who are Doing Well

	CHILDHOOD		ADULTHOOD		
Case	Adversity	Sources of Strength	Role and Style	Maturity of Defenses**	Vulnerability *(Latent)*
Danny	Manic-Depressive mother, narcissistic father	Mother's self-discipline, father's dynamism, uncle's support	Restaurateur, husband, enthusiastic, forceful	High Adaptive (Level 7)	Desires recognition, wife depressive like mother
Reba	Mother over-controlling and self-involved	Father's generosity, older sibling, family stability	Exemplary parent, wife, forthright, thoughtful	High Adaptive (Level 7)	Anxiety, stress-related asthma
Dafna	Father manic-depressive, mother over-stimulating	Mother's optimism, family support, psycho-therapy, husband	Store manager, wife, forthright, thoughtful	High Adaptive (Level 7)	Anxiety, mood swings, substance abuse
Lorna	Parents brisk and mechanical	Family stability and support	Mechanical engineer, wife, conformity	High Adaptive (Level 7)	Sexual identity conflicts, perfectionism, emotional restriction
Donald	Father unavailable, mother controlling, unempathic	Family stability, mother's support, parents' self-confidence	Sales manager, loyal son, serious conformity	High Adaptive (Level 7,6)	Inhibition with women, emotional restriction, shame
Lainey	Parents closed, mechanical, self-certain	Family stability, parents'energy and self-confidence	Mother, wife, hair stylist, enthusiastic, hypomanic, rebelliousness	High Adaptive (Level 7)	Insecurity, denial
Carole	Parents financially stressed, chaotic; child parentified	Parents' hard work and support, mother's self-confidence	Teacher, husband, union officer, forceful, hypomanic, conformity	Mental Inhibitions, Minor Image Distorting (Level 6,5)	Insecurity, denial
Deborah	Mother detached in feeding, father withdrew when anxious	Family stability, parents' support and success	Administrator, wife, forthright	High Adaptive (Level 7)	Separation anxiety, anxiety over assertiveness
Roxanne	Father absence, mother lonely, angry and detached	Parents' hard work	Mother, wife, real estate agent, forthright	High Adaptive (Level 7,6)	Anxiety, limited inner resources, simplistic view of people

- Median Global Assessment of Functioning (GAF) for this group = 94 (No symptoms, superior functioning) For all study participants GAF = 81.2. All in this group had Secure Adult Attachment Interview (AAI) (Dafna Earned-secure) except Roxanne.
- ** Mean defense level for all project participants = High Adaptive/Mental Inhibitions (Level 7,6)

Most of the families of children who did unexpectedly well provided a basic stability for their children, which gave the children a sense of predictability, security, and relative mastery in their childhood worlds. For some stability was not rock solid: Dafna suffered from her father's manic-depressive crises, Carole from her family's economic insecurity, Roxanne from the parents' bad marriage, and Danny from his mother's recurring depressions. Some of the participants who did better than expected benefited from important support from people other than their parents, such as Dafna from her psychotherapist and her second husband; Danny from his uncle and housekeeper; and Reba from an older brother and sister who helped her see that her mother's selfishness was not the child's doing.

Another striking correlate with success in the face of adversity is being a woman. In the group of nine, seven were women; in general in the project, boys who received less than optimum parenting in early childhood were less likely to be doing as well in adulthood as women with correspondingly difficult backgrounds. Clinical investigators (S. Freud, 1905; A. Freud, 1965; Blos, 1979) have described a boy's early emotional development as more arduous than a girl's. A boy has to detach himself from his initial identification with his mother and transfer it to a father who can then become the primary parent with whom the boy identifies. A girl's development follows a straighter trajectory, a directness which may allow for more emotional firmness and less vulnerability. Additionally, social and cultural pressures on boys to be strong, assertive, achieving, and self-sufficient compared to those on girls to be supportive, attractive, personable, and competent (each gender also urged to suppress qualities in conflict with the norm) may be more arduous for boys. Both of the two boys in the group of nine who did better than expected had stronger elements of bisexuality in their makeup than most of the males in the project—Donald with his very close tie to his mother, and Danny with his pleasure in the kitchen and in feeding others.

Surveying coping style, the group's defenses are largely at the mature, High Adaptive level, though not uniformly. Carole has a panoply of less mature defenses—projection, disavowal of troubling emotions and perceptions, identification with the aggressor, and self-compensation with personal attainments for feelings of inadequacy. Her defense mechanisms labor to protect her against the underlying insecurity engendered in her by her family's less than adequate early nurturing and economic marginality. While Carole's defenses help her cope, they also impart a rigidity to her personality unlike mature defenses which impart greater emotional flexibility.

Close conformity to parents' and societal expectations helped three participants. Their compliance allowed them to identify with good qualities in their parents and sublimate or suppress their angry and aggressive impulses. Nonetheless, these conforming children were more emotionally restricted than others in the group who exceeded expectations. Rebellion, the obverse of compliance, played a significant role in one participant's adaptation (Lainy), although her rebellion was more in her appearance and choice of work than in a rejection of her family's underlying values.

A hypomanic personality style may have assisted three in the group with achieving their success. This style is characterized by an unusual degree of enthusiasm, optimism, and energy for life. The potential downside is that this manner of being may involve considerable use of emotional energy to protect the self against inner sadness and mourning, as well as denial of uncertain, conflicted feelings and troubling perceptions. People who cope with enthusiasm and optimism often have under-developed personality qualities of seriousness and self-reflection, perhaps the case with Lainy, Danny, Dafna and Carole.

A clear marker for those who did better than anticipated was having, as an adult, a mental representation of a secure attachment in childhood. Eight of the nine in the group had Secure classifications (Dafna's was Secure-earned-secure) on their Adult Attachment Interview. Only Roxanne, the child of a bitter marriage and divorce, was Insecure.

Table 5.2 (Protective Influences in the Face of Troubled Parenting) summarizes family, community, and gender circumstances that lent themselves to the children's favorable outcome. Nonetheless, the overall findings from this group should dispel the notion that people emerge unscathed from adversity. No potion protects fully. People can indeed triumph against adversity in the sense of doing well with their lives and feeling good about themselves. However at the same time that unfortunate family experiences may not show in an individual's outward comportment, their effects are woven into the unconscious and into the character of the person, governing the range of behavioral and emotional freedom, and making the person vulnerable to emotional symptoms. There is a price to be paid for resilience. Thus, Danny and Carole propel themselves to be important and recognized; Danny repeats his childhood family experience by picking a wife with depressive moods like his mother's; Reba, Dafna, Deborah and Roxanne may be prone to symptoms of anxiety; and Donald struggles with hidden shame.

Chapter 5. Table 5.2 Protective Influences In the Face of Troubled Parenting

(Parents who were depressed, manic, overcontrolling, overstimulating, self-involved, not empathic, inconsistent providers.)

Some effective parent role modeling
Good work ethic
Energy
Self-confidence
Optimism
Enthusiasm
Generosity
Parents committed to child
Parents fond of each other
Absence of Trauma
No physical abuse, severe neglect, abandonment, or divorce in early childhood
Other sources of support
Siblings
Relatives
Housekeepers
Neighbors
Spouses
Psychotherapy
Being female

Our participants embody what historical and literary fictional figures repeatedly show, that there are no heroes without their shadow. Othello, a brave and passionate general, doesn't understand the ways of the heart and succumbs to jealous insecurity. Cordelia, loving and generous, takes so much pride in her virtue that it becomes an arrogance which prevents her from speaking of her love to her father lest she sound like her manipulative sisters, driving the old man to distraction and death. Odysseus, the Greek leader whose name is synonomous with a journey through life, leaves his home to conduct the affairs of his state, but becomes a stranger to his family. So too, the paths of those in the project who have outstripped early misfortune are colored by the ambiguous duality of weakness and success.

Chapter 6

FAMILY COUNTS: Continuity, Discontinuity, Coherence, and Symptoms from Birth to Age 30

What's past is prologue.
Shakespeare, The Tempest

SHORTLY AFTER ALL the participants in the study had been interviewed, we found ourselves one fall day walking along a little-used country road and wondering what we would discover when we looked at the childhood films and read the histories of the people we had just met. As we were walking, we noticed suddenly that there were apples lying in the ditch at the edge of the road. In clumps of two or three, or just one or two every few feet, some still red and others turning gold, the apples glowed as they softened in the sun. There were no apple trees in sight, however, just a steep hill that rose from the side of the road. Curious, we climbed up the hill and at its crest found a meadow with an old abandoned orchard. The apples along the road had rolled all the way down from the trees at the edge of the orchard. Further back where the ground was flat, fallen apples lay neatly under the trees, their sweet cider smell saturating the air on that hot day. We were reminded of the adage, "The fruit does not fall far from the tree." To our minds that saying previously had meant that children turn out much like their parents. On this day in the country, we also saw how the fruit can roll a very long way from the tree, especially if the tree itself is leaning or on uneven ground.

Our experience in the country presaged what we learned from the 76 participants after we had connected their present with the past. Family counts. It counts in ways that we had not foreseen, and for ways we had anticipated. We now have a fuller appreciation of how children's emotional development unfolds stepwise in a timely, smooth fashion by intricately interweaving family influences, chance, and our species' inborn biological dependence on parents' care, security and predictability.

Sometimes it even seems that family doesn't count much at all, that circumstances beyond parents' influence are more powerful, until closer examination reveals the familial imprint. By imprint, we do not mean DNA, even though genetic patterning assuredly connects children to their parents. Rather we mean the stamp of events both brief and repetitive that occur within a home. In studying the 76 lives, we see family experience reveal itself over and over again in children's personalities. Their wishes, fears, and unconscious fantasies control, like a boat's big invisible keel, much of their course in life. Family experience shows strikingly in children's anxiety, depression, and disturbed behavior, and as well as in their psychiatric difficulties as adults. Were it not for being able to look at individuals closely from birth to age 30 and see how coherent their lives are, how their strengths and weaknesses make sense in terms of what they have lived through, we would have greater need to rely on purely hereditary explanations for their behavior.

For example, Nick (chapter one, Successes) shows the power of family experience in his description of his mother, "She just comes into a room full of people and she'll get excited and suggest something to do or talk about and her enthusiasm has a contagious effect." Nick grew up basking in his mother's contagious enthusiasm—which we know to be present because the researchers filmed it and also felt it—and at 30, Nick radiates it himself.

Kandis's mother (chapter two, Childhood Distress Externalized) radiated a far different contagion. When Kandis was but a few days old, her mother said, "I will get rid of a child who doesn't mind me." As the weeks passed, the mother didn't let her baby play if it meant disorder, and distastefully scrubbed away every mess Kandis made, whether on herself or in the home. "Indulging children is a weakness and they will find you out," the mother said.

Kandis internalized her mother's distaste for her and said when she was a schoolgirl, "I'm the most unpleasant thing I can think of because I'm mean to myself." As a teenager she said, "It was not as if I felt deprived of love as a kid because I didn't know what it was to have any." Dr. Brody echoed, "She has a loving, gentle quality but her will has been squashed. She is emotionally starved and doesn't know how to get out of it, her feelings are so tied up in rage and sadness." As a lonely, melancholy adult, Kandis responded, "I try to smile. I try to treat people better than my parents ever did me." In Kandis's case the mother's ill nature enveloped her daughter with a feeling of unworthiness.

Studying lives across time affirms parents' sobering, humbling power in shaping their children, but the surprises we encountered give new perspectives on child development and adult emotional vulnerability. Most striking was the cumulative, damaging force of traumatic experiences in childhood such as physical abuse, illness in a family, and divorce on later emotional health. Startling also was how fully formed the personalities of most of the children were by six or seven years of age (formed in terms of their basic moods, style of behavior, defenses, sense of self as, for example, competent, sociable, shy, insecure, etc.) and how pliable and susceptible to influence their personalities were until three or four. We were also impressed with how hard children labor internally to make sense of their families. Connected with their hard work is their marvelous inner inventiveness in using chance experiences and finding external supports to construct their psychological life and manage confusion or distress. Surprising has been the ubiquity of children's identifications with different aspects of their parents, whether it be with their parents' professions, a parent's favored psychological defense mechanism, or a parent's prevailing mood. Striking have been the unforeseen ramifications of choices parents made—places to live, jobs, roles in the family—on some of the children.

Revelations some participants made at 30 of hidden histories when they were growing up (such as severe physical abuse in a handful of families) impressed, even shocked the researchers. These were events which several of these children themselves suppressed from thinking about (even at 18 years of age) until they were free physically and relatively free psychologically from their parents. Understanding this suppression provides new understanding of the workings of memory over time—its potential for accuracy, distortion, recapture, and longstanding influence on mental functioning. For the first time, we have seen clearly how in some cases psychiatric symptoms in childhood crystallize and endure into adulthood, and how in other cases these symptoms transform into new psychiatric syndromes. Ultimately, we now understand how much is determined by early life and how little; how much is predictable and how little; how much sense it all makes when you look back.

Plasticity and Fixity in Early Personality Formation

In the group of families, neither the initial team of researchers documenting the babies' first weeks of life, nor we, reviewing the records and films, could tabulate traits that persisted. Truculent newborns turned peaceful; passive, listless infants became active and forceful; crying babies were later happy and sociable; cuddly, early smilers changed to irritable, and so on. But by the last months of the first year and early in the second, moods and behaviors started to endure—all other things being equal. That caveat "other things being equal" is extremely important. As people's lives showed, unbidden bad experiences and unforeseeable good influences had the power to bend the trajectory of development *at any age,* even though the greatest vulnerability was early in life. If the trajectory was bent by trauma or adversity, the children were vulnerable to further bad experiences, even willfully re-exposing themselves to painful situations that caused the same distress in order to try to force a better outcome.

For most of the babies, however, in the first twelve months of life the core sense of who they were to be was emerging from the matrix of their relationship with their mothers. This relationship—which gives birth to the child's personality—was transpiring on three levels: *the microkinesic level* of second-by-second mother-infant reciprocal interactions; *the global level* marked by both the mother's moods and her caretaking; and *the neurophysiological level,* where the nurturing an infant receives effects its establishment of neurotransmitter and stress hormone responses, in turn effecting a person's ability to regulate emotions.

Attempts in our study and in other recent longitudinal research projects to describe a child's mental and emotional nature *in the first weeks of life* don't predict what a child may be like later; however, by six to 12 months of life, it is often possible to characterize a child's temperament on the basis of his level of activity, emotional reactivity, curiosity, and shyness—traits that generally persist into later life. This is not always so, as many of our case studies have shown profound changes taking place in the following years under the impact of circumstances in children's lives. Although activity level, emotionality, curiosity, and shyness toward the end of the first year may indicate inherited temperament in some children, in others they may already be responses to the shaping that occurs in the mother-infant relationship. Further, although part of personality, temperament tells little about how a person manages relationships, feelings, or investment in day-to-day activities, the essential human qualities about which our study has been most interested.

Recent findings from studies by Waters (1995), Hamilton (1995), and the Minnesota Child Development project (Sroufe, 1997; Sroufe, Carlson, and Shulman, 1993) that document infants' earliest behaviors and interactions with their mothers, and follow the children to adolescence, are similar to the Brody study's: a child's experience with its principal caretaker and its security of attachment with that parent at the end of the first year and into the second are measurable, and they strongly predict important aspects of a child's behavior later in childhood such as ability to form friendships and work competently in school. In fact, inner security may well be the strongest index of a person's mental and emotional nature. But trust is not inherited, though babies are biologically predisposed to develop it. Experience molds them. Behavioral and emotional evidence of internal working models of security appear, for example, in the profound mistrust and withdrawal in the second six months of life of infants who have lost their mothers, as Spitz (1965) recognized almost half century ago, and in the different types of reactions babies show at the end of the first year when briefly separated from their mothers during the Strange Situation Test (Ainsworth, et al, 1978).

Given the initial plasticity of very young children, it is startling how relatively fully formed most of the children in the Brody study had become by six or seven years of age. By kindergarten or first grade, we see patterns of behavior, thought, motivation, and feeling that enduringly define their personality. Relatedly, Emde (1981) has described empirically how children at about seven years of age begin to feel they are the same person they were at a younger age. The following years enrich their personality with knowledge and experience, grounding and embellishing their lives with choices of work and partners. However, the Brody case studies showed how the individuals' organization of self around relatively discrete ways of thinking, feeling, and acting has been there for the better part of 25 of their 30 years.

This continuity was not true for everybody; although our species has many inborn rules for the progressive evolution of characteristics and capabilities, emotional development can be warped, stymied, even sent into disarray by unfavorable family circumstances and trauma. To elaborate, there are several fundamental, highly interrelated emotional developmental sequences in early childhood that unfold stepwise at relatively fixed ages in all children. These sequences are: 1) The child's basic mood, mental representation of itself, and working model of security internalized from its relationship to its primary attachment figure, usually the mother, between six and 24 months of age, 2) the child's representation of its self as distinct from a permanent representation of its mother, between one and two years, 3) the child's struggle for control of its own body and impulses in relation to its parents and immediate environment between the ages of two and three, 4) the emergence of rivalrous feelings with the parent of the same sex for the affection of the parent of the opposite sex, between the ages of three and five years, and the ensuing working through of these feelings—a process that is closely connected with learning to express affection, manage aggression and rivalry, experience the sense of right, wrong, and guilt, and erect psychological defenses to channel each of these emotions, and 5) the establishment of basic identifications with attributes of the parents, including their emotional styles, habitual defense mechanisms, and behavioral mannerisms, in the first five years of life, usually largely with the parent of the same sex.

As we have seen, first identifications and a sense of security emerge from the interaction with the mother in the first year of life. The other steps unfold from experiences with the father and mother together, with additional influences from siblings, other caretakers, and relatives in the child's life. If there is no father in the family to draw the child out of its exclusive orbit with the mother, the child may turn to others to broaden its experience. Families that have one parent due to the absence of a father or loss of a father or mother due to death or divorce in the very early years of a child's life offer children considerably different emotional balances than do two parent families. In the families we studied, divorces occurred after the children's pre-school years so that we were not able to differentiate the impact of parental separation in the earliest years from that in subsequent childhood. Yet even when parenting is less than favorable, most children's inborn flexibility allows their basic development to unfold on schedule, although their life stories show how early experiences stamped and colored their personalities by accentuating impulsivity, increasing anxiety, heightening sadness and anger—all leading to defensive attempts to manage these states.

A few children whose families were extremely disturbed did not develop like the others, or even on schedule emotionally, and at age seven it was impossible to see the outlines of who they would become as adults. We highlighted two: the first was Ulla (chapter three, Childhood Distress Internalized), at seven passive, shy, awkward, and sad. "A frightened, lost soul appealing to her mother for help . . . as if she is holding herself together for fear she will fall apart." Slow to develop, immature for her age, and unhappy, Ulla had been manipulated and neglected by her parents in her earliest years. When she was seven they divorced, and Ulla began a gradual transformation into the beautiful, poised, self-promoting fitness instructor and aspiring film-maker she was at 30. Along the way she had fitful contact with her father who shared illegal drugs with her when she was an adolescent and on more than one occasion beat her. She herself vandalized property as a teenager. Now an adult, Ulla is very narcissistic, lacking a solid identity and emotional core, and trying to compensate by playing roles and winning adulation which brings her alive.

Danny, the restaurateur, was also unusually unformed by school age. His mother was a hard-working, overly-disciplined, depressed physician with periods of manic excitement who took her life when Danny was in college. His father was a hearty but inconsistent, exhibitionistic drama professor. They were not neglectful parents, and each in their own way was a forceful and sometimes positive presence in Danny's early life. Indeed, they were so forceful and different from each other that Danny struggled to make sense of the cross-currents of their influences and become his own person. His teacher described him in school as "The ablest of diplomats, the rudest of companions." Well into his youth, his emotional life was replete with contradictions. Dr. Brody feared "the seeds of manic-depression in him" because of his efforts to contain anxiety with denial and exaggerated confidence, while the psychologist at 18 saw in him the "potential to become a creative powerhouse." At 30, Danny's successful restaurant was an embodiment of creativity and prodigious energy.

Ulla's and Danny's early immaturity and developmental vacillations were exceptions to the relatively straight developmental lines of the great majority of participants. Tatiana (chapter one, Successes) is representative. Her school observer said of her, "She has one of the sweetest faces I have ever seen. Her schoolroom is incredibly regimented, run by a woman with an abrasive voice and chastising manner which subdues all the kids. Tatiana handles this the best, with the longest attention span, the best behavior, and an impressive ability to work on her projects. She has an intense desire to impress the teacher and is somewhat too goody-goody. Though at times too didactic with her classmates, she is also generous and helpful." At age 18 Sylvia Brody wrote, "This is a girl of uncommon worth. Her relations with people are sound and reflect a pious, loving home. There is an unassuming simplicity and giving quality that is uncommon these days. I cannot but feel that there are strong repressions of feelings, fantasies and impulses in her but they are wholesome repressions and may allow her to use her energies productively and with much gratification because her relationships with people are so positive." Tatiana's repressions and obsessive-compulsive personality style and defenses were well formed by the time she was in first grade—the legacy of a well-structured and loving upbringing, her parents' similar defenses, and an extended separation from her parents in the second half of the first year that created a need to bind underlying anxiety with repression. Her personality from childhood still guides her today in a successful, contented life as a wife, consumer-advocate agency staffer, and law student. In her work she looks out for the well-being of people and corrects those who would take advantage of others.

A somewhat different, but no less coherent path to adulthood occurred for some participants whose personalities were well discernible by seven, and who have accentuated or attenuated these personality tendencies with the passage of time. Thus by seven years of age, Frank (chapter two, Childhood Distress Externalized), was extremely restless, which was a manifestation of his inner emptiness, his need to generate excitement to ward off depression, and angry rebelliousness. However, he was also beginning to subdue his restlessness with obsessive-compulsive defenses. Now in adulthood, his obsessive—compulsiveness has clamped down so firmly on his emotions that he has lost his inner life All that remains of his childhood restlessness is his run-on speech and his inability to stay with any vocational path. He has pathologically turned his aggressiveness inward and against himself in the form of psychosomatic preoccupations and latent suicidal impulses. Conversely, Dafna (chapter two, Childhood Distress Externalized), hyperactive like Frank in childhood, has attenuated her early tendencies as an adult. She continues to manage her inner tension by keeping busy and with lively verbal expressiveness but has found peace from her former "sense of a storm always brewing," first through psychotherapy, then by distancing herself from a childhood family that was "always on the verge of disaster," and finally by marrying a man who is "not a kid like my father or first husband . . . and practical like my mother but calmer."

The Internal Work of Childhood

Family counts so much that it preoccupies children all their years of growing up. Children are constantly working to understand not only their mothers, fathers, brothers, sisters—even pets—but also the feelings these figures arouse, and their own place in the constellation. The sense children make of their family says as much about a child's own self-concept as it does about the people with whom they are living. We can somewhat grasp how children work at understanding themselves in their family by thinking about our own childhood, but ordinary memories may not reveal the unceasing bewilderment, struggle, fear, triumph, and intensity of emotional work, especially in the early years of life. The participants in the study, on the other hand, revealed tremendous mental family toil. Through interaction with researchers who helped them express and explore their feelings and experiences, the children gave uniquely repetitive windows into their psyches at different stages of life.

The stories children told about animals were central to revealing their preoccupation with their families. The Children's Apperception Test pictures animals of different ages engaged both in human-like activities (e.g. riding bicycles) and in the wild (e.g. sleeping in a cave or stalking another animal), and when shown to children helps them suspend normal reticence. Our participants told stories about each of the pictures at four, five, six and seven years of age, and at 18 responded to a more advanced set of images. Their families were so present in the children's thinking that they almost always told a story about family members and their feelings about them. The children's stories depicted family relationships that strikingly replicated and enriched the researchers' observations of family members' behavior. Emotions of child figures in the stories were often similar to feelings the researchers themselves experienced interacting with these same parents. Story events also correlated closely with real-life family experiences the parents had reported, such as birthday parties, accidents, illnesses, or fights.

Rarely was a child's reaction to a picture unfathomable, but one such instance occurred when Luke (chapter four, Promise Lost) angrily pushed away the picture of a kangaroo family bicycling along a path and refused to make up a story about it. He did this at three, four, and five years of age. Some 25 years later he clarified his mysterious reaction by telling his interviewer that he had started playing the violin when he was four, and that it had been isolating and lonely growing up as a child prodigy, isolation that continues to this day. He recalled his parents trying to stimulate him, as was their habit, by decorating his childhood room with natural history scenes. On one wall, they put pictures of kangaroos. Paradoxically, he remembered how he envied the animals contentment together, imagining himself in a pouch in his mother and feeling angry at her because of his discomfort. Significantly, Luke's childhood record revealed that his parents had overstimulated him with too much sexual information at a very young age, bringing him into the delivery room when his sister was born. It is likely that Luke's refusal to look at the kangaroos was also connected with sexual fantasies and fears, a sense of exclusion from other children, and a flight from feelings. The original research team did not know about the actual pictures on his wall. With the advantage of hindsight, we see in Luke's phobic reaction to the pictures his pain in dealing with his overstimulating parents, and by the time he was in school, his already fixed sense of isolation and discomfort with emotion.

Children's play also demonstrated their incessant focus on family. For example, Frank's story telling illustrates how play can reveal a child's central preoccupation. Frank placed a male and a child figure in a doll-room, saying, "This is daddy and this is me. I'm making a room for daddy where I can keep him with me to play with me." In real life, his austere father was little able to share pleasures with his son. Bereft of companionship and regularly spanked for his restlessness, Frank by five was "plagued with much underlying aggression and a poor-self image." When he played fantasy games he was a monster or robot from outer space; in real life, he tried valiantly to be good. Judging from the vividness of his play, if Frank had been given the opportunity to engage in play therapy as a child, it is likely that he would have been able to make very effective use of it. In play with a therapist, he could have effectively expressed his unhappiness and received support and relief from it. If this had occurred, it is likely that he would be far freer with emotion and more engaged in life today.

Family members figure constantly in dreams. The "royal road" to understanding thoughts and feelings—Freud's (1900) phrase—were the dreams participants recalled at 30. They could still remember striking nightmares from childhood, or dreams that had kept coming back over and over again. Almost always about feelings originating in their families, dreams showed how the process of working out feelings about parents and siblings is lifelong. Frank's dream of being chased by a monster and his gun not going off has four likely meanings: 1) his sense of himself as monstrous because his father won't play with him, 2) his sense of being monstrous because he displeases his parents with his restlessness, 3) his misfired aggressiveness, and 4) his stifled sexuality.

Chuck's triumphant, recurring hockey dream (chapter two, Childhood Distress Externalized) ("I shoot with all my might. The puck goes in as time runs out. We win the game. The crowd erupts. I'm famous. I'm rich . . . but I'm too exhausted to enjoy it.)" encapsulates his lifelong attempt to prove and justify himself to his mechanical and controlling mother.

Nolan (chapter three, Childhood Distress Internalized) still remembers a nightmare he had in elementary school. In the dream, a teacher gives him a problem. When he can't solve it, the teacher takes him to a haunted house and " . . . dumps me off in the black of night." He's terrified and suddenly realizes he's standing in front of his own house. He thinks he should go to his brother's bedroom but then hears a noise from the basement. "A voice out of nowhere says, 'don't go down there. It's dangerous.' My hand turns the doorknob and I descend slowly. It's bright and there are friends down there." The dream freezes in time the panic he really once felt when his mother forced him against his will onto a summer camp bus. It also captures his attempts to connect with people, which continue to this day. Nolan added that he was sure the teacher also represented his domineering father and classroom teachers he felt he couldn't please, as well as his mother. Additionally, the teacher probably also represents Nolan's harsh, critical conscience—already firmly established in childhood—which has blocked his spontaneity and made it difficult for him to enjoy himself.

Earliest memories in life were graphic apertures into children's early emotions. In the project, contented, successful people with effective parents and no exposure to trauma were much less likely to remember childhood nightmares or recurring dreams. Their earliest memories spoke to the pleasure of early family experience. Nick's first memory (chapter one, Successes) went back to his second or third year: "I'm running down a hill with my father. The thrill of doing it was like a daydream. It was like flying over the ground." The recollection captures a little boy's exhilaration that he can do wondrous things in the company of his father. Nick's other earliest memories were more ambiguous. He remembered getting separated from his mother at the playground when he was about three, and panicking. He wandered around looking for her, getting more and more scared until, "All of a sudden I saw her and had this tremendous sense of relief. She picked me up and hugged me and the whole thing was over."

Nick went on, "There was also the time when we were driving and there was one of those real dramatic hail storms pounding on the roof of the car . . . I don't recall my mother's reactions but I do remember a very strong sense of her presence that made things all right." This memory is likely a screen memory, condensing like a dream multiple experiences and feelings. In the memory, Nick expresses both the "hail" of anxiety (his own and his mother's) and the sense of calm as his parents made life secure for him in general, containing their anxiety over his possible kidney illness as a very small child. The hail possibly symbolizes his unconscious perception of his mother's frozen or suppressed tears over the threat of his kidney condition.

People work on their "internal working models of security" for at least the first 30 years of their life. A person's internal working model of security is their strategy for physical safety in their environment, as well as emotional safety in intimate relationships. As Bowlby (1969) described years ago, people first assure their safety as very young children, even babies, by staying close to their mothers upon whom they depend for survival. Thus, bonding between an infant and its primary caretaker, a predetermined phenomenon in our species, flows into a psychological attachment to the caretaker, usually the mother. If the baby can count on its mother to protect it from pain, cold, and hunger, as well as foster a sense of pleasurable well-being, the child becomes securely attached to its parent. In turn, the child and later the adult anticipates that both relationships with other people and experiences in the world, will follow dependable patterns, and that he or she will be safe. We all know, of course, that life does not necessarily run smoothly, but a person with the security of initial emotional stability has the flexibility to make choices that will provide the best chance for ongoing emotional and physical safety. Ensuring security does not include crawling into a fortified hole either literally or figuratively, a view which implies that the world is pervasively dangerous and human connections are to be avoided.

What is impressive is the dual nature of human beings. On the one hand, our initial working model of security casts a permanent stamp on our personality—gives us joy, condemns us to caution, makes our feelings unruly, whatever the case may be. On the other hand, unless all hope has been wrung out of us by chronic deprivation or catastrophe, we do seek to improve our life and can revise an initial insecure working model of security. First revisions occur in the family. After the initial attachment to the mother gives the child a pattern for interacting with others, the child attaches psychologically to the rest of the family, usually beginning with the father who, like the mother, affords protection and ensures survival. Siblings and even pets come next; they too offer feelings of comfort and safety in successful families. A child's psychological strategies of attachment to the different people who play an important role in its life may be quite different, each one "nesting" within the other like the plastic nesting eggs young children like to assemble and disassemble. The relationship with the mother may be seen as the interior-most or core emotional system, radiating its influence outward, while other affiliations wrap around the core, coloring emotional experience and providing the child with its first opportunity to modify—for better and for worse—its internal working model of security.

In order to feel safe with other people while also obtaining from them the support it needs, by the time the child is about five years of age he or she has developed a generalized strategy of closeness, approach, and withdrawal in relationships. However, encounters with particular people—a teacher or classmate, for instance—may activate specific feelings and behaviors similar to those engendered by a father or sibling, a transference reaction in the terminology of psychodynamic psychotherapy. As the years go on, people can find outside of their family many other forces for internal change, among them acceptance from friends, mentors, and helpmates such as spouses; assurance from a supportive peer group; hope based in religious faith; insight from psychotherapy; even the disciplined application of one's own powers of introspection. These resources also can layer a person's mental images of attachment as the inner work continues

In our study we had two specific windows for measuring our participants' mental representations of their attachment to their parents. The first window was the psychodiagnostic testing the children received at four through seven years, in particular the Children's Apperception Test and family drawings. The representations of parents and parent-child relationships that the children created on these tests provided views of their trust versus mistrust, affection versus anger, independence versus dependence and self-doubt, and initiative versus guilt in their relationship with their parents and in themselves—all indices of the youngster's security of attachment in very early childhood.

This categorization, based on projective test psychological probes, parallels Ainsworth's benchmark, observational, Strange Situation laboratory test for security of attachment to the mother, which had not yet been created when Brody and Axelrad began their project. In the Strange Situation mothers and their babies first come into a playroom. After a short time the mother leaves, and the child remains behind with a stranger or is alone until the mother returns in a few minutes. On the basis of children's ability to use their mother's presence and soothing on her return to calm their normal distress, children fall into three basic groups: Secure, Insecure/anxious-avoidant, and Insecure/ambivalent. Like infants categorized by the Strange Situation, indices of security of attachment in our study correlated with the kind of care-taking the children had received earlier: Mothers of more secure young children were more likely to be Group A mothers (those who had more effectively managed their babies' distress, exhibited better control in childcare, shown more empathy, and been more playful with their babies) than mothers of children who were less secure (Brody and Axelrad, 1978).

Since most children maintain their status, change in security of attachment from the emotional point of view does not come easily but it can occur. For example, Waters (1985) found that some insecurely attached 12-month-olds from impoverished, homeless families became securely attached on the Strange Situation by 18 months if their family circumstances changed for the better. After toddler-hood, *behavioral* measures of security of emotional attachment become cloudy because children's reactions are so much more complex and because psychological defenses have become available to mediate and obscure anxiety. Therefore, beyond infancy, researchers emphasize mental representations to assess an individual's attachment to parents. The contemporary standard is the Berkeley Adult

Attachment Interview (AAI) (George, Kaplan, and Main, 1985), useful once a person reaches late adolescence.

As Mary Main, one of the interview's creators, says, the AAI "surprises a person's unconscious" by first asking the interviewee to give adjectives that describe their parents while growing up, and then asking them to give specific experiences that illustrate the adjectives. Some people describe their parents as loving and have many specific memories to illustrate it; other interviewees describe a mother or father as rejecting, and have clear memories of them acting this way; another group fumbles for memories, can't illustrate their adjectives for their parents, contradict themselves, or express few if any feelings about painful events. Taking into consideration descriptions of parents, experiences involving threats of loss or safety during childhood, and the manner in which a person talks about attachment related events, the Adult Attachment Interview provides a picture of an individual's psychological connection to the parents. The test classifies people into Securely Attached and Insecurely Attached, categories which can be further subdivided into Insecure-dismissive of attachment, Insecure-enmeshed attachment, and Insecure-unclassifiable. In several investigations (Diamond and Blatt, 1999) these categories show correlations with emotional health in adulthood and people's effectiveness as parents with their own children.

The Adult Attachment Interview at 30 years of age was our second specific window into the nature of our participants' internal working model of attachment. In keeping with the dual nature of the human personality (fixity and plasticity in early development), and people's ongoing internal work, our findings show that most of our participants who indicated secure attachment by psychodiagnostic testing in early childhood continued to do so on the AAI at age 30, but many also reworked their representations of attachment becoming less or more secure. As our case studies showed, the more time that passes after infancy, the more opportunities there are for people to have corrective experiences which open the way for more emotional freedom. At the same time, our participants showed in raw numbers and in individual life studies how the passage of time meant more chances for bad experiences to take their toll on inner security.

Continuity, Discontinuity, and Coherence in Lives Over Time

Sometimes years later in adulthood when you meet a classmate from grammar school, you recognize him and marvel how much people remain the same. It is equally possible that you may not at all recognize the classmate until you see his name tag or are introduced. Only then you may recall that he was one of the first people with whom you had regular sleepovers, for example, starting back around fourth grade. If a conversation ensues, only glimmers of the childhood friend and echoes of the relationship may occur. But whatever changes have taken place in both of you—profound or slight—much of what both of you were and where you both came from, psychologically speaking, is still there. Statistical findings (see Appendix) from our 30 year followup, like the individual biographies, highlight this.

When we look at which group of parents in infancy a child came from (more effective versus less effective mothers, fathers, and mothers and fathers together) and compare their outcome as adults on the basis of our several scales (Global Assessment of Functioning, Erikson Psychosocial Development Scale, Defensive Functioning Scale, and Security of Adult Attachment), children who had more effective parents *tended* to do better on each measure. However, the strongest and only statistically significant correlation occurred between the quality of mothering the participant received in very early childhood and the participant's score on the Defensive Functioning Scale. That is, children who had the most effective mothering as measured in infancy, quality parenting that for most children continued throughout their childhood, as adults had the most mature defense mechanisms.

A parsimonious explanation for the connection between style of defense mechanisms of a grown child and mothering received in infancy is that the mother's care of a child functions to mediate the baby's inner states of arousal, quiescence, contentment and distress; and her care also mediates between these internal states and the effects of the environment that impinge on the infant in their myriad ways. The mother does this unceasingly in so many ways that include (but are not limited to) putting the baby to sleep, waking the baby, feeding, keeping the child warm, touching, smiling, talking, staying close, moving apart, making and breaking eye contact, restraining the child. In essence the child internalizes how the mother comforts him, fulfills needs, and diminishes discomfort.

What is central is that the *mother's own defense mechanisms mediate how she cares for her child* in going about all of these activities. As time passes the baby achieves the ability to regulate itself emotionally—its internal states and reactions to events in its environment. The child does this through a linked combination of physiological maturation and internalization of, and identification with the mother's ministrations. Her mediation of his early childhood emotional regulation becomes his own mode of managing unpleasant thoughts, feelings, stress, and maintaining equilibrium—in essence the mother's defense mechanisms are taken in by the child and become the child's. This is an essential part of psychological structuralization. As many of our individual case studies showed, psychic structuralization—be it healthy or unhealthy—seems significantly established by early childhood and persists into adulthood. The mother's manner of care—discernible in infancy and continuing in the same mode in her interactions with her child throughout childhood in most of the study families—appears instrumental in her child's intrapsychic development and style of psychological adaptation.

The statistically significant connection between infancy mothering and a child's maturity of defenses in adulthood is a remarkable reminder of the enduring impact mothers have on children. Defenses in many ways define a person's character, the style and stability of their adaptation in life, as Vaillant (1977, 1992), the developer of the scale, has well shown. A person's mobilization of psychological defenses—their day-to-day and moment-to-moment ability to manage pleasant and unpleasant internal feelings, thoughts, and urges, and to some extent external unpleasantness—*is* their psychic functioning in so many respects. Indeed, if a mother is to determine something specific about her child's intrapsychic structure, it is likely to be the shape of his major ego function of mediating internal conflicts through psychological defenses because the mother herself, beginning in infancy, has been the principal person who mediated the child's inner emotional storms as well as adjustment to the demands of external reality.

Two of the other outcome measures (GAF, Erikson scale), while connected with a person's stability, are likely to be more influenced than the Defense Scale by a person's past *and present* circumstances such as losses of friends, encounters with violence, job satisfaction or loss, gratifying partnerships, and fulfillment with children. They are composite pictures of behavioral functioning and satisfaction in life, which appears more evanescent, fluid and fluctuating than the more enduring intrapsychic defensive functioning. Nonetheless psychological structure also has some potential for shifting. Individuals can cross-over from Insecure responses on the Strange Situation to Secure in their toddler years, and from Insecure on the Strange Situation to Secure mental representations of attachment on the AAI at age 30, and vice versa. Defensive functioning, though relatively fixed by middle childhood, may shift to lower or higher levels in the face of favorable or buffeting circumstances, as shown in our and Vaillant's longitudinal studies.

Choice and Chance

Families are like the proverbial pot of simmering soup to which a little something is added each day, gradually changing the flavor. Sometimes parents made decisions to add a new ingredient at odds with the soup, or chance intervened like an inadvertent spice, triggering an alchemy which changed everything in ways nobody could anticipate. Families in the project made moves from one community to another, took new jobs, parents switched bread-winner and homemaker roles—decisions which not only altered the adults' lives but also the children's, profoundly influencing the kind of people they became. Sometimes fate also intervened, forever affecting its victim or beneficiary.

For instance, when Oscar (chapter five, Promise Lost) was seven his parents *elected* to leave New York City to run a mission in the shantytowns outside Lima, Peru. There Oscar encountered unbidden death four times by the time he was 18—a young man's body in a trash pile, a woman jumping in front of a bus, his sister's boyfriend shot by police, and his own friend knifed in a fight. With his parents unaware of the traumatic effect of these encounters, losses, and his emotional needs, Oscar threw up psychological barriers against trusting that relationships could be permanent or his future rosy. He became a wry cynic. However, his characterologic defensive style has only been partially effective in helping Oscar suppress the impact of his childhood encounters with death and get through his days. He suffers chronic anxiety and anxiety-related physical symptoms. He longs for a permanent relationship with a woman, but post-traumatic images of bodies and the death of his friend continue to flash into consciousness when he contemplates intimacy with a girlfriend. As a result, he mentally links sexual assertiveness with harmful aggressiveness and loss, inhibiting his own normative assertiveness for fear that harm and betrayal might come from it.

In other families, Frank's (chapter two, Childhood Distress Externalized) parents' decision to move to a new community took him away from friends who had felt like a surrogate family to him and were the source of brightness in his life; and Luke's parents' (chapter four, Promise Lost) bittersweet choice to foster his musical talent substituted a cloistered conservatory education for the rough-and-tumble of regular school. Today, Luke feels painfully awkward socially.

More auspiciously, Victor's parents (chapter one, Successes) made a brave and selfless decision to save their marriage. The father—putting his family before his career—gave up his dream of being a successful, admired New York City writer and became a homemaker and part-time artist in a small town, which allowed the mother to work full-time outside the home and earn a regular income. The parents' choices made them unusual role models on which Victor capitalized in creating his own winning personality, mixing his mother's pragmatic competence with his father's nurturing and creativity.

A child's capacity to sculpt a lasting mental response to chance experiences is prodigious. Olive's reaction (chapter four, Promise Lost) to her father's removal of her falling-down swim suit top during a backyard party when she was seven wove in her mind as a form of sexual assault that continues to this day, anger which in turn repetitively leads her into acrimonious relationships with men. As researchers, however, we understand that the sources of her reaction went even further back. At the time of the party, Olive's relationship with her father was charged with too much intensity because her sister's untimely birth when she was 14 months old—the conception itself a matter of chance—had displaced her at too young an age from her closeness with her mother. Then the mother also became sick. Olive turned to her father for nurturing, and he tried to respond. So when he removed her swim suit top at an age when modesty is usually not a big issue for children, she was emotionally predisposed to read and feel too much into it.

Reba was lucky that (chapter five, Expectation Exceeded) her older brother and sister counseled her when she was in kindergarten that she was not to blame for her mother's self-involved selfishness. This enduringly liberated Reba from the kinds of self-doubt, self-recrimination, and inhibition of assertiveness that occur when a child spends the formative years of life trying to understand a parent's coldness and criticism. Under such circumstances self-inhibition saddled Frank, and to a lesser extent, Reba's older brother and sister.

To give them meaning, children's minds assimilate chance events into their pre-existing web of experience. If the meaning is powerful, it can permanently change emotional functioning. Eddy's encounter with the woman with an eye patch (chapter four, Promise Lost) is another such chance moment. When Eddy was four, while his parents were vacationing he stayed with a baby-sitter who was wearing an eye patch prior to surgery for a splinter in her eye, and heard her husband ask her, "When will it come out?" Eddy took this to mean the eye, not the splinter. His confusion would have been innocent enough even though it understandably filled him with fright, but in an amazing mental feat, he sexualized the misunderstanding, so that to this day his most intense sexual arousal is in connection with images of women who have an eye patch or are blind. How did this concatenation of overheard words, vision of mutilation, sexual arousal, and permanent emotional attachment to a fetish image of a woman with a patch over her eye come about? What we saw on film was that Eddy had an unusually sensual relationship with his mother in infancy, as well as an unusually fond, stimulating relationship with his father, too. We also had good evidence from a recurring dream he reported during his followup that he was anxious about being separated from his parents while staying with the babysitter. Because of his especially loving, stimulating home, Eddy was probably predisposed to feel affection for the woman with the patch. Thus the fearsome image of the woman losing an eye—a snapshot that incorporated his state of ongoing erotic arousal with fears of body mutilation and separation anxiety—imprinted itself in his mind in connection with his simultaneously aroused state of affection toward the babysitter and anxiety over being separated from his parents.

Eddy's encounter with the woman with an eye patch during a state of heightened emotional arousal, like Olive's sister's conception while her mother was still nursing, illustrate the variety of chance occurrences that can mark any person's life, and which neither wisdom nor carefulness can foresee or prevent. That they have had powerful and not altogether good impacts on the emotional life of both people, especially Olive, is true. But chance also provides the potential for the rich and startlingly intricate psychological development that characterizes human beings.

Trauma and Sustenance

Families were the source of most of the adversity that the children experienced, even though their parents envisioned providing their children a safe, nurturing oasis when they were born. Many parents simply couldn't live up to their good intentions because of external circumstances such as poverty or their own psychological limitations. For other families, unpredictable events usurped parental control. Sometimes not chance but a choice—such as moves—changed the course of children's lives in unanticipated ways. Many of the chance events became traumatic, but also the opposite—sustaining, supportive, rescuing, and protective experiences. In a broad sense, anything that threatens the security of a child's attachment to its parent in early life is traumatic, and threatened security leads children to truncate their futures. They participate in relationships at school and work in self-protective ways that range from anxious, depressive coping to combative, counterphobic adaptations. In addition to experiences that threaten a child's feeling of secure family relationships, exposure to physical danger can be emotionally damaging, especially when it involves physical harm to the body, fear of injury, pain, and shame.

Our participants experienced five kinds of family-based traumas in their first 18 years: 1) Losing parents through divorce, 2) physical abuse by a parent, 3) severe emotional abuse by a parent in the form of ongoing denigration, 4) severe mental illness in a parent, typically depressions or alcoholism, and 5) physically handicapping or life-threatening illnesses or accidents in a parent, sibling, or oneself. With the exception of a sibling's illness, these are the threats to the security of a child's attachment to its parents which Bowlby recognized would affect a child's emotional development. In our study specific traumas outside the family were sexual molestation (one boy) or sexual assault (one girl), and witnessing deaths or severe accidents (one boy and one girl). In all instances, the experiences still reverberate 20 years later as shivers of danger in their bodies, and as guilty, anxious thoughts that they could have done more to prevent the event or help others more afterward.

All told, 23 of the 76 participants (30%) had at least one of these traumas, and eight of the 23 had more than one trauma. Encountering more than one damaging experience was not just bad luck; the events were often intrinsically connected. For example, alcoholism, abuse, and divorce often went together in families; handicapping physical illnesses created so much strain that the risk of divorce was high; and parents' mental illnesses characterized by depression, drinking, or erratic behavior were linked to the child being sexually molested or assaulted by strangers or acquaintances outside of the home. Thus, one participant described how as a boy he felt neglected by his mentally ill father and turned to another man as a surrogate father. This man then took advantage of him sexually. The girl who was sexually assaulted had identified with her overly passive, helpless, and depressed mother. Unable to recognize danger, she was taken advantage of by a casual acquaintance.

As our participants' histories and others' research shows (Wallerstein, Lewis, and Blakeslee [2000] found a continuing effect of divorce on children even when parents manage a separation amicably; and Terr [1990, 1994] described the long-term mental impact of relatively brief, random traumatic events) even one traumatic experience has a lasting influence on an individual. Children must weave their personality around it. Most do this weaving reasonably, and the event remains but a small, though detectable rent in the seam of their being. From the statistical point of view *there was no significant difference in the Global Assessment of Functioning of the 15 who experienced one trauma and 54 who did not.* The 15 had no more psychiatric symptoms than did the non-traumatized individuals. However, *the eight who encountered two or more traumas growing up did not fare as well.* As a group, the multiply-traumatized had a median Global Assessment of Functioning of 72.6, significantly below the mean for all the participants (81.2). The multiply traumatized mostly function adequately but are prone to psychological symptoms and problems in their work and interpersonal relationships. They have not fully compensated for their bad encounters.

These findings are consistent with historical investigations of trauma (Khan, 1963) and contemporary studies (van der Kolk, MacFarlane, and Weisaeth, 1996) that point to the cumulative effect of trauma on the mental apparatus—*repeated adversity breaches an individual's capacity to maintain emotional balance, and symptoms and/or characterologic distortions emerge.*

Families can't prevent some traumas. On the other hand, there were ten children who experienced physical abuse by one parent, or regular, harsh emotional denigration and/or rejection by one or both parents, trauma that was theoretically preventable (Chapter Two: Kandis, Farley; Chapter Three: Ulla; Chapter Five: Nita). Their severe maltreatment markedly scarred their emotional growth: their mean GAF at age 30 was 69 (significant symptoms and impairment); defense level immature; psychosocial attainment low; rate of psychiatric diagnosis very high (80%); and incidence of Insecure attachment high (59%). They were making lives for themselves with some success, but all suffered a degree of joylessness, and either symptoms such as depression and anxiety, or personality problems such as pathological narcissism, schizoid isolation, or poor self-esteem.

Encapsulating trauma so that it does not create a major handicap involves finding compensatory sources of sustenance. Children with their relative development flexibility and drive to make a good life for themselves actively work at using assistance when they encounter it. This pattern is not just true for those who were traumatized but also applies to the even larger group who grew up with adversity in the form of less than favorable parenting. Sustenance sometimes came out of the blue, just as misfortune does; sometimes in other cases, help was readily available for the child to assimilate while developing. Dafna's identification with her mother's quality of upbeat denial, her use of psychotherapy, and a second husband's grounding calmness helped her compensate for the chaos her father's manic-depressive disease and mother's over-activity had brought to her childhood household. Farley's identification with his parents' work ethic has allowed him to partially encapsulate his father's physical abuse. The abuse's residue continues nowadays in the form of his occasional anxiety attacks and subdued range of emotions.

Nolan's closeness to his supportive older brother has been life-saving. Danny's ability to discern and identify with his father's ebullience and his mother's self-discipline—while at the same time jettisoning his father's immature exhibitionism and mother's depression—has been of immeasurable value. Additionally, Danny found a role model in his uncle who so appreciated good food and wine. Reba found enduring sustenance in a brief exchange with her older brother and sister when they explained to her that her mother's maltreatment was not Reba's fault. Reba, Danny, Kandis, and others also found support in the presence of gentle housekeepers or parents of friends who provided them with reassurance, encouragement, tranquil voices, and asylums from commotion and unhappiness. For example Reba and Danny internalized their housekeepers' lullabies, soothing themselves as small children by humming to themselves.

Significantly, *experiencing two or more traumas growing up was more likely to lower an individual's Global Assessment of Functioning than having parents who were less than optimal in early childhood.* We have learned that having the best parents makes it easier to become a contented, competent, and emotionally stable adult, but even ideal parents are not an inoculation against trauma. Conversely, traumatized children, or youngsters grappling with ongoing adversity, sometimes find sustenance in their extended family and in their community. Despite parents' limitations and despite the pain some parents inflict, these less favored children even manage to use their parents' good qualities to make a better life for themselves. Finally, many traumas—like abuse and divorce—are potentially avoidable.

Impaired Parenting

What is the meaning of the finding that only one-third of the mothers in the project met the original researchers' direct observational criteria for effective parenting (Group A), and less than one-third of the father's gave positive impressions of their parenting during their interviews (on the basis of their pleasure, thoughtfulness, activities, and knowledge in regard to their children)? To investigate the maternal groupings, Bahadur (1998) independently reanalyzed the archival infancy films with contemporary measures of mother-infant interaction, which validated Brody's 1964 classification. Families came to the study in response to notices in their doctors' offices seeking volunteers for a study of child development. Their motivations for volunteering differed, but troubled parents seeking support may possibly have been over represented. The original research design might alternatively have specified a random selection process, or have explicitly chosen parents from a clinical psychiatric population balanced against an equal number of parents from a non-clinical population, in which case the correlations between infancy mothering and adult outcome may well have been stronger.

Nonetheless, the study's approximate distribution—that one-third of the infants received favorable mothering versus two-thirds less favorable—may be a realistic indicator of the general population. Rampant external pressures (e.g. economic, inconstant fathers, social unrest) and internal pressures (e.g. inhibitions, aggression, projection, self-involvement) can thwart mothers' innate desire and capacity for nurturance. It is not too great a leap to speculate that the same forces that conspire against effective mothering in a significant percentage of the population are also those that make human beings unable to coexist peacefully in many parts of the world, and less than able to nurture the natural environment that sustains humankind. More extensive and deeper pursuit of the epidemiology of troubled parenting awaits future research.

Family Memories

Much that we know about the study children we know to be true because observers saw it and recorded it more than a quarter century ago, because families reported it, and because we saw it on the old 16 mm research films. Like journalists, we have multiple sources. Many of the memories the participants *now* have of their early life give a different picture from the one provided by multiple sources from the past. Unlike static family photograph albums, memories are organic: people revise their recollection of events in different epochs of their life. What changes their recall is the emotion the individual infuses into the memory, emotion that is colored by feelings a person has for the family, feelings which also alter with the passage of time.

What happens to memories is not simply a matter of intellectual curiosity but an urgent issue for many people because their ability to make a better life for themselves and their children depends to a great extent on having coherent feelings about at least mostly accurate recollections. Growing up in many respects is the process of achieving this state of being able to view the past, not with detachment, but with a realistic appraisal of former feelings and events. Many things—such as independence from parents—can facilitate this process. Husbands and wives can help each other revisit their pasts, and psychotherapy can make an important difference.

Examples of memories linked to the emotional context in which they originally occurred are Olive's "memory" of her father "sexually molesting" her by "tearing off her swim suit top," and Eddy's adult sexual arousal by images of a woman with an eye patch, actually a memory of an event when he was four years old and of his feelings at the time. Eddy had "lost" the full memory until his 30-year interview, at which time a concurrence of associations both to a recurring scary dream about ascending a dark staircase, and to thinking about his fetish-like pleasure in one-eyed women allowed him to recover the full memory of the woman with an eye patch and the words "when will it come out," complete with the memory of a smell of the medicine-coated bandage.

After his interview, Eddy confirmed with his parents that he had indeed been cared for by a family friend with a bandage over her eye. He wondered toward the end of his followup if he would lose his sexual arousal in connection with the eye patch fetish now that he knew its source. For Eddy, it was not a particularly pressing issue if the fetish lost or retained its power; though he enjoyed the excitement of the image, he could accept it either way.

For Olive, on the other hand, clearing up what appears to be her distorted memory of her father's action is central to her future. Her rage at her father—anger which she most likely considerably displaces onto him from her disappointment with her mother who put Olive aside when her sister was born—prevents her from forming the kind of relationship with a man she desires. Olive and her psychotherapist are currently trying to understand her anger at her father and its role in her adult relationships.

Other examples of people's memories of their families show how recollections are multiply determined by context, psychological defenses, and the age at which an event occurs. To illustrate his memory that his mother "took good care me," Chuck (chapter two, Childhood Distress Externalized) said at age 30 that when he was five his mother caught him climbing over his apartment's balcony railing to reach for a balloon and scolded him for endangering himself. The actual incident, which the mother and father had reported to the project staff when Chuck was three, was far more frightening and dramatic. The mother had become so upset by her son's self-endangering move that she lost control and kept hitting him until the father heard the screaming and ran to stop her. Similarly, Dafna (chapter two) has no memory as an adult of having been physically punished, even though her parents spanked her often until she was about seven. However, she does have accurate memories that go back to even younger ages of her father's bouts with mania-induced alcohol abuse, including his being found unconscious and hospitalized, and her brother's falling down a bluff. Thus, children relegate some experiences to forgetfulness, experiences that occur well past the stage of infantile amnesia that comes to an end at about three. Their selective forgetfulness seems to be in the interest of protecting their view of their parents, or to put it differently, the amnesia helps disengage them emotionally from their parents by minimizing unpleasant events. Chuck, and to a lesser extent Dafna, are prone to a hypomanic personality style characterized by denial of unpleasant affects.

Writers on and students of development have offered various characterizations about adolescence, each one capturing an aspect of that age. For example, Erikson (1950, 1968) pointed to adolescence as the period during which young people consolidate their identities; Anna Freud (1969) was impressed by the inner turmoil of the age (its *sturm and drang* [storm and urgency]); and Offer and Offer (1971) countered by emphasizing the smoothness with which most teenagers appear to go about the task of loosening their ties to their parents, forming other bonds, and making vocational choices outside their families.

However, for most of the participants in our study, what stood out was that adolescence was an age of denial, blinders, and forgetfulness about what their childhood families had been like. Though closer in time to their childhoods at 18 than at 30, they gave glossed over pictures of growing up with their parents, reporting "I was treated okay," "my parents were responsible," "I could count on my parents." Twelve years later, the same people, now adults, gave far fuller descriptions of their parents, replete with specific memories that showed good and bad qualities. The emotional work they had done in the intervening years allowed most participants to resolve their dependency on their parents and think more analytically about family relationships.

In adolescence, avoiding thinking carefully about families had been central to the process of disengaging from their parents. Teenagers literally had much to hide from their mothers and fathers and almost universally told lies about mediocre school grades, lackluster effort, and with whom or where they had been spending time in order to manipulate more freedom for themselves. They almost universally experimented with marijuana, alcohol, and sex—activities they wanted to hide and keep private even if their parents were permissive. Their process of concealment contained in it a reciprocal pulling the wool over their own eyes about their parents' real attributes. Thus, our participants as teens most resembled Anna Freud's adolescents, struggling mightily between a desire to unleash their impulses, and the need to restrain and channel them, desires and needs that came from within themselves as well as from their families and society. It is teenagers' need to hide their inner life from themselves and others that may give the illusion of relative peace.

We had some knowledge about their true struggles because of our prospective information about their families, and some of the participants themselves only gained understanding of themselves and their parents for the first time when they looked back as grownups without the need for either self-concealment or dissimulation toward their parents. As adults, most reflected with apology for their teenage self-centeredness, untruthfulness, rule-breaking, and anger at their parents. They not only were less secretive about themselves, they were also more clear-eyed about their mothers and fathers.

Although as grownups their memories of life with their parents were less distorted by defensiveness, there is a major area about which adults have no verbal memories. Participants are amnesic about the way their parents cared for them during the first two or three years of life. The absence of memories for this time is not the result of psychological defenses against painful affects or a part of the process of separation and individuation from parents. Nor does the concept of repression do justice to the phenomenon. Rather, the amnesia is there because experiences during this preverbal period are "remembered" implicitly rather than explicitly. Because they do not yet have words to label events, thoughts, and feelings, babies register them preverbally or somatosensorily in their musculature and in the organization of their stress hormone and neurotransmitter responses. As van der Kolk (1996, 2002)) has said about traumatized individuals, when ordinarily verbal children and grownups can't find words to describe traumas they encounter, "Their body keeps score." We know from our earlier case discussions and from the data of the whole project that a baby's interactions with its mother in the first year or two have a shaping effect on the emerging personality of the child. In contrast to the fluctuating though explicit memories of the years that follow, nobody ever consciously recalls what this first relationship was like.

When Dafna as an adult said her mother was playful, comforting, practical, but not calm when she was growing up, she, like many of the participants, can't convey a different but equally important reality about her mother: During her infancy, Dafna's mother was brusque, overly active, and often insensitive. The mother's behavior likely had as important an effect in shaping Dafna's childhood inner tension and hyperactivity as her father's periodic emotional crises, though it is not consciously recalled nor as amenable to numerical measurement as the later trauma of her father's illness. When we wrote about Dafna in Chapter Two, we questioned whether her appraisal of her mother as playful and comforting was based on a mature understanding that her mother was well-meaning and did the best she could. Other reasons suggested themselves: the fact that her mother provided for her in a far more stable way than her father; the mother's quality of upbeat denial; limited contact with other mothers who nurtured differently; or protecting her mother from criticism and herself from guilt that would come if she devalued her mother. Having considered memory more fully, it is likely that each of these mechanisms operates, but the most significant influence in her forgetfulness is her normative amnesia for the first two or three years of life—a lack of explicit registration in words for experiences which, encoded preverbally, remain among the most profound (Massie and Szajnberg, 1997; Fonagy, 1999).

This primal forgetfulness poses a great barrier and dilemma in the treatment of psychiatric conditions that are linked to these forever forgotten early events. For example, many of the participants in the study suffer chronic anxiety, depressions, and personality disturbances marked by defensive grandiosity, pathological narcissism, counterphobic behavior, and unnatural optimism—all connected to disturbed relationships with their caretakers in the very first years of life. In treatment, the patient can't recall what transpired in these early times, and his or her retrospective imaginings and accounts may contain the seeds of truth or mistruth. The therapist must consider both possibilities, and search the posture, muscle tone, voice, and facial expression of the patient for clues to the accuracy of remembrances while he or she recounts past events. What memory exists of the first three years is stored more in the body than in words.

If a patient has a secure and ongoing relationship with a therapist, patient and therapist together can reexperience essential emotions from the patient's past and connect these emotions with words, thus giving *conscious* meaning to past experiences. This naming may make it possible for the patient to disconnect present-day emotional reactions to situations from the past. For instance, the patient may be able to exploratorily revisit past fears of losing an attachment to a caretaker and in doing so, revise his or her internal working model of security in a way that allows more emotional freedom and effectiveness in daily life. Our therapeutic work, and the project case histories, indicate that treatment is most effective and favorable changes most likely to occur in people's lives when we understand the childhood roots of adult anxiety and depressive symptoms, and individuals themselves also understand them.

Sometimes it is therapeutically impossible to undo trauma, particularly if it occurred in the preverbal era of life; then the most effective treatment may be a supportive psychotherapy that helps the patient contain anxiety, limit depression, and make adjustments for personality problems. If damage cannot be undone, psychiatric medications may also be useful for treatment of symptoms, especially those rooted in this earliest period. Psychotropic medications do not cure, but may ameliorate neurotransmitter and neurophysiologically based components of emotional regulation previously made imbalanced—or rendered vulnerable to imbalance—as early as the first year of life.

On the Threshold

We have watched the participants now for 30 years, and one group stands out as having matured the best. It was a shared sentiment we felt after we interviewed them and locked at the tapes of the interviews, and still felt after we reviewed all the information about the participants. But how do we render our pleasurable reaction to these outstanding people into precise words and concepts, we asked ourselves? We knew their attainment and our reaction to them went beyond measurement by scales, although their success was not inconsistent with measurement. All the people to whom we reacted very favorably were in the top rank on the Global Assessment of Functioning, the Erikson Psychosocial Development Scale, the Defensive Functioning Scale, and Secure on their Adult Attachment Interviews. This uniformity reassured us that our reaction was not simply personal or our own value judgment. We knew that their attainment was deeper than even contentment, freedom from symptoms, and education or incomes which, in fact, were often modest.

After much review, it came to us that what we were responding to in the most successful participants was their quality in common of vivid personal appeal. We would have like them as friends and colleagues. We further pondered the group's personal appeal and elaborated 12 components: 1) They had a great deal of available affect—a broad range of emotion. They could laugh, be sad, and be serious. 2) They interacted with us, shared readily, and trusted—a reflection of their good personal relationships in general. 3) They were thoughtful about others and society. Their thoughtfulness contained an empathy and altruism that was mature and did not stem from a defensive reaction against feelings of anger or personal neediness. 4) They had an area of ambitiousness or aspiration in their lives that was not simply aggressiveness or a need for power and control, but did involve being able to muster assertiveness and focus energy. 5) They took care to make themselves physically attractive in keeping with their basic physical endowment. This attention to appearance was a function of healthy narcissism or self-investment as opposed to pathological narcissism that seeks to repair feelings of inadequacy or to manipulate others. 6) They treated us well and graciously, also reflective of their relationships in general.

7) They spoke believably, a function of their honesty, investment in communication, and personal ideals. Effective expressiveness showed the intactness of their cognitive processes. 8) They were decent people in the sense of having strong ethical values, indicative of a well developed conscience. 9) Related to their aspirations, they had in psychoanalytic terms

a well developed ego ideal. That is, they carried within themselves, as part of their identity, an image of an admired person they aspired to be like. The image was connected with a loved person they had internalized, usually a parent or parts of both parents, who softened internal self-demands away from harsh guilt or shame as a guiding force, but also gave them a sense of personal ideals, direction and purpose. 10) Their education and accomplishments were consistent with their intellectual endowment. 11) they were thoughtful about themselves, able to think critically about themselves in an objective way—referred to as having a good observing ego. 12) They had an area of creativity in their lives. For some, it existed in the recreation they enjoyed as adults (e.g. sports, hobbies); for others creativity was inherent in their work and in raising their children. Active expression of these gifts and interests was possible because they were not hobbled by emotional conflicts. Conflicts in certain areas of their emotional life remained limited or were successfully sublimated in work, play, and family life.

Drawing upon Anna Freud's (1965) developmental lines and metapsychological stages, and Erikson's (1959) psychosocial stages of development, we ordered the components of adult personal appeal according to the ages of childhood by which the traits or components appear in the course of growing up (Table 6.1. Adult Personal Appeal and Age Quality First Appears in Childhood). The ages are not precise for there is a range, and many components reappear at later developmental stages to be reworked and further elaborated. Additionally, we know from study of children whose development does not go well that certain traits are precursors of later appearing traits. For example, the capacity for empathy often appears first in children's story-telling play with dolls, figures and toys, and in such situations as asking their mother to help a crying child in a grocery store. Empathy grows from the earlier capacity for trust that appears in infancy, and is itself a precursor for later cooperative play with peers in school. Ironically, although normatively established by approximately three years of age, empathy may be obscured by children's normal assertiveness, push for autonomy, oppositional behavior toward parents, and by sibling rivalry, all of which emerge within the same approximate time frame of three years of age. Similarly, creativity—emerging as a distinct personality trait usually in later childhood or adolescence—links back to earlier childhood imaginative play and industriousness. If children are too inhibited to play in early childhood and too insecure to be industrious in middle childhood, they are unlikely to complete the linkage and become creative adults.

Chapter 6. Table 6.1 Adult Personal Appeal And Age Quality First Appears in Childhood

Adult Personal Appeal	Age Manifest in Childhood
Available affect Socially interactive, sharing, trusting Considerate of others, empathic	Infancy—Toddler-hood (0-3)
An area of ambition and energy in life Care to be physically attractive	Early Childhood (4 - 6)
Treats others well and graciously Believable	Middle Childhood (7 - 9)
Decent, ethical Well developed ego ideal Accomplishment and education consistent with intellectual endowment	Later Childhood—Adolescence (10 - 18)
Thoughtful about oneself, others and society An area of creativity in life	Adolescence (13 - 18)

The men and women with strong personal appeal are typified by the participants described in chapter one (Successes) particularly in the bedrock of favorable parenting from which they come. This group have had the good fortune to escape trauma and have favorable current circumstances in their lives. Some others also come from the group who overcame adverse early family circumstances (chapter five). Sylvia Brody (1978) addressed the sources of their early success in her report on their first seven years, "The children's characters have been determined in part by the intensity and duration of their anxieties; their cultivation of perceptual, cognitive and imaginative abilities; and the depth and stability of the internalizations achieved during infancy and early childhood." If the children were doing well at seven, we found in our adult followup that, they were likely to be still doing well unless they encountered difficult circumstances later.

Recently, while sharing the results of the 30 year followup of her now grown 76 children with Dr. Brody (personal communcation, 2000), we asked her what the 23 additional years of the study had taught her, what it had shown that was new. This time she abjured technical language and answered simply, "Children aren't raised by parents. Their parents don't teach them how to grow up. Children catch it from their parents," a pithy reduction of a lifetime's worth of scientific data. Other investigators have also offered their wisdom. The child psychiatrist Robert Coles (1999), drawing from his career of interviewing children and youth, recently wrote, "Bringing up children is a long, sometimes trying haul for any of us. What really matters of course, is decency, sound judgment, goodness of heart—a capacity for restraint with respect to some of one's impulses and an ability to help a daughter or son to know the need for, the satisfactions that go with, a constraint applied directly and for an understanding reason." Sylvia Brody would not disagree, for this in essence is what children "catch" from their parents.

In writing about development, one encounters a dialectical process at work in which abstractions about processes turn us back to individual lives to learn more and more—and vice versa—to summarize what we learn. We thus think back now to Vicki, the infant who galvanized us during our psychiatric training when we saw the movie of her mother twisting her head around and forcing a spoon into her mouth, over and over again. That image set us on a journey, eventually connecting us with Dr. Brody and then to conducting the 30 year followup of the longitudinal study. It was Vicki who at seven was sad-eyed and too restless and nervous to play with the dollhouse while her mother sat by impassively in dark glasses. It was Vicki who raged at her parents as a teenager and drank herself into unconsciousness at night when she was alone, but who also had a retreat in her kindly aunt's room where she curled up under the bedcovers.

When she was 30, Vicki was thin, with a poor appetite, and suffered from migraine headaches and anxiety. She refused to look at the camera because she said it was "cold." She had been divorced for some time from a youth to whom her aunt had introduced her. She was nonetheless an impressive person. She no longer drank alcohol and was articulate, thoughtful, gentle—the office manager of a dog and cat hospital. She had said, "My parents never should have had children . . . They had the mistaken notion that they could just have us and then they wouldn't have to do anything, that we would just grow up while they ran their business." In Sylvia Brody's words, Vicki had "caught" her parents' coldness, hostility and neglect, transfigured it into anxiety in childhood, rage in adolescence, and back to anxiety in adulthood. As we interviewed her at age 30, she had started dating again and hoped that the good feelings she had shared recently with a man might flower into a relationship. Having children was a long way from her mind.

Recently reconsidering "the myth of infant determinism," the developmentalist Kagan (1998) writes, "Many early ideas and habits either vanish or undergo such serious transformation that they cannot be retrieved in later life, any more than the first strokes of a seascape can be discerned from the larger scene, once a painting is complete." Vicki's life points to the effort she has put into transforming herself into a successful person in the face of great family odds, yet in contradistinction to Kagan's statement, her early childhood insecurity **is** discernible in adulthood in her persistent anxiety, her psychophysiologic symptoms, and her belief that she is not strong enough to make it through veterinary school as she would like. Although Vicki is a very appealing person and is doing far better than anticipated, we could not include her in the chapter six group that exceeded expectations because of her significant emotional symptoms, her unmet desire for a partner, her stymied ambition, and mistrust of the camera that was unique among participants. Unlike the most successful individuals, her strength of character does not come from a fortuitous blending of good experiences, but from enduring adversity with hope and self-discipline so that her appeal is also that of a survivor.

Vicki never returned her take-home psychological test after her 30 year interview. Five years passed. Then one day, out of the blue, in the midst of our writing and data analysis, she called to ask if we were still interested in her tests which she had completed but never mailed. She was 35. What had happened was that she was marrying the man she had just met prior to her 30 year interview and was in the process of moving to his house. While packing up her apartment, she found the un-mailed envelope with the tests in it. We talked by telephone for some time. It was clear that not just finding the envelope led to her call, but also the fact that she had become more comfortable than the camera shy person she had been at 30, and ready to reveal more of herself. Her fiance has been of great help to her in this She said also that for the first time in her life, she thought she might be able to have children, a thought that had terrified her in the past because she feared that she might mistreat a child of her own the way her parents had mistreated her.

She has been in psychotherapy for several years, and with arduous work is learning that the coldness she saw in her mother's eyes growing up was not because of her, not reflecting off herself, but came from her mother's chilling self-involvement. A baby normally looks in her mother' eyes and sees warmth and love, introjects it into herself, where it becomes the baby's sense of herself. When Vicki was small she saw nothing but anger and emptiness of feeling for her in her mother's eyes. We saw it too. This unpleasant void became Vicki's introjection. At 30, she had feared seeing herself as damaged in the camera's eye, as if the camera would seek out an inner mark. Five years later, Vicki said on the phone that she is becoming convinced that she can be an altogether different person from her mother.

Vicki's sister continues to have severe troubles and remains mostly dependent on her parents, at times depressed and erratic, at times excited and hopeful. She has not had a psychiatric hospitalization for some time and goes to therapy regularly. A kind of mentor to her younger sister, Vicki shares with her insights about how she had been affected by their parents as she gains them herself, so as to help her sister speed up her treatment. Along with her own take-home psychological tests, Vicki forwarded a copy of her sister's psychological testing from her sister's first hospitalization when she was a teenager to help us better understand her family. It read in part, "She has severe body anxieties and confusion about how things fit together in a cohesive whole. Her female drawing is of a witch with a broom. Her male representation is a Picasso-like fragmented man with frightening characteristics . . . Severe emotional deprivation of long duration has had a devastating effect on her maturation."

Family counts for good and for bad, but if need be it is possible to make an emotional journey a long distance away from home, rolling like the puzzling apples we found by the side of the road with no orchard in sight. Both the fact that family counts and that healing journeys are possible are the lesson of the Brody study. The playwright Sam Shepard (2001) has written, "It's very strong, the connection between physical territory and inner territory. In America we've run out of the former . . . Now, the spiritual notion talks about something that's even more hopeful because the inner search doesn't come to some Pacific Ocean . . . It's a never ending process . . . Lostness can be profoundly rejuvenating in a way—it's a desperate time but being really lost can start something that's brand new." Or speaking of his characters, he says, their "language is a veil, hiding demons and angels which the characters are always out of touch with. Their quest in the play is the same as ours in life—to find those forces, to meet them face to face and end the mystery."

Perhaps some of "our characters" say it just as well. People like Reba: "Being a real person, becoming a person is a hard job. I still work at it. I ask myself, 'Are you listening to yourself? Can I understand myself? Can I work at changing?' "Or Nick's mother and father: "We didn't spoil what was there." All babies have tremendous capacity, and Nick's parents helped him flourish by knowing when to engage and when to step back. For many parents, this sense does not come so easily. If the lives in this book shed light on any of these mysteries of development and parenting, then we have done our work.

Appendix

METHODS AND MEASUREMENTS

The Statistical Relationship between Mothering in Infancy, Childhood Experience, and Adult Mental Health in the Group of 76

Introduction

In THE EARLIER followups of the participants—at 1 year of age, 7 years, and 18 years—Brody and her colleagues reported that children who received the most satisfactory parenting showed more robust emotional growth than their counterparts who received less satisfactory parenting. But as the children grew older the statistical relationship between parenting and outcome became attenuated.

This appendix provides the **core findings** from the 76 now adult participants relevant to the question of **how infancy nurturing, childhood family experience, and traumatic experiences prior to age 18, relate to adult mental health.**

Methodology from Birth to Age 18

In 1963 and 1964 parents-to-be responded to requests for volunteers for a study of child development in their prenatal clinics and doctors' offices. The families came from all socioeconomic groups and a wide range of ethnicities, the majority being middleclass (Hollingshead and Redlich, 1958) and Caucasian.

Appendix. Table A.1 Procedures from the Third Trimester Through Age 18

Child's Timeline	**Procedures**
3rd Trimester	Interviews with mother (from pregnancy to child's age 7)
Birth	(1964) Neonatal assessment
6 Weeks:	Filmed feedings
6 Months	Developmental assessments
1 Year	Maternal classification; child observations
3, 4, 5 Years	Filmed mother-child play Psychodiagnostics (WISC, CAT, human figure drawings)
6	School observations
7	Teacher reports

Interviews with fathers from ages 4-7 covering same questions as with mother: attitudes to child, hopes, anxieties, routines, child's training, education, events in life, sibling and spouse relationships, parent's childhood.

18 Years (1982) Interviews with youth (family, health, education, goals, leisure, friendships, attitudes to self, others and society, anxiety, conflicts, symptoms, early memories) Psychodiagnostics: WAIS, TAT, Rorschach, Bender, Human Figure drawings.

The original team of researchers classified the mothers into six groups on the basis of ratings of the films with scales for the observationally and clinically derived characteristics of the mother's empathy, control, efficiency, consistency, organization, thoughtfulness, love, friendliness, playfulness, didacticism, and aggression in feeding her infant in the first year (Brody and Axelrad, 1970). For statistical reasons and predictive purposes they clustered the six into a More Effective Mothering Group (Group A) and a Less Effective Mothering Group (Group B). We refer to Group A and Group B parents with such relatively equivalent phrases as "more favorable parenting," "less favorable parenting," "better," "less adequate," "optimum," "less than optimum." Table A.2 summarizes the maternal groups of the 76 children followed to age 30. The demographics of the 76 were similar to those of the original 132 except for a higher proportion of men.

Appendix. Table A.2 Characteristics of Maternal Groups in the First Year Of Life and Numbers of Adult Children

Group A Mothers (n=26):
Empathy: moderate to high
Control/organization: moderate to high, thoughtful
Affect: loving, tolerant, if didactic also friendly.

Offspring at age 30 = 12 women, 14 men

Group B Mothers (n=50):
Empathy: uneven, moderate, low
Control/Organization: uneven, too high or low, inept, peremptory, dominating, overactive
Affect: restricted, inhibited, depresssed, aggressive, hostile, detached, mechanical, impersonal, passive, withdrawn, self-conscious, childish

Offspring at age 30 = 22 women, 28 men

Earlier research by Brody (1956) showed how mothers' interactions with their infants during feeding captured the quality of their overall care for and responsiveness to their children in infancy. In a reanalysis of a subset of the original first year of life films, an independent investigator blind to outcome (Bahadur, 1998)—using the present-day Global Rating of Infant-Mother Play (GRIMP) (Elmore, Cohn, and Zlochower, 1995)—reported that the original researchers' Group A (more effective) mothers received significantly better scores than the Group B mothers.

Table A.3 is a flow chart of the 30-year followup procedures. All interviews—videotaped and audiotaped—were semistructured, allowing participants to associate to their thoughts, feeling and memories; and allowing the interviewers to explore areas of a subject's life that appeared important, affect laden, or defensively warded off. Additionally, subjects who had children of their own were videotaped either feeding their children or playing with them for comparison with the standardized scenes of their mother feeding and playing with them a generation earlier. Interviews occurred in professional offices in New York City, Berkeley, CA, and Boston unless it was too difficult for participants to travel to an office or if they had children of their own, in which case interviews took place in subjects' homes. Participants were reimbursed their out-of-pocket expenses. Interviews were conducted by Henry Massie, M.D., a psychoanalytically trained Board Certified child/adolescent and adult psychiatrist, or Carl Norris, Ph.D., a psychologist, both blind to earlier data on the participants. The review of psychiatric symptoms was drawn from the Structured Clinical Interview (Spitzer, 1989).

Appendix. Table A.3 Flow Chart of the 30-Year Followup Procedures

3-Hour Semistructured Interview

Adult Attachment Interview (AAI)	**Ages 18-30 Interview**
Focuses on security, loss, trauma in career first 18 years of life.	Family relationships,education, health, relationship, leisure, sexuality, children, psychiatric history, early memories, recurrent/ striking dreams, future wishes

House-Tree-Person Drawings

Analysis and Scoring of Interviews
Defensive Functioning Scale: Maturity of defense mechanisms
GAF: competence, contentment, adjustment, impact of symptoms, if any.
Psychosocial functioning: attain Erikson's psychosocial stages.
AAI:Mental representation of security in childhood family.
Diagnosis: DSM IV Axis I or II (if any)

Psychodynamic synthesis of outcome and archival record of childhood history.

Data Analysis

Table A.3 shows the five principal outcome measures used in the 30-year data analysis: 1) Global Assessment of Functioning (GAF) (American Psychiatric Association, 1994), 2) Measures of Psychosocial Functioning (Erikson Scale) (Hawley, 1980), 3) Defensive

Functioning Scale (Vaillant, 1994; Vaillant 1999), 4) Adult Attachment Interview, and 5) presence or absence of a psychiatric diagnosis according to the Diagnostic and Statistical Manual of Mental Disorders (DSM-IV) American Psychiatric Association, 1994). The GAF (condensed in Table 4) rates overall life adjustment, satisfaction, competence, and freedom from, or impairment with emotional and behavioral psychiatric symptoms. The Measures of Psychosocial Function rates the attainment of psychosocial developmental stages as promulgated by Erikson (1950): trust vs. mistrust, autonomy vs. shame/doubt, initiative vs. guilt, industry vs. inferiority, identity vs. identity diffusion, intimacy vs isolation, generativity vs stagnation, and (in later life) ego integrity vs despair.

Appendix. Table A.4 Global Assessment of Functioning (GAF)

91-100:	*Superior functioning*
81-90:	*Good functioning, absent or minimal symptoms*
71-80:	*Slight impairment, transient and expectable reactions to psychosocial stressors*
61-70:	*Mild symptoms, some difficulty in social, occupational and school functioning.*
51-60:	*Moderate symptoms, moderate difficulty in social, occupational and school functining*
41-50:	*Serious symptoms, serious impairment of functioning.*
31-40:	*Some impairment of reality testing or communication, or major impairment in several areas.*
21-30:	*Behavior considerably influenced by delusions or hallucinations.*
11-20:	*Some danger o hurting self or others.*
0-10:	*Persistent danger of severely hurting self or others.*

(Adapted from DSM IV, American Psychiatric Association, 1994)

The Defensive Functioning Scale identifies and classifies into seven groups the prevailing defensive and adaptational maneuvers (conscious and unconscious, healthy and otherwise) an individual uses, starting with Level 7 (highest maturity and emotional health) and descending to Level 1. *High Adaptive* defenses (Level 7) maximize gratification, allow conscious awareness of feelings, ideas and consequences, and promote an optimum balance among conflicting motives (e.g. anticipation, self-observation, assertion). *Mental Inhibitions* (Level 6) keep potentially threatening ideas, feelings, memories, wishes and fears out of awareness (e.g. displacement, isolation of affect). *Minor Image Distorting* defenses (Level 5) involve distortions in the image of the self, body and others to regulate self-esteem (e.g. devaluation of others, omnipotence). *Disavowal* (Level 4) works to keep unpleasant or unacceptable stressors, impulses, ideas, affects, or responsibility out of awareness with or without misattribution of these to external causes (e.g. denial, projection, rationalization). *Major Image Distorting* defenses (Level 3) are marked by gross distortion or misattribution of the image of the self or others (e.g. autistic fantasy, projective identification, splitting). *Action Level* defenses (Level 2) deal with internal or external stressors by action or withdrawal (e.g. acting out, passive-aggression, apathy). *Defensive Dysregulation* (Level 1) is characterized by failure of defenses to contain an individual's reaction to stressors, leading to breaks with reality (e.g. delusional projection, psychotic denial). Table A.5 summarizes defense levels according to the Defensive Functioning Scale. Table A.6 is a glossary of defenses that provides succinct definitions of the mechanisms.

Appendix. Table A.5 Defense Levels

Level 7: High Adaptive: anticipation, affiliation, altruism, humor, self-assertion, self-observation, sublimation, suppression.

Level 6: Mental Inhibitions: displacement, dissociation, intellectualization, isolation of affect, reaction formation, repression, undoing.

Level 5: Minor Image-distorting: devaluation, idealization, omnipotence.

Level 4: Disavowal: denial, projection, rationalization.

Level 3: Major Image-distorting: autistic fantasy, projective identification, splitting of slef-image or image of others.

Level 2: Action Level: acting out, apathetic withdrawal, help-rejecting complaining, passive aggression.

Level 1: Defensive Dysregulation: delusional projection, psychotic denial, psychotic distortion.

(Adapted from Vaillant (1999) and DSM IV, A.P.A. (1994))

Appendix. Table A.6 Glossary of Defense Mechanisms

Acting out: action rather than reflection or feeling.

Affiliation: turning to others for help or support.

Anticipation: experiencing emotional reactions in advance of, or anticipating consequences of future events, and considering alternative responses.

Autistic Fantasy: excessive day dreaming as a substitute for human relationships, effective action or problem solving.

Denial: refuse to acknowledge some profound aspect of external reality or subjective experience. Not the gross impairment in reality testing seen in psychotic denial.

Devaluation: attributing exaggerated negative qualities to oneself or others.

Displacement: transferring a feeling about, or a response to one person or event onto another.

Dissociation: breakdown in integrated functions of consciousness, memory, perception of self or environment, or physical sensation and actons.

Help rejecting complaining: complains or makes repeatd requests for help that disguise hostility toward others, which is then expressed by rejecting the help others offer. The complaints may involve physical or psychological symptoms or life problems.

Humor: emphasizing the amusing or ironic aspects orf a conflict or stressor.

Idealization: attributing exaggereated positive qualities to others.

Intellectualization: excessive use of abstract thinking or generalizing to control or minimize disturbing feelings.

Isolation of affect: separating ideas from the feeling originally associated with them.

Omnipotence: feeling or acting as if one possess special powers or abilities and is superior to others.

Passive aggression: indirect, unassertive espressoiin of aggression toward others, with a facade of overt compliance masking covert resistance, resentment, or hostility.

Projection: falsely attributing to another one's own unacceptable feelings, impulses, or thoughts.

Rationalization: substituting behavior, thoughts or feelings that are diametrically opposed to one's own unacceptable thoughts or feelings.

Repression: expelling disturbing wishes, thoughts, or experiences from conscious awareness. The feeling component may remain conscious, detached from its associated ideas.

Self-assertion: expressing feelings and thoughts directly in a way that is not coercive or manipulative.

Self-observation: reflecting on one's own thoughts, feelings, motivation and behavior and responding appropriately.

Splitting: compartmentalizing opposite emotional states and failing to integrate positifve or negative qualites of oneself or others into cohesive images.

Sublimation: channeling potentially maladaptive feelings or impulses into satisfying and socially acceptable behavior.

Suppression: intentionally avoiding thinking about disturbing problems, wishes, feelings or experiences.

Undoing: words or behavior designed to negate or to make amends symbolically for unacceptable thougths, feelings, or actions.

(Adapted from DSM IV, APA, (1994))

Nathan Szajnberg, M.D., a board certified child and adolescent and adult psychiatrist and psychoanalyst, rated the videotaped interviews of all participants for the outcome measures and for diagnoses, blind to prior project data. Dr. Massie, still blind, reviewed the diagnoses and when disagreements occurred a consensus rating was reached. Erik Hesse, Ph.D. independently provided AAI ratings, and showed high agreement (Chi Square=11.4, $p<0.01$) with Szajnberg's ratings for the major categories of Secure vs. Insecure.

In the statistical results that follow, we report correlations between maternal infancy groups A and B and outcome because the documentation of the mother-child relationship was more complete and verifiable contemporaneously through the original research films. We did, however, review all of the interviews with the fathers at ages four to seven (blind to outcome of the children) and group the fathers into a More Effective Fathering Group (A) and a Less Effective Fathering Group (B) on the basis of the original researchers' descriptions of the fathers' attitudes, insight, knowledge and behaviors with respect to their children. When statistically significant correlations between parental groups and outcome occurred, they came from maternal groups. Adding the paternal groups to the calculations (either singly or in combination with maternal groups) did not change the trends or direction of the findings.

Table A.7 (Correlations Among Outcome measures at Age 30) shows that all measures—Defense Level, Global Assessment of Functioning, Psychosocial Development, Adult Attachment Interview (AAI) secure vs. insecure classification, and presence or absence of DSM-IV diagnosis—were significantly related to each other ($p=<.01$), with the exception of diagnosis with AAI. Participants who had high GAFs were likely to have mature defenses, higher psychosocial attainment, and secure images of childhood attachment to their parents. The converse was also true. Additionally, those adults free of a psychiatric diagnosis had significantly higher GAF scores, defense levels, and psychosocial attainment, with the converse also true ($p<.01$). On the other hand, insecure status on the AAI did not significantly correlate with the presence of specific DSM-IV psychiatric diagnoses and vice versa ($p>.05$), although a slightly higher proportion of insecurely attached adults do have a psychiatric diagnosis (Chi Square =.266, $p=.61$). The disagreement between representation of attachment and presence or absence of a psychiatric diagnosis at age 30 may reflect the fact that the AAI marks relative internal security (and thus vulnerability to stressors), but is not an indictor of psychopathology *per se*.

Appendix. Table A.7 Correlations between Outcome Measures at Age 30

GAF and Defense	r = .77, p<.01*
GAF and Psychosocial level	r = .87, p<.01*
GAF and AAI	r = .33 p<.01*
Defense and Psychosocial level	r = .76, p<.01*
Defense and AAI	r = .39, p<.01*
Psychosocial level and AAI	r = .43, p<.01*
GAF and Diagnosis	r = ..67,p<.01*
Defense and Diagnosis	r = .50, p<.01*
Psychosocial level and Diagnosis	r = .51, p<.01*
AAI and Diagnosis	r = .06, , NS

Figure A.1 shows the distribution of Global Assessment of functioning Scores in the group of 76; and Figure A.2 illustrates the distribution of defense levels in the group of 76.

Appendix. Figure A.1
Distribution of Global Assessment of Functioning (GAF) Scores

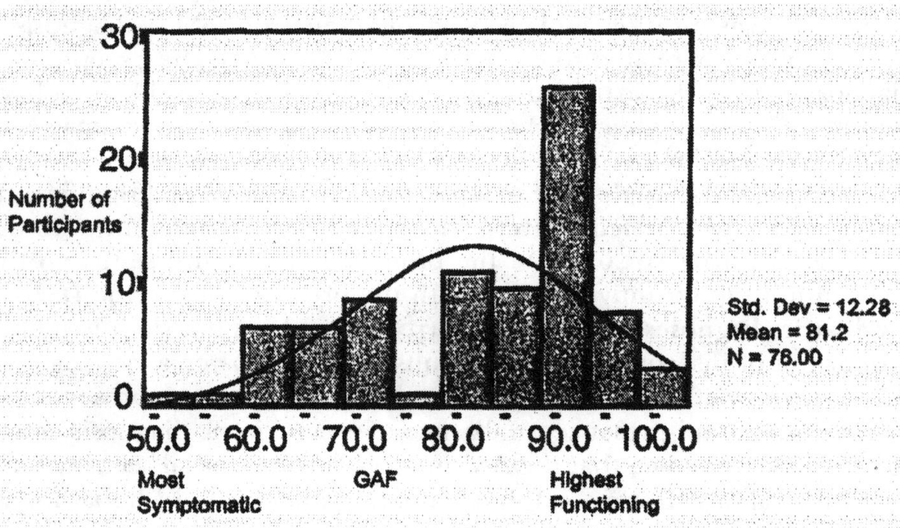

Appendix. Figure A.2 The Statistical Relationship between Mothering in Infancy and Adult Outcome

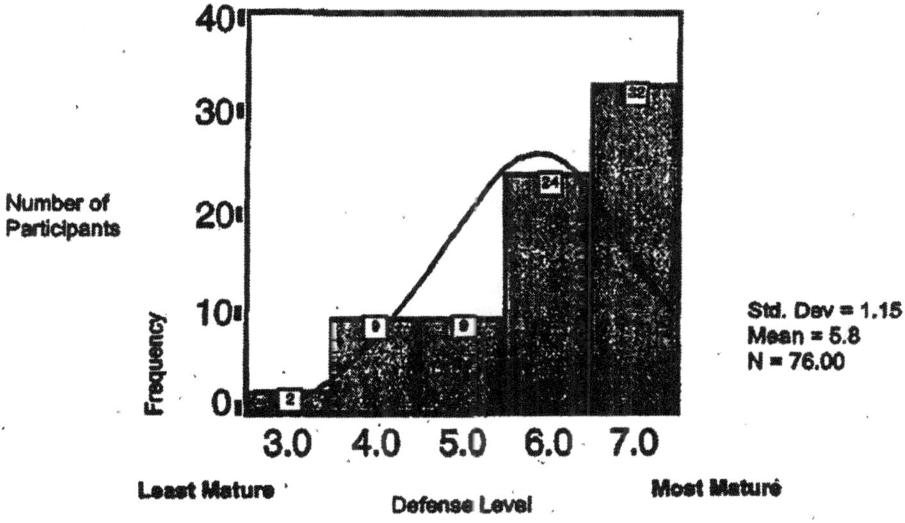

The Statistical Relationship between Mothering in Infancy and Adult Outcome

Table A.8 shows the ratings of five outcome measures according to maternal group. **For defense levels, there is a statistically significant relationship between effectiveness of mothering in infancy and adult outcome**. Children of Group A mothers had more mature and healthy defense mechanisms as adults than children of Group B mothers. For the other outcome measures—GAF, Psychosocial Development, AAI, and diagnosis—there is a statistical trend in the predicted direction. If the Brody study population were larger, or if the sample had been selected from a high risk group of disadvantaged families or from a clinical population of mothers with psychiatric diagnoses, it is possible that the trends would have become statistically significant.

Appendix. Table A.8 The Adult Outcome of Children with More Effective Mothering in Infancy (Group A) Compared to Children With Less Effective Mothering (Group B)

MATERNAL GROUP	OUTCOME Means and Standard Deviation				
	Defense	GAF	Psychosocial	AAI	Diagnosis
Children of A (n=26)	6.19, SD.9	83.8, 12	33.4, 5.6	Sec. 19/73% Insec, 7/27%	No: 18/69% Yes: 8/31%
Children of B (n=50)	5.62 1.2	79.8 12	31.2 6.4	Sec, 30/60% Insec, 20/40%	No: 32/64% Yes: 18/36%
	t=2.34 p=0.02*	t=1.53 p=0.18**	t=1.53	chi sq=0.91 p=0.131**	chi sq=0.21 p=0.65**

* Signif. diff.
** Not Signif. diff.

As seen from Table A.2, approximately one-third of the mothers of the followup group of 76 had been classified in the more effective group by the original researchers, as was the case 30 years earlier with the original 132 families. At followup, the psychological defenses of the adult children of more favorable mothers straddled the highest level (High Adaptive) and the next level (Mental Inhibitions), whereas the children of less effective mothers had defenses straddling Mental Inhibitions and the next lower level (Minor Image Distorting) (t=2.34, p=.02).

Global Assessment of functioning means hovered in the low 80s for the children of Group A mothers (good functioning, absent or minimal symptoms) and in the high 70s (virtually 80) for the offspring of Group B mothers (slight impairment, transient and expectable reactions to psychosocial stressors), not a significant difference (t=1.35, p=.18). On the Erikson scale of psychosocial attainment, scores were again close with both children of Group A mothers and Group B mothers achieving largely favorable resolutions of psychosocial task (trust, autonomy, initiative, industry, identity, intimacy, generativity) with mean scores in the low 30s out of a possible high of 40, with children of Group A mothers scoring slightly higher, not a significant difference (t=1.53, p=.13).

The Adult Attachment Interview suggests that a higher percentage of children who had experienced more effective mothering in infancy

(Group A) were Secure in the psychological representations of attachment as adults, a nonsignificant trend in the predicted direction (chi square=.91, p=.34). Importantly, the AAI shows that children can crossover from favorable mothering in early life to insecure states as adults. There is movement in the other direction also, with children whose mothers were less effective (Group B) able to achieve internal images of valued and secure attachment to their parents by adulthood.

When we look simply at the relationship of infancy mothering and the presence or absence of a DSM-IV psychiatric diagnosis at age 30, we find that 30.8% of children of more effective mothers (Group A) had diagnoses, compared to 36% of children of Group B mothers, a nonsignificant trend (chi square .208, p=.65).

Factoring in paternal groups did not change the trends or significance. The absence of numerical correlations with fathers' groups may be mistakenly interpreted to suggest that fathers have a secondary ("not statistically significant") role in child development. In reality this statistically demeaned role is misleading for, as numerous individual family histories in the project show, fathers profoundly affect a child's growth and adult adaptation. The positive presence of a father during and after a child's infancy facilitates the mother's care; his absence changes the inner nature of a child's emotional evolution, especially when oedipal triadic feelings arrive in the third and fourth year of life. From a data analytic point of view, it may well be that the father's role in project families appears indirectly in the very fact that the GAF, Erikson, psychosocial measure, AAI, and diagnosis are less strongly correlated with maternal group. In essence, these four categories are more composite measures of past and present experience. That is, the father's contribution comes in complementing, enhancing, diffusing, or disturbing the mother's influence in childhood. The father typically is the child's first encounter with the animate world apart from the dyadic mother-child relationship; he goes on to powerfully shape the child's future response to the world apart from the family.

Trauma, Adversity, and Abuse in Childhood and Adult Outcome

Although the numerical data did not point as powerfully to the protective influence on emotional growth of infancy mothering, it did point directly to the cumulative effect of trauma on growth. Table A.9 lists the kinds of adverse circumstances children faced.

Appendix. Table A.9 Traumas and Adversities in the Life Of 76 Children Prior to Age 18

Trauma/Adversity	Number of case
Divorce	9
Alcoholic parent	8 fathers, 1 mother
Severe psychiatric parent illness	3 fathers, 1 mother
Life threatenting physical illness or injury in parent or sibling	3
Life threatenting physical illness or injury or handicap in child	2
Abusive parent(s) (physical or emotional)	9 fathers, 4 mothers (10 families)
Witnessing death or severe injury	2

The mean Global Assessment of Functioning scores of adults who experienced one childhood trauma/adversity are marginally lower than the scores of children with none, a non-significant difference. However the accumulation of adversity (multiple traumatic circumstances in childhood) strikingly depressed adult GAF scores. Children with two or more traumas or adverse circumstances prior to age 18 had significantly lower GAF scores at 30 than children with fewer than two such experiences (t=2.195, p=.03) (tables A.10 and A.11)

Appendix. Table A.10 Adult Outcome of Children with One Trauma/Adversity Compared to Children with None

Divorce, alcoholic parent, parental illness, injury to self or in family, handicapping condition, molestation, abusive parent, witnessing, violence death or injury.

Families with No Trauma (n=53) : Mean GAF = 82.4, SD 12.3
Families with One Trauma (n=15): Mean GAF = 81.4, SD 11.6 No signif. diff.

Appendix. Table A.11 Adult Outcome of Children with Two or More Trauma/Adversity Compared with Children with None or One

Families with 0 or 1 Trauma: n = 68 : Mean GAF = 82.2 SD 12.1
Families with Two or More Traumata n =8: Mean GAF = 72.2, SD 11.3

t = 2.195, p = 0.031: Signif Difference

With respect to psychiatric diagnosis, children suffering two or more childhood trauma/adversities had a higher proportion of diagnoses at age 30, but the numbers were very small for statistical calculation and a chi square test (chi square .990, p=.32) was not significant. On the other hand, isolating the subgroup of ten children who were physically abused by a parent or severely emotionally denigrated/rejected by one or both parents (a maltreatment group) showed striking statistically significant depressions of Global Functioning and Defense Level, and much higher incidence of psychiatric diagnosis compared to non-maltreated children (Table A.12).

Appendix. Table A.12 Adult Outcome of Maltreated Children Compared to Non-Abused Children

		GAF	Defense	Psychosocial	Diagnosis	AAI
Abused n=10		69.1	4.83	27.8	8(80%)	2(20%) Secure
	SD:	9.3	1.3	6.2		
	t=	3.39	2.06	2.38	chi sq 10.73	5.34
	p=	.001	.003	.02	.002	.02

All differences are statistically signif. between groups.

It is noteworthy that children whose mothers and fathers were more effective (Group A) were equally likely to encounter traumatic/adverse circumstances as children of less effective parents (Group B), though this finding is tempered by the small number of cases with two or more traumas when groups A and B are looked at separately. This is not the case with abuse, however, for only one parent (a mother) of the ten maltreated children was in the effective group. *With respect to trauma/adversity, the presence of one such circumstance in a family (e.g. mental illness or alcoholism in a parent) made a second adversity, such as divorce more likely.* Likewise, alcoholism made child abuse more likely.

Additional Findings

Table A.13 shows the DSM-IV Axis I and II conditions in the 76 participants. The overall incidence of psychiatric illness in adulthood is 32%, which is in the same range as the results of recent community mental health epidemiological surveys (Murphy, Tohen, and Tsuang, 1999). Because of the small numbers of individuals with each diagnosis we could not statistically analyze the relationship of specific diagnoses with specific etiological circumstances or with the Adult Attachment classification.

Appendix. Table A.13 Primary Diagnoses at Age 30 In the Group of 76

24 Individuals (32%). Six with more than one diagnosis.

Dysthymia	10
Major Depression	3
Cyclothymia	1
Anxiety disorders	5
Obsessive-Compulsive Personality	2
Narcissistic Personality Disorder	1
Borderline Personality Disorder	2
Marijuana Dependence	2
Sexual Paraphilia	2

Parents from higher socioeconomic groups were not more likely to be Group A parents, and higher childhood socioeconomic level did not make good adult mental healthy more likely. Further, there was no correlation between measures of intelligence in childhood and adult mental health. Children with higher intelligence, however, did go further in school, and at age 30 had higher incomes than their less educated counterparts. There was a general modest movement in the study population toward higher socioeconomic status from the parent to the present generation. This may be reflective of the economy, of the parents' interest in their children (signaled by their volunteering for the project in the first place), and perhaps most reflective of the current generation's postponing marriage and childbearing to focus on careers, education, and personal growth to an age well beyond when their parents married and started having children.

Conclusion

The mean GAF scores for the group of 76 indicates good, though not superior functioning. However eight children of Group A mothers (31% of 26) had GAF scores at 30 years of 80 or below (impairment), and nine children of Group B mothers (18% of 50) had GAF scores of 91-100 (superior functioning). Thus 17 (21%) of the 76 children changed to better or worse outcomes than the original hypothesis had predicted for them. Clearly, trauma and adverse circumstances were main factors depressing outcomes, and encounters with favorable influences inside and outside of families enhanced emotional growth.

With respect to genetic inheritance, the study did not systematically track possible generational transmission of syndromes, nor did it formally offer a psychiatric diagnosis for all parents. The original researchers were most interested in the parents' behaviors with, and feelings for their children. But in the process of documenting them, they readily noted when parents were, for example, depressed, anxious, hostile; and noted the parents' own self-observations and explanations for their moods and behaviors, which parents typically traced to their own childhood experiences and current life stresses. In the Brody study, for instance, parental moods appeared to have a contagious effect on children's development: happy, extroverted parents typically raised contented, expressive children; depressed parents typically raised children with subsued and dysphoric affects; and angry, rejecting parents raised anxious angry children—phenomena described by us in earlier research (Massie, Bronstein, Afterman, and Campbell, 1988; Massie, Bronstein, and Afterman, 1996; Massie and Szajnberg, 1997) and by others (Murray et al., 1996; Murray and Cooper, 1997). The data from the Brody study does not allow us to distinguish the possible role of genetics in mediating these processes. None of the project participants as of age 30 had experienced a psychotic illness, a condition in which genetic factors may be more likely to play a significant role.

The data analysis has provided comparisons between groups and correlations between early experience and outcome, but it cannot convey the rich course of psychological life in the same way that individual life histories have in the preceding chapters. The earlier detailed individual case studies of the 76 participants, while consistent with the data analysis, amplify the intricate processes by which children internalize their early experiences with their parents, establish emotional regulation, establish identifications with aspects of their parents' personalities, and in some cases experience childhood symptoms, gradually transforming them into adult psychiatric symptoms and personality styles.

In sum, *project findings underline the 30 year old subjects' own beliefs that their childhood and parents exerted profound influences on their emotional lives; that development is continuous from early experience to adulthood, and it is discontinuous.* Misfortune (trauma and adversity such as changes in a parent's effectiveness, illness, domineering siblings) distort life's course; by contrast, unanticipated positive influences (teachers, siblings, partners, therapists, relatives, even housekeepers) can ameliorate emotional disturbance. People do change for better and for worse. Effective nurturing in infancy makes emotional security most likely, and this appears to offer some protection against mental illness later, but clearly does not inoculate against it. With enough information, we can see how events in people's lives interdigitate with their psychological structuralization across time, and that emotional life is not simply continuous or discontinuous, it is also coherent.

References

Ainsworth, M., Blehar, M., Waters, E., & Wall, S. (1978), *Patterns of Attachment.* Hillsdale, NJ: Erlbaum.

Alexander, F., French, T., & Pollack, G. (1968), *Psychosomatic Specificity,* Vol. 1. Chicago: University of Chicago Press.

Amaya-Jackson, L., Mesco, R., McGough, J., & Cantwell, D. (1992), Attention-deficit/ hyperactivity disorder. In: *Neurobiological Disorders in Children and Adolescents,* ed. E. Peschel, R. Peschel, R. Howe, & J. Howe. San Francisco: Jossey-Bass, pp. 45-50.

American Psychiatric Association (1994a), *Diagnostic and Statistical Manual of Mental Disorders,* 4th ed. (DSM-IV). Washington, DC: American Psychiatric Press.

______(1994b), Global Assessment of Functioning Scale. In: *Diagnostic and Statistical Manual of Mental Disorders,* 4th ed. (DSM-IV). Washington, DC: American Psychiatric Press, pp. 30-32.

Anthony, E. J., & Cohler, B., Eds. (1987), *The Invulnerable Child.* New York: Guilford Press.

Apted, M. (1999), *42 Up.* Documentary movie. Granada Television production for the BBC. Produced and directed by Michael Apted.

Bahadur, M. (1998), *Continuity and Discontinuity of Attachment from Age 1 to Age 30.* Unpublished doctoral dissertation. New York University.

Barrie, J. M. (1947), *When a Man's Single.* New York: Harper & Brothers, p. 2.

Bateson, G., Jackson, D., Haley, J. & Weakland, J. (1956), Toward a theory of schizophrenia. *Behav. Sci.,* 1:251.

Bellak, L. (1975), *The Thematic Apperception Test (TAT) and Children's Apperception Test (CAT) in Clinical Use.* New York: Grune & Stratton.

Bios, P. (1979), *The Adolescent Passage.* New York: International Universities Press.

Bowlby, J. (1909), *Attachment and Loss,* Vol. 1: *Attachment.* New York: Basic Books.

______(1973), *Attachment and Loss,* Vol. 2: *Separation.* New York: Basic Books.

______(1980), *Attachment and Loss,* Vol. 3: *Loss.* New York: Basic Books.

Bretherton, L., & Waters, E. (1985), Growing points of attachment: Theory and research. *Monographs of the Society for Research in Child Development,* 50:(1-2)298-S18.

Breuer, J., & Freud, S. (1893-1895), Studies on Hysteria. *Standard Edition,* 2, London: Hogarth Press, 1955.

Brody, S. (1956), *Patterns of Mothering.* New York: International Universities Press.

______(2002), *The Development of Anorexia: The Hunger Artists.* Madison, CT: International Universities Press.

Axelrad, S. (1967-1984), *Maternal Behavior and Child Development.* Seven educational films. Archives of the History of American Psychology, University of Akron, Akron, OH. Also available through the Media Center, Pennsylvania State University, University Park, PA.

____________(1970), *Anxiety and Ego Formation in Infancy.* New York: International Universities Press.

____________(1978), *Mothers, Fathers, and Children.* New York: International Universities Press.

Siegel, M. (1992), *The Evolution of Character.* New York: International Universities Press.

Buck, J. (1966), *The House, Tree, Person Technique.* Los Angeles: Western Psychological Services.

Carlson, E., Jacobvitz, D., & Sroufe, L. A. (1995), A developmental investigation of inattentiveness and hyperactivity. *Child Develop.,* 66:37-54.

Chiland, C., & Young, J. G., Eds. (1984), *Children and Violence.* Northvale, NJ: Jason Aronson.

Chodorow, N. (1978), *The Reproduction of Mothering.* Berkeley, CA: University of California Press.

Coles, R. (1999), Review of *The Velveteen Father,* Jesse Green. *Books of the Times,* October 17, p. 27.

Derogatis, L. (1993), *Symptom Checklist—90—Revised.* Minneapolis: NCS Assessments.

Diamond, D., & Blatt, S., Eds. (1999), *Psychoanalytic Theory and Attachment Research,* Vol. 1. Hilkdale, NJ: Analytic Press.

Dinesen, I. (1958), Interview by H. Arendt. In: *The Human Condition.* Chicago: University of Chicago Press.

Eliot, T. S. (1936), Introduction, *Nightwood* by D. Barnes. London: Faber & Faber, p. 3.

Elmore, M., Cohn, J., & Zlochower, A. (1995), A comparison of micro-analytic and rating scale methods. Paper presented at the Society for Research in Child Development, Indianapolis, IN, March.

Erode, R., & Hewitt, J., Eds. (2001), *The Transition from Infancy to Early Childhood: Genetic and Environmental Influences in the MacArthur Longitudinal Twin Study*. New York: Oxford University Press.

Erikson, E. (1950), *Childhood and Society*. New York: W. W. Norton.

______(1959), *Identity and the Life Cycle*. New York: International Universities Press.

______(1968), *Identity: Youth and Crisis*. New York: W. W. Norton.

Escalona, S., & Leitch, M. (1952), Early phases of personality development—A non-normative study of infant behavior. *Monographs of the Society for Research in Child Development*, 17.

Exner, J. (1974), *The Rorschach: A Comprehensive System*. New York: Wiley.

Fonagy, P. (1999), Memory and therapeutic action. *Internal. J. Psycho-Anal.*, 80:215-223.

Fraiberg, S. (1959), *The Magic Years*. New York: Scribners.

Freud, A. (1936), *The Ego and the Mechanisms of Defense*. New York: International Universities Press, 1966.

______(1965), *Normality and Pathology in Childhood*. New York: International Universities Press.

______(1969), Adolescence as a developmental disturbance. In: *Adolescence: Psychosocial Perspective*, ed. G. Caplan & S. Lebovici. New York: Basic Books, pp. 5-10.

Freud, S. (1893), Charcot *Standard Edition*, 3:7-23. London: Hogarth Press, 1962.

______(1894), Neuro-psychoses of defence. *Standard Edition*, 3:41-68. London: Hogarth Press, 1962.

______(1900), The Interpretation of Dreams. *Standard Edition*, 4&5. London: Hogarth Press, 1953.

______(1905), Three Essays on the Theory of Sexuality. *Standard Edition*, 7:123-243. London: Hogarth Press, 1953.

______(1915), Instincts and Their Vicissitudes. *Standard Edition*, 14:109-140. London: Hogarth Press, 1957.

______(1933), New Introductory Lectures on Psycho-Analysis. *Standard Edition*, 22:1-182. London: Hogarth Press, 1964.

______(1940), An Outline of Psychoanalysis. *Standard Edition*, 23:139-207. London: Hogarth Press, 1964.

George, C., Kaplan, N., & Main, M. (1985), *An Adult Attachment Interview*, Unpublished manuscript, Department of Psychology, University of California, Berkeley.

Gilligan, C. (1982), *In a Different Voice: Psychological Theory and Women's Development,* Cambridge, MA: Harvard University Press.

Ginsburg, B., Becker, R., Trattner, A., & Bareggi, S. (1984), A genetic taxonomy of hyperkinesis in the dog. *Internal,]. Develop. Neurosci.,* 2:313-322.

Guthrie, W. (1954), Don't you push me down. In: *Rise Up Singing,* ed. P. Blood-Patterson. Bethlehem, PA: Sing Out Publications, p. 108.

Hamilton, C. (1995), Continuity and discontinuity of attachment from infancy through adolescence. Paper presented at the Society for Research in Child Development, Indianapolis, IN, March.

Harlow, F. H. (1961), The development of affectional patterns in infant monkeys. In: *Determinants of Infant Behavior,* Vol. 1, ed. B. M. Foss. New York: Wiley, pp. 75-80.

Hawley, G. (1980), *Measures of Psychosocial Development (MPD).* Odessa, FL: Psychological Assessment Resources.

Herzog, J. (2001), *Father Hunger Explorations with Adults and Children.* Hillsdale, NJ: Analytic Press.

Hinshaw, S., March, J., Abikoff, H., Arnold, L., Cantwell, D., Conners, C., Elliott, G., Halperin, E., et al. (1997), Comprehensive assessment of childhood attention-deficit hyperactivity disorder in the context of a multisite, multimodal clinical trial. *J. Attention Disord.,* 1:217-254.

______Owens, E., Wells, K., Kraemer, H., Abikoff, H., Arnold, L., Conners, C., Elliott, G., Greenhill, L., et al. (2000), Family processes and treatment outcome in the National Institute of Mental Health collaborative multimodal treatment study of children with ADHD (the MTA study), *J. Abnorm. Child Psycho.,* 28:555-568.

Hirsch, E. (1999), *How to Read a Poem.* New York: Harcourt Brace.

Hollingshead, A., & Redlich, F. (1958), *Social doss and Mental Illness: A* Community *Study.* New York: Wiley.

Horowitz, M. (1998), *Cognitive Psychodynamics: From Conflict to Character.* New York: Wiley.

Jellinek, M., & Herzog, D. (1999), The child. In: *Harvard Guide to Psychiatry,* ed. A. Nicholi. Cambridge, MA: Belknap/Harvard University Press, pp. 586-610.

Kagan, J. (1998), *Three Seductive Ideas.* Cambridge, MA: Harvard University Press.

Khan, M. (1963), The concept of cumulative trauma. *The Psychoanalytic Study of the Child,* 18:286-306. New York: International Universities Press.

Krall, V., & Szajnberg, N. (1995), Projective personality traits of children with Irritable Bowel Disorder. *Perceptual & Motor Skills,* 80:1341-1342.

Laing, R. D. (1959), *The Divided Self.* London: Tavistock.

Levy, IL, & Blatt, S. (1999), Attachment theory and psychoanalysis: Further differentiation within insecure attachment patterns. *Psychoanal, Inq.*, 19:541-575.

Mahler, M., Pine, F., & Bergman, A. (1975), *The Psychological Birth of the Human Infant,* New York: Basic Books.

Malone, C. (1963), Some observations on children of disorganized families and problems of acting out. *J. Amer. Acad. Child. Psychiatry,* 2:22-49.

Massie, H., & Campbell, B. K. (1983), The Massie-Campbell Scale of Mother-Infant Attachment During Stress (ADS Scale) . In *Frontiers of Infant Psychiatry,* ed. J. Call, E. Galenson, & R. Tyson. New York: Basic Books, pp. 394-412.

______Bronstein, A., & Afterman, J. (1996), The role of depressive affects in close maternal involvement with children: Inner themes and outer behaviors in child development, 2. *Psychoanal. Psycho.*, 13:54-80.

______Campbell, B. K. (1988), Inner themes and outer behaviors in early childhood development: A longitudinal study. *The Psychoanalytic Study of the Child,* 43:213-242. New Haven, CT: Yale University Press.

______Rosenthal, J. (1984), *Childhood Psychosis in the First 4 Years of life.* New York: McGraw-Hill.

______Szajnberg, N. (1997), The ontogeny of a sexual fetish from birth to age & 30 and memory processes. *Internal. J. Psycho-Anal,* 78:755-771.

______(2002), The relationship between mothering in infancy, childhood experience and adult mental health: Results of the Brody prospective longitudinal study from birth to age 30. *Internal. J. Psycho-Anal.*, 83:35-55.

Mrazek, D., Klinnert, M., & Mrazek, P. (1991), Prediction of early onset asthma in genetically at risk children. *Pediatr. Pulmonol.*, 27:85-94.

____________________& Macy, M. (1991), Early asthma onset Consideration of parenting issues. *J. Amer, Acad. Child Adol. Psychiatry,* 30:277-282.

Murphey, J., Tohen, M., & Tsuang, M. (1999), Psychiatric epidemiology. In: *Harvard Guide to Psychiatry,* ed. A Nicholi. Cambridge, MA: Belknap/ Harvard University Press, pp. 752-777.

Murphy, L., & Moriarty, A. (1976), *Vulnerability, Coping and Growth Jrom Infancy to Adolescence.* New Haven, CT: Yale University Press.

Murray, L., Cooper, P. (1997), The role of infant and maternal factors in post-partem depression: Mother-infant interactions and infant outcome. In: *Post-Partum Depression and Child-Development,* ed. L. Murray *Sc* P. Cooper. New York: Guilford Press, pp. 111-135.

______Fion-Crowley, A., Hooper, R., & Cooper, P. (1996), The impact of post-natal depression and associated adversity on early mother-infant interactions and later infant outcome. *Child Develop.*, 67:2512-2526.

Ng, F. M. (1994), *Bone.* New York: Harper Perrenial.

O Cadhain, M. (1981), *The Road to Bright City.* Dublin: Poolberg.
Offer, D., & Offer, J. (1971), Four issues in the developmental psychology of the adolescent. In: *Modern Perspectives on Adolescent Psychiatry,* ed. J. Howells. Edinburgh: Oliver & Boyd, pp. 28-44.
Pearson, J., Cohn, D., Cowan, P., & Cowan, C. (1994), Earned and continuous security in adult attachment: Relation to depressive symptomatology and parenting style. *Develop. Psychol.,* 6:359-S7S.
Petrill, S., Saudino, K., Cherny, S., Erode, R., Hewitt, J., Fuller, D., & Plomin, R. (1997), Exploring the genetic etiology of low general cognitive ability from 14 to 36 months. *Develop. Psychol.,* 33:544-548.
Rexford, E. (1963), A developmental concept of the problems of acting out. *Amer. Acad. Child Psychiatry* 2:6-21.
Roiphe, H., & Galenson, E. (1981), *Infantile Origins of Sexuality,* New York: International Universities Press.
Sappho (6th Century B.C.), In: Part One: *Lyrics in the Original Greek,* tr. M. Barnard. Berkeley: University Press of California, 1989.
Shakespeare, W. (1623), *The Tempest,* ed. N. Frye. Baltimore, MD: Penguin, 1959.
Shepard, S. (2001), Program note, Magic Theater production, *True West.* San Francisco, CA.
Smith, Z. (2001). *White Teeth,* New York: Vintage.
Spitz, R. (1965), *TheFirst Year of Life.* New York: International Universities Press.
Sroufe, L. A. (1996), *Emotional Development: The Organization of Emotional Life in the Early Years.* Cambridge, UK: Cambridge University Press.
______(1997), Psychopathology as outcome of development *Develop. &Psychopathol,* 9:251-268.
______Carlson, E., & Shulman, S. (1993), The development of individuals in relationships: From infancy through adolescence. In: *Studying Lives Through Time,* ed. D. Funder, R. Parke, C. Tomlinson-Keasey, & K. Widaman. Washington, DC: American Psychological Association, pp. 315-342.
Szajnberg, N., & Crittenden, P. (1997), The transference refracted through attachment. *J. Amer. Acad. Psychoanal.,* 25:409-438.
______Krall, V., Davis, P., Treem, W., & Hyams, J. (1993), Psychopathology and relationship measures in children with irritable bowel disease and their parents. *Child Psychiatry & Hum. Develop.,* 23:215-232.
______Waters, E. (in preparation), Disturbed attachment in mothers of children with irritable bowel disorder compared to cancer and renal disease.
Terr, L. (1990), *Too Scared to Cry: Psychic Trauma in Childhood.* New York: Harper Se Row.

______(1994), *Unchained Memories: True Stories of Traumatic Memories Lost and Found.* New York: Basic Books.

Thomas, A., Chess, S., & Birch, H. G. (1968), *Temperament and Behavior Disorders in Children.* New York: New York University Press.

Tolstoy, L. (1873-1876), *Anna Karenina,* tr. C. Garnett New York: Modern Library.

Vaillant, G. (1977), *Adaptation to Life.* Boston: Little, Brown.

______(1992), *Ego Mechanisms of Defense: A Guide for Clinicians and Researchers.* Washington, DC: American Psychiatric Press.

______(1994), The defensive functioning scale. In: *The Diagnostic and Statistical Manual of Mental Disorders,* 4th ed. (DSM-IV). Washington, DC: American Psychiatric Press, pp. 751-757.

______(1999), The defense mechanisms. In: *Harvard Guide to Psychiatry,* ed. A. Nicholi. Cambridge, MA: Belknap/ Harvard University Press, pp. 196-202.

van der Kolk, B. (200S), The body keeps score. Presentation at the Esalen Institute, Esalen, CA, February.

______McFarlane, A., & Weisaeth, L. (1996), *Traumatic Stress.* New York: Guilford Press.

Wallerstein, J., Lewis, J., & Blakeslee, S. (2000), *The Unexpected Legacy of Divorce.* New York: Hyperion Books.

Waters, T., Hamilton, C., & Weinfield, N. (2000), The stability of attachment security from infancy to adolescence and early adulthood: General discussion. *Child Develop.,* 71:708-706.

______Treboux, D., Crowell, J., Merrick, S., & Albersheim, L. (1995), From the Strange Situation to the Adult Attachment Interview: A 20-year longitudinal study of attachment security in infancy and early adulthood. Paper presented at the Society for Research in Child Development, Indianapolis, IN, March.

Werner, E., & Smith, R. (1992), *Overcoming the Odds: High Risk Children from Birth to Adulthood.* Ithaca, NY: Cornell University Press.

Winnicott, D. W. (1951), Transitional objects and transitional phenomena: A study of the first not-me possession. In: *Collected Papers: Through Paediatrics to Psycho-Analysis.* London: Tavistock, 1958, pp. 229-242.

______(1962), *The Maturational Processes and the Facilitating Environment.* New York: International Universities Press.

Index

Depression: 28 35 70 74 79 82 84 95 108 113 116 118 120-3 127 130 137 148-9 155 173-4 178 180 193-4 200 216 220 223 226 231 235 240-1 252-4 260 283-4 291.

Prepublication Reviews of LIVES ACROSS TIME/GROWING UP

"A momentous project. There are few long-term studies of individual lives, and fewer still that combine sophisticated psychological observations with psychoanalytic understanding and span the entire period from the earliest mother-infant relationship to adulthood. Henry Massie and Nathan Szajnberg, building on the earliest mother-infant studies of Sylvia Brody, tell us of the lives of 76 individuals over the course of 30 years. Their accounts are richly detailed, finely textured, highly individual and extraordinarily human. They emphasize both continuities and discontinuities, how major themes can be identified in the earliest months, and how intervening events can make immense differences. The reader learns how some children grow up much as predicted, some better and some worse, and in the course of doing so comes to know 79 extraordinary people—the 76 subjects and the 3 who studied them."
— **Robert Michels, M.D.**, Walsh McDermott University Professor of Medicine and Psychiatry at Cornell University.

"A tremendous piece of work! I read the whole book through without stopping. It was too fascinating to put down. Life-long stories are the best of stories. Danny, the restaurateur, Lorna, the engineer, and Lainy, the purple-haired cosmetologist are just a few of the interesting 30-year olds we get to know. The best part, however, is that we also get to meet these people as babies, as toddlers, as kindergartners, second-graders, and teens finishing high school. And we see them and their families through the eyes of different researchers including Sylvia Brody and her team who originated the study."
— **Lenore Terr, M.D.**, Author of *Too Scared to Cry*; Clinical Professor of Psychiatry, University of California School of Medicine, San Francisco.

"A marvelous, humane journey of exploration and interpretation of people's lives across time. The book is like a symphony where different themes appear, recede, and reappear, expanded and reworked. I read the book twice. I was transformed by it."
— **Stella Acquarone, Ph.D.**, Director, London School of Infant Mental Health; author of *Infant-Parent Psychotherapy*.

"An important work that illuminates one of the most important psychological issues of the day, how much continuity is there in the child's journey from infancy to maturity. The authors explore how the child's early and later relationships combine with the events and crises of life to shape adult expectations and disappointments."
— **Judith Wallerstein, Ph.D.,** Author of *The Unexpected Legacy of Divorce* and *Surviving the Breakup*; Faculty, School of Social Welfare, University of California, Berkeley.

"The study of 76 individuals from birth to age 30 is a remarkable success. A tremendous amount of interview, observation, psychological testing, and mother-child interaction film data about each of the participants has been so well organized and written in a clear style that the book reads like a novel.
— **Colette Chiland, M.D.**, Professor Emerita, School of Medicine, University of Paris; Honorary President, International Association of Child and Adolescent Psychiatry and Allied Professionals.

Lives Across Time/Growing Up provides us with a psychoanalytic research gem: A longitudinal study of child and adolescent development capped by interviews when the subjects hit 30. The issue of the effects of early mothering is addressed in intimate and individual detail, connecting the hypotheses to a sense of how we each live. This makes for a volume that is rich and easily read by all."
— **Mardi Horowitz, M.D.**, Author of *States of Mind*; Professor of Psychiatry, University of California School of Medicine, San Francisco.

The Authors

Henry Massie, M.D. is a child, adolescent and adult psychiatrist practicing in Berkeley, California; a Clinical Associate Professor of Psychiatry at the University of California School of Medicine, San Francisco; and a researcher who has made fundamental contributions to the understanding of patterns of mother-infant interaction and their implications for children's emotional development. He is also the author with Judith Rosenthal of *Childhood Psychosis in the First Four Years of Life.*

Nathan Szajnberg, M.D. is a psychoanalyst and child, adolescent and adult psychiatrist practicing in San Francisco. He is Clinical Professor of Psychiatry at the University of California School of Medicine, San Francisco, and the Wallerstein Research Fellow in Psychoanalysis. He is a longterm investigator in psychoanalysis child psychiatry and child development. His earlier book is *Educating the Emotions: Bruno Bettelheim and Psychoanalytic Development.*

The Authors

[illegible] California School of Medicine [illegible]

Nathan Szajnberg [illegible] San Francisco [illegible]

BVG

For Product Safety Concerns and Information please contact our EU representative GPSR@taylorandfrancis.com
Taylor & Francis Verlag GmbH, Kaufingerstraße 24, 80331 München, Germany

www.ingramcontent.com/pod-product-compliance
Lightning Source LLC
LaVergne TN
LVHW011116300926
849160LV00008B/405

* 9 7 8 1 8 5 5 7 5 5 1 7 8 *